GOD'S Truth.......

For Those Who Love Him

Charleston, SC
www.PalmettoPublishing.com

God's Truth
Copyright © 2021 by Joseph De Capite

Second Edition

Hardcover ISBN: 978-1-63837-097-0
Paperback ISBN: 978-1-63837-098-7
eBook ISBN: 978-1-63837-099-4

All Scripture quoted is from the New King James Version (NKJV) unless otherwise noted.

New King James Version®. Copyright © 1982 by Thomas Nelson. Used by permission. All rights reserved.

Scripture quotations marked (NIV) are taken from the Holy Bible, New International Version®, NIV®. Copyright © 1973, 1978, 1984, 2011 by Biblica, Inc.™ Used by permission of Zondervan. All rights reserved worldwide. www.zondervan.com. The "NIV" and "New International Version" are trademarks registered in the United States Patent and Trademark Office by Biblica, Inc.™

Scripture quotations marked (KJV) are taken from the King James Version of the Bible.

SECOND EDITION

GOD'S

Truth.......

For Those Who Love Him

JOSEPH DE CAPITE

*To my wife, Regina, and to our children, Juliana Marie, Steven Joseph,
and Valerie Ann, and our grandchildren, Edwin, Reagan and Leo*

Have you ever wondered why there are so many Christian denomina-tions and why there is so much confusion as to what the Bible says? It is because people have opinions about what they think the Bible says. Finally, now you can learn true answers. This book does not contain my thoughts, ideas or opinions about the important topics presented; it only contains provable truths from your Bible.

Contents

CHAPTER 7
GOD'S TRUTH ABOUT THE KINGDOM OF GOD

Author's Statement

There are **three** fundamental principles to keep in mind regarding proper understanding of the Holy Bible.

> The **first** principle is that the Bible is a coded book. Many people today do not know that the Holy Bible is coded. It is coded because it is unlike any other book ever written in that it was divinely inspired by God Himself. Notice **2 Timothy 3:16**, "All Scripture is given by inspiration of God, and is profitable for doctrine, for reproof, for correction, for instruction in righteousness." The Holy Bible provides, for those "who hunger and thirst for righteousness," revealed knowledge scattered throughout its text. Notice what **Isaiah 28:10** says: "For precept must be upon precept, precept upon precept, line upon line, line upon line, here a little, there a little."
>
> The **second** principle is that the Bible interprets itself through the use of other related Scriptures. I found out many years ago that the Bible does not require human interpretation in order for a specific topic therein to make sense. Through the ages, God inspired holy men and women to write His Word and made certain to preserve it through time for our knowledge and admonition in today's society. As for interpreting the Bible, **2 Peter 1:20** clearly states, "Knowing this first, that no

prophecy of Scripture is of any private interpretation." (Take time out right now to get your Bible and study this Scripture. Please do not take my word for it; study and search out truth for yourself.)

The Scripture above clearly states that a person should not place his or her own interpretation into any prophecy or any Bible Scripture! Yet, that is precisely what many modern-day theologians, clergy, and lay Christians have done or have been taught to do. They have used their own preconceived beliefs and have twisted Scripture to fit their beliefs.

Notice what **2 Peter 3:15–16** says, "And consider that the long-suffering of our Lord is salvation—as also our beloved brother Paul, according to the wisdom given to him, has written to you, as also in all his epistles, speaking in them of these things, in which are some things hard to understand, which untaught and unstable people twist to their own destruction, as they do also the rest of the Scriptures." Again, the end result of placing one's interpretation into Scripture is exactly what Christianity has today—total religious chaos and confusion. Everyone's doing what seems right in his or her eyes. This was prophesied long ago in **Deuteronomy 12:8**, "You shall not at all do as we are doing here today—every man doing whatever is right in his own eyes." It is unfortunate that instead of putting various Scriptures properly and sensibly together, it has become common practice and customary for people to individually interpret Scriptures to say what they have already learned or have been taught, without biblical proof. In other words, a person places his or her own interpretation into Scripture, which may be different from another person's interpretation. This practice most certainly leads to utter confusion and chaos in personal beliefs. And isn't that what we have today in the Christian religion? Everyone doing and teaching what he or she believes to be right.

Private interpretation takes place by either adding or taking away Scripture to fit a personal belief. But once again, take a look at what the Holy Bible clearly tells us about adding or taking away from Scripture: "For I testify to everyone who hears the words of the prophecy of this book: If anyone adds to these things, God will add to him the plagues that are written in this book; and if anyone takes away from the words of the book of this prophecy, God shall take away his part from the Book of Life, from the holy city, and from the things which are written in this book" (**Revelation 22:18–19**). Notice also **Deuteronomy 12:32**, which says, "Whatever I command you, be careful to observe it; you shall not add to it nor take away from it."

> The **third** principle is that the Bible is like a giant jigsaw puzzle with literally thousands of pieces that require putting together. Just like any real jigsaw puzzle, the pieces can only be put together one way—in proper order—to see the picture that God is showing us. Only then can the true picture of the puzzle emerge and become crystal clear to the person who not only believes in God but also is willing to believe what He says. Once the pieces of the picture puzzle are put together correctly, you can clearly see the beautiful overall picture of God saving His creation. You may experience seeing this wonderful picture by thoroughly reading and studying your Bible. This book was designed to help you clearly see the salvation plan through God's mighty words.

Notice what the Bible says about confusion: "For God is not the author of confusion but of peace, as in all the churches of the saints" (**1 Corinthians 14:33**).

Many people believe in God; very few believe what He says in the Holy Bible. Even sincere and well-meaning men and women in the clergy have inadvertently assumed that someone else's teachings came from the Holy Bible. They never bothered to prove for themselves what they were taught. But the Scriptures tell us to prove what is being taught. "These were more fair-minded than those in Thessalonica, in that they received the word with all readiness, and searched the

Scriptures daily to find out whether these things were so" (**Acts 17:11**). Also, "Test all things; hold fast what is good" (**1 Thessalonians 5:21**).

When it comes to the things of God, we should "test all things" and not rely on careless assumption, wishful thinking, or someone else's opinions.

The purpose of this book is to place the many pieces of the giant jigsaw puzzle together on various topics so that you can clearly see and understand God's truth, using your own Bible to answer questions. The full explanation about any one subject is seldom made complete and clear using only one Bible passage. As the Holy Bible clearly states, "For precept must be upon precept, precept upon precept, line upon line, line upon line, here a little, there a little" (**Isaiah 28:10**). A true and full understanding of any biblical subject can be obtained only when all pertinent Scripture scattered throughout the Bible are correctly placed together.

Please note that the subjects presented in this book do not contain my ideas or opinions but come from God, directly to you through His inspired Word, the Holy Bible. As you read, study, and meditate on these subjects, you may discover new knowledge or be shocked to find that what you have been taught is not in the Bible. You might also observe things you might not have seen or clearly understood before. And you may find, in many instances, that the Bible really does answer your questions, if you ask God for guidance. Remember that the Holy Bible does not require human interpretation.

As you read this book, ask God in prayer with a sincere heart to clear your mind of any beliefs that you have not thoroughly proven. Ask God to open your heart, mind, and eyes to His truths. Also, be sure to constantly compare the presented Scriptures in this book with your own Bible. This book will make a lot of sense to you, as nothing ever did before. Most truths systematically outlined herein are either unknown or have been intentionally kept secret by mainstream Christianity but are now, finally, made available to you.

Weigh carefully the facts presented in this book, and be sure you reference each Scripture presented herein with your own Bible. I hope and pray that this book will clearly present vital truths and answers the majority of your questions on the conditions for inheriting God's kingdom, which is your awesome destiny.

I have desired to write this book for a long time; I want to share with those who care to know the true answers to difficult biblical questions, straight from God's Word, His Holy Bible. By reading this book, I hope that God will open many eyes to His wonderful truths on the various topics. Therefore, be prepared for some startling new truths that you may not have thought about or read anywhere else. Many facets of your life and many topics are not covered herein. Please read the chapters in sequence to avoid confusion.

A special thanks to my wife, Regina, for proofreading each chapter of this book prior to publication. Thanks also to our children, Juliana, Steven and Valerie—my personal cheering squad.

As you read this book, may you be richly blessed—physically, mentally, and spiritually—by our loving creator God. Remember: "Blessed is he who reads and those who hear the words of this prophecy, and keep those things which are written in it; for the time is near" (**Revelation 1:3**).

Chapter 1
GOD'S TRUTH ABOUT THE BIBLE

1.1   WHAT EXACTLY IS THE HOLY BIBLE?

The vast majority of people today own a copy of the Holy Bible. Many people own several copies. As the *Wall Street Journal* (December 13, 2008) commented in an article titled "Profit Sharing: The Good Book Is the Best Seller,"

> It's an astonishing fact that year after year, the Bible is the best-selling book in America—even though 90% of the households already have at least one copy. The tremendous sales volume, an estimated 25 million copies sold each year is largely driven by innovation in design, color, style on the ultimate niche marketing.

Even though it is the most-printed, most-purchased, and most-translated book, with over forty companies printing it, it's the least understood and most talked about book in the world. *What exactly is the Bible, and why is it important?*

These are good questions that need to be answered. But not just any answers will do. Remember the analogy of the giant jigsaw puzzle mentioned in the Author's Statement. The correct answers must come straight from the pages of the Holy Bible and must be properly placed so that God's awesome picture emerges.

You owe it to yourself to know what the Holy Bible is all about. *Why?* Because it's the only book that is inspired by God, contains God's mind, and offers salvation to humanity.

What you are about to read is not my opinion or my interpretation of the Bible, because as you will find out for yourself throughout this book, the Bible interprets itself. Notice again: "Knowing this first, that no prophecy of Scripture is of any private interpretation, for prophecy never came by the will of man, but holy men of God spoke as they were moved by the Holy Spirit" (**2 Peter 1:20–21**).

This may come as a new truth to you, but no man or woman—no pastor, no reverend, no bishop, and no pope—can or has the authority to interpret the Bible. No one! That's what you just read. Your complete understanding of the Bible must come straight from the pages of your Bible, and each truth that you prove will have a deep impact on the way you live.

You need to prove what the Bible is for yourself. Many people base their religious beliefs on upbringing, hearsay, peer pressure, rumors, and false traditions. Most people do not take the time to really study into the matter for themselves and prove what is true. If you make the effort to thoroughly prove the subject matter for yourself and ask God for guidance, you will find and prove the truth. (We will discuss the word "truth" a little bit later in this book.)

If you do not own a Bible, I recommend that you purchase one. I personally use the New King James Version. Don't let the word "version" scare you. All Bibles say the same thing but in various ways, using different words, although the New International Version omits over 1,500 words. I prefer the New King James Version because it is written in modern English and is the closest translation to the original Hebrew in the Old Testament and Greek (mostly) in the New Testament. It makes for easy reading, but I do have copies of practically all other versions.

The word "Bible" comes from the ancient Latin word "Biblia" meaning "book" or "a collection of books." The word "Scriptures" also comes from the Latin derivative "scriptura," meaning "writings."

"Sacra" is also a Latin derivative, meaning "sacred." "Sacra" is often associated with "scriptura." Used together, they mean "sacred writings."

The Bible contains God's sacred writings, consisting of sixty-six books. It is divided into **two** main parts. **Part one** is called the Old Testament and contains thirty-nine books. It begins with the book of Genesis and ends with Malachi, although they are not in chronological order. The Old Testament was written in Hebrew. Hundreds of copies of the Old Testament have been found over time, with the most recent being the Dead Sea Scrolls, found circa 1947–1948. All texts are with little or no deviation of text from the Bible we have today.

Part two is called the New Testament and contains twenty-seven books. The New Testament is thought to have been written in Greek, although back around 1987, Professor George Howard of the University of Georgia began translating a version of the book of Matthew, found by archeologists, written in Hebrew. The Hebrew Matthew, as it is called, was preserved by a fourteenth-century Jew named Shem-Tob (*The Gospel of Matthew According to a Primitive Hebrew Text*, Howard, 1987). The New Testament begins with the book of Matthew and ends with Revelation.

The first English Bible translation was initiated by John Wycliffe in 1382 and completed by John Purvey in 1388. It takes about seventy hours to read the entire Bible, from Genesis to Revelation.

I challenge you to pick up your Bible and check for yourself what I've stated in this chapter. Remember that the Holy Bible challenges us to test its content! Read again **1 Thessalonians 5:21**, and believe what it says: "Test all things; hold fast what is good." The King James Version renders it, "Prove all things; hold fast that which is good." Both translations mean the same thing. We are to prove what the Bible says. That's what the Bible says about itself—"Prove me!"

The Holy Bible wants you to test it. And in this book, put it to the test we will. From the Bible's own pages, I have found **seven** important points on what the Bible is.

1. The Bible is the inspired Word of God. "All Scripture is given by inspiration of God, and is profitable for doctrine, for reproof, for correction, for instruction in righteousness, that the man of God may be complete, thoroughly equipped for every good work" (**2 Timothy 3:16–17**).

The phrase "inspiration of God" means the Bible was and is God-breathed or God-uttered. God inspired men like Moses, David, Isaiah, Daniel, Paul, and many others to write doctrine and instruction on how to properly live according to God's way of living, not man's way. Yes, the Bible was written by men but not just any men—only those who were specifically chosen and inspired by God to write exactly what He told them to write; Nothing more and nothing less and certainly without their own added interpretation (Reference **2 Peter 1:20–21**).

2. The Bible is God's written Word. It was written down by chosen people of God through time. God had them write the Bible for our learning and benefit. "For whatever things were written before were written for our learning, that we through the patience and comfort of the Scriptures might have hope" (**Romans 15:4**). *What hope should we have?* The hope of someday receiving eternal life from God. Take a look at **Titus 1:2**, which says, "in hope of eternal life which God, who cannot lie, promised before time began."

3. The Bible is truth. **John 17:17** further defines what God's Word is: "Sanctify them by Your truth. Your word is truth." To sanctify means "to set apart for a special purpose." God's people are set apart by His Word, and His Word is truth. The Holy Bible is written in ink and contains God's truths. There are no lies, cover-ups, or half-truths.

Now look at **Psalm 119:160**, "The entirety of Your word is truth, and every one of Your righteous judgments endures forever." God's entire Word, His entire Bible, is the truth. No other book contains

God's truth. That is what your Bible says. It is not what I say or believe that matters; it is what God says that matters. "All Scripture is given by inspiration of God, and is profitable for doctrine, for reproof, for correction, for instruction in righteousness" (**2 Timothy 3:16**).

Pilate, during Christ's trial, did not know what truth was, but you will know what truth is after reading it from your own Bible. The preceding clearly tells us that all Scripture is God's truth, and all Scripture is inspired by God. By the way, God can only tell the truth; He cannot lie. *Do you believe that?* Take a look at **Hebrews 6:18**, "That by two immutable things, in which it is impossible for God to lie, we might have strong consolation, who have fled for refuge to lay hold of the hope set before us." **2 Peter 1:21** tells us, "For prophecy never came by the will of man, but holy men of God spoke as they were moved by the Holy Spirit." Only holy men, called and chosen by God Himself, wrote His truth.

In addition to all Scripture being truth, Christ clearly stated that He was the way, the truth, and the life. "Jesus said to him [Thomas], 'I am the way, the truth, and the life. No one comes to the Father except through Me'" (**John 14:6**). This means that when Christ first came to earth, He lived by all the laws and principles found in the Bible. Christ personified the entire Bible by living by all of its principles, thereby living a perfect, sinless life. Christ lived, walked, and breathed the truth. The whole Bible is God's written truth, and His Son, Christ, personified that truth. Hence, Christ is the way, the truth, and the life. Furthermore, the Bible states that no one can come to know the Father except through Christ.

Even today, God tells humans that His truth is found in the Holy Bible and in studying the person of Christ, but most people still refuse to believe what He says. Remember **Titus 1:2**, "in hope of eternal life which God, who cannot lie, promised before time began."

Our hope, which will happen sometime in the future, is to be given the gift of immortal life through a resurrection (expounded upon later in this book). Since we do not have immortal life right now, we can only hope for it.

You may be thinking, *If God cannot lie, where did lying come from, and who spoke the first lie?* Turn to **John 8:44**, where Jesus is speaking to the scribes and Pharisees. "You [the scribes and Pharisees] are of your father the devil, and the desires of your father you want to do. He was a murderer from the beginning, and does not stand in the truth, because there is no truth in him. When he speaks a lie, he speaks from his own resources, for he [Satan, the Devil] is a liar and the father of it." Satan spoke the first lie to Adam and Eve and is therefore the father of lies. God cannot lie.

4. Since God is Holy, His written Word, the Bible, is Holy. That's why it is called the Holy Bible. Turn to **1 Peter 1:16**, which reads, "Because it is written, 'Be holy, for I am holy.'" Also, at the burning bush, God called Moses to speak with him on Mount Sinai. God told him to take off his shoes because the ground where he was standing was holy ground. *Why was the ground holy?* It was holy because God's presence was there. What God proclaims in His Holy Bible is also holy because His presence is in there too. "Then He [God] said, 'Do not draw near this place. Take your sandals off your feet, for the place where you stand is holy ground'" (**Exodus 3:5**).

5. God's Word, His Holy Bible, stands forever. This means that the Bible was never done away with, nor will it ever be. "The grass withers, the flower fades, But the word of our God stands forever" (**Isaiah 40:8**). Remember the Holy Bible is a very up-to-date old book. *Don't you find it surprising that it is still with us today, even after having been around for thousands of years?* Think of the people who lost their lives so that you and I could have a copy of the Bible! God does not want us to live without His "owner's manual," and He made sure that we have it. "Heaven and earth will pass away, but My words will by no means pass away" (**Matthew 24:35**). "For assuredly, I say to you, till heaven and earth pass away, one jot [a dot] or one tittle [the crossing of the letter "t"] will by no means pass

from the law till all is fulfilled" (**Matthew 5:18**). These are powerful words from a powerful God whose truthful words last forever!

6. God's Word, whether written or verbal, always accomplishes its mission. God compares His Word to rain coming down from heaven. Take a close look at the beautiful Scripture in **Isaiah 55:9–11**:

> For as the heavens are higher than the earth, so are My ways higher than your ways, and My thoughts than your thoughts. For as the rain comes down, and the snow from heaven, and do not return there, but water the earth, and make it bring forth and bud, that it may give seed to the sower, and bread to the eater, so shall My word be that goes forth from My mouth; It shall not return to Me void, but it shall accomplish what I please, and it shall prosper in the thing for which I sent it.

As the rain water's the earth, so God's Word waters us. It refreshes and allows us to grow spiritually. Both God's Word and rainwater always accomplish the mission they were sent for. Both never return empty to God.

7. God's Word is living and powerful. It is not dead or weak. God's Word is like a sharp two-edged sword that can discern our inner-most thoughts. "For the word of God is living and powerful, and sharper than any two-edged sword, piercing even to the division of soul and spirit, and of joints and marrow, and is a discerner of the thoughts and intents of the heart" (**Hebrews 4:12**).

As you can see, God's Holy Bible is the only book that offers us any hope for the future that we can truly count on. No man, no church, no organization, no science, no religion, no human government, and no technological advances can give us real hope, only Almighty God! The Holy Bible always tells us the truth, even if the truth hurts sometimes. The Holy Bible is God's instruction manual on how to live properly on this earth. The Holy Bible tells us how to nurture a strong relationship with the maker of the universe and humanity.

May God bless you as you seek God's instruction, revelation, and truth, which can only be found in your Holy Bible.

1.2 WHY SHOULD THE BIBLE BE IMPORTANT TO YOU?

Contained herein are **five** important **external** reasons and **internal** proofs (there are many more) on why the Bible should be important to you and why it is so different from other religious books. An external reason compares the Bible with all other books ever written. An internal proof measures the validity of the Bible's own content. Let's find out for ourselves, objectively, why this "book of books" is premier among all other books and why it should be important to you.

1. The Bible is considered first in literature. In other words, in the huge field of literature, the Bible stands alone—by far—among all other books ever written, both ancient and modern. The Holy Bible remains unsurpassed. The poetry, symbolism, various writing styles, prophesies, and accurate historical accounts add much to its literary genius, authenticity, and credibility.

2. The Bible is first in circulation. The Bible has been read by more people in more languages than any other book in human history. It has been translated in its entirety into more than four hundred languages, and portions of it have been translated into nearly 2,500 languages. According to the United Bible Society Scripture Language Report (2000), organizations distributed 633 million portions of Scripture in the year 2000. In 2001, Gideon International distributed more than 56 million complete copies of God's Word worldwide. That averages to more than one million

per week—that's 107 copies per minute. With a total circulation well past the ten billion mark.

3. The Bible is first in its influence—an influence on other books that is incalculable. More books have been written about the Bible and its content than on any other book ever written. More authors and poets quote the Bible more than any other source.

4. The Bible is first among religious writings. If you are wondering about the books on Eastern religions, let me quote Professor M. Montiero Williams from Oxford University. Dr Williams spent forty-two years of his life studying all of the Eastern religious books. His ultimate conclusion is this: "The Bible is preeminent. There is no book on the face of the earth that comes anywhere close. Saying that any book, anywhere, written by anyone, could on any level compare to the Bible would be a statement of ignorance" (theChristianExpositor.org). These are enlightening words from an expert in Eastern religions.

What about the Koran? The Koran is the Muslim holy book and consists of 113 chapters. It contains standards for personal, social, economic, religious, and political behavior. It is not a totally religious book. Muslims believe that the Koran supersedes all other revelation, including the Bible, although they do consider the first five books of the Bible as sacred. The Islam religion rejects Jesus as the Son of God, as well as rejecting His crucifixion, His resurrection, the forgiveness of sins, and that salvation is only available through Jesus, the Christ. **Acts 4:10–12** clearly says, "Let it be known to you all, and to all the people of Israel, that by the name of Jesus Christ of Nazareth, whom you crucified, whom God raised from the dead, by Him this man stands here before you whole. This is the 'stone which was rejected by you builders, which has become the chief cornerstone.' Nor is there salvation in any other, for there is no other name under heaven given among men by which we must be saved." The Koran clearly contradicts the Holy Bible.

What about the Book of Mormon? The Mormons use four standard works: The Book of Mormon, Doctrine and Covenants, the Pearl of Great Price, and the King James Bible. Out of these four works, only the Bible is considered by the Mormons to have corruptions and is accepted with qualifications. But notice what the Bible says in **2 Timothy 3:16**, "All Scripture is given by inspiration of God, and is profitable for doctrine, for reproof, for correction, for instruction in righteousness." *Where is all Scripture found?* All Scripture is found in your Holy Bible. Also, consider **Isaiah 40:8**, "The grass withers, the flower fades, but the word of our God stands forever." And **Isaiah 55:11**, "So shall My word be that goes forth from My mouth; It shall not return to Me void, but it shall accomplish what I please, and it shall prosper in the thing for which I sent it." No person or religion can add to or take away from the Holy Bible. "Whatever I command you, be careful to observe it; you shall not add to it nor take away from it" (**Deuteronomy 12:32**). "For I testify to everyone who hears the words of the prophecy of this book: If anyone adds to these things, God will add to him the plagues that are written in this book; and if anyone takes away from the words of the book of this prophecy, God shall take away his part from the Book of Life, from the holy city, and from the things which are written in this book" (**Revelation 22:18– 19**). Finally, **Matthew 24:35**, "Heaven and earth will pass away, but My words will by no means pass away." Clearly the god described by the Mormons, Muslims, and Eastern religious books is **not** the God of the Bible.

5. The Bible and archeology. Notice these comments by the famous archaeologist Nelson Glueck: "The manner in which archaeology has verified the historical accuracy of the Bible has been nothing short of remarkable!" Glueck continues, "It may be clearly stated categorically that no archaeological discovery has ever controverted [gone against] a single biblical reference. Scores of archaeological findings have been made which confirm in clear

outline or exact detail historical statements in the Bible" (Glueck, *Rivers in the Desert*, 136).

Glueck's comments echo the words of another prominent archaeologist, William F. Albright, who stated, "There can be no doubt that archeology has confirmed the substantial historicity of the Old Testament tradition ... the excessive skepticism shown toward the Bible by important historical schools of the 18th and 19th Century has been progressively discredited" (Glueck, 24–25).

Empires like Babylon, Medo-Persia, Greco-Macedonia and Rome have all been confirmed by historical references. Towns and cities like Nineveh, Jericho, Jerusalem, and Bethlehem have all been confirmed by historical references. Names of kings like Nebuchadnezzar of Babylon, Cyrus of Persia, King Darius of Media, King David of Israel, and many others have been confirmed in archeological finds. There are many more confirmations, too numerous to mention here, but you can research the matter yourself in countless Bible dictionaries, encyclopedia, atlases, and handbooks, such as the *Biblical Archaeology Review*. There, you will find confirmation of biblical accounts from many external sources.

Now let's take a close look at **five** of the **internal** proofs of why our Bible is more important than the rest of the religious books of the world. I encourage you to read the Scriptures found herein from your own Bible.

1. The Bible and prophecy. Prophecy means to prophesy a future event well in advance, before it comes to fruition. God inspired His prophets to write prophecy on important upcoming events. Prophecy is not a human lucky guess; rather, it's a circumstance or an event that God tells us is sure to happen. It may happen quickly, or it may take years for that prophecy to be fulfilled. Some prophecies were written many years before they came to pass.

There also is a duality in almost all prophecy in the Bible. This means that a prophetic event may occur two times. An example of this is the first man, Adam; then there is the second Adam, Christ. "For since by man [Adam] came death, by Man [Christ] also came the resurrection of the dead. For as in Adam all die, even so in Christ all shall be made alive. But each one in his own order: Christ the first fruits, afterward those who are Christ's at His coming" (**1 Corinthians 15:21–23**).

When God's Word says it, an event will take place regardless of whether or not you believe His Word. In **2 Peter 1:19-21**, God inspired Peter to write: "And so we have the prophetic word confirmed, which you do well to heed as a light that shines in a dark place, until the day dawns and the morning star rises in your hearts; knowing this first, that no prophecy of Scripture is of any private interpretation, for prophecy never came by the will of man, but holy men of God spoke as they were moved by the Holy Spirit."

There are many prophecies throughout the Old and New Testaments. We will analyze **four** prophecies, all having to do with Jesus the Christ. Notice especially how precise and specific each of the prophecies came to be fulfilled.

A. In **Isaiah 9:6**, it states that the Christ, the Messiah, would be born as a boy. The book of Isaiah was written about one thousand years before Christ's birth. Yet look at the startling accuracy of this prophecy. This is a well-known Scripture, but I wonder how many people understand its significance. "For unto us a Child is born, unto us a Son is given; And the government will be [future tense] upon His shoulder." Notice that a Son is to be born, and the government will be on His shoulders. *Which government will be on His shoulders?* The government or kingdom of God will be on Christ's shoulders. Christ will have direct responsibility to set up a future world-ruling government right here on earth! Amazing!

"And His name will be [future tense] called Wonderful, Counselor, Mighty God, Everlasting Father, Prince of Peace. Of the increase of His government and peace There will be no end, upon the throne of David and over His kingdom, to order it and establish it with judgment and justice from that time forward, even forever. The zeal of the LORD of hosts will perform this" (**Isaiah 9:6–7**). Notice the duality: Christ was born [past tense]; Christ will come again [future] to fulfill His leadership role in God's kingdom, mentioned above.

B. The Bible states precisely that the Messiah would be born of a virgin. "Therefore, the Lord Himself will give you a sign: Behold, the virgin shall conceive and bear a Son, and shall call His name Immanuel" (**Isaiah 7:14**). "Immanuel" means "God with us." Christ was miraculously conceived by the Holy Spirit and born of Mary, a virgin. While living on earth, Jesus was both God and man and was living with or among us. Hence, the name Immanuel.

C. The Bible tells us that Christ was to be born in Bethlehem. "But you, Bethlehem Ephrathah, though you are little among the thousands of Judah, yet out of you shall come forth to Me the One to be [future tense] Ruler in Israel, whose goings forth are from of old, from everlasting" (**Micah 5:2**). Notice that a future world ruler—Christ—would be born in the small, insignificant little town of Bethlehem. His goings forth were of old, and yet He is everlasting.

D. David prophesied that Christ would be worshipped by kings and those who dwell in the wilderness by bringing Him gifts. "Those who dwell in the wilderness will bow before Him, and His enemies will lick the dust. The kings of Tarshish and of the isles will bring presents; The kings of Sheba and Seba will offer gifts. Yes, all kings shall fall down before Him; All nations shall serve Him" (**Psalm 72:9–11**). This prophecy was partially fulfilled at Christ's birth by the wise men bringing gifts but won't be completely fulfilled until He returns to earth as King of Kings and Lord of Lords.

"And He shall live; And the gold of Sheba will be given to Him; Prayer also will be made for Him continually, and daily He shall be praised" (**Psalm 72:15**). Consider where Christ will stand at His return. "And in that day [the day of His second coming] His feet will stand on the Mount of Olives, which faces Jerusalem on the east. And the Mount of Olives shall be split in two, from east to west, making a very large valley; Half of the mountain shall move toward the north and half of it toward the south" (**Zechariah 14:4**).

Are all of these prophecies about Christ lucky guesses or just coincidences, or was the Bible really inspired by Almighty God, who declares the "end from the beginning?" Take a look at **Isaiah 45:21**, "Tell and bring forth your case; Yes, let them take counsel together. Who has declared this from ancient time? Who has told it from that time? Have not I, the lord? And there is no other God besides Me, a just God and a Savior; There is none besides Me."

2. The Bible is the one and only book that speaks with the authority of God Himself. Reread **Isaiah 45:21**, above. God tells us that He is God and that there is no one else but Him. These are powerful words that speak with full authority. "'I am the Alpha and the Omega, the Beginning and the End,' says the Lord, 'who is and who was and who is to come, the Almighty'" (**Revelation 1:8**). Not only is God all-knowing, all-powerful, and everlasting, but He says, through His Holy Bible, that even His words are everlasting and will not pass away. His words last forever and cannot be broken. Talk about authority. "Heaven and earth will pass away, but My words will by no means pass away" (**Matthew 24:35**). The Bible is the one and only Holy Book in the entire world that speaks with great supernatural authority.

3. The Bible and its authors are in total agreement with one another. Forty separate people—with various backgrounds, personalities, and characteristics—were inspired by God to write His Holy Bible, and they all are in agreement! Some were shepherds; others were kings, tax collectors, physicians, fishermen, and true prophets of God. That these people lived over a span of 1,500 years makes the Holy Bible truly important and remarkable. Today, it's difficult to get two people who witnessed an accident at the same time to agree on the details. Think about that. *How do you get forty different people, from various walks of life, separated by over fifteen hundred years, to write a book and agree on the religious subject matter?* Two people who go to the same church often can't agree on church doctrine. *How did all the Bible writers agree?* The answer is that all the chosen authors were writing down things that came from one source—Almighty God!

4. The Bible is the only book that offers the gift of everlasting life.

> Jesus answered and said to her, "If you knew the gift of God, and who it is who says to you, 'Give Me a drink,' you would have asked Him, and He would have given you living water." The woman said to Him, "Sir, You have nothing to draw with, and the well is deep. Where then do You get that living water? Are You greater than our father Jacob, who gave us the well, and drank from it himself, as well as his sons and his livestock?" Jesus answered and said to her, "Whoever drinks of this water will thirst again, but whoever drinks of the water that I shall give him will never thirst. But the water that I shall give him will become in him a fountain of water springing up into everlasting life" (**John 4:10–14**).

Notice that Christ tells the woman that if they drink of His water (walk His way of life and obey His commandments), they will never thirst again, meaning they will be given everlasting life. As humans, we all require water, but as spirit beings, we will never thirst again!

5. The Bible can have a positive impact on the quality of your life, if you approach reading and studying it with a sincere heart. "For the Word of God [the Holy Bible] is living and powerful, and sharper than any two-edged sword, piercing even to the division of soul and spirit, and of joints and marrow, and is a discerner of the thoughts and intents of the heart" (**Hebrews 4:12**). When you pick up your Bible with a sincere heart to learn what God has to say to you, it will grip you and change your life for the better.

Have you been gripped by the Bible? Have you opened your heart and allowed God's truths to penetrate your thinking and change you? If you read it, believe it, and do what God says to do, you will see positive changes in your life.

I will end this section of the book with **two** timely Scriptures—one from the New Testament and one from the Old Testament—that I hope you will take to heart. "But He [Christ] answered and said, 'It is written, "Man shall not live by bread alone, but by every word that proceeds from the mouth of God"'" (**Matthew 4:4**). The words that proceed from the mouth of God are found only in the Holy Bible. "The fear [respect] of the LORD is the beginning of wisdom; A good understanding have all those who do His commandments. His praise endures forever" (**Psalm 111:10**). *Aren't God's commandments found in the Holy Bible? Are you doing them?*

1.3   WHY IS THE BIBLE GOOD FOR YOU?

By now you should have clear biblical answers as to what the Bible is. But maybe the real questions you have been wrestling with are *"Why should the Bible be important to me?"* and *"Can the Bible really help me in everyday living?"*

As you begin reading, studying, and understanding the Bible, you'll find almost every facet of information essential to human living in God's Word. This is because God loves you and does not want you to be without anything you need to experience a happy, wholesome life. "So that the servant of God is equipped for every good work" (**2 Timothy 3:17**). What you need to know to live an abundant life is found in the Holy Bible. "For God so loved the world [people] that He gave His only begotten Son, that whoever believes in Him should not perish but have everlasting life" (**John 3:16**). It is important to note that God loved us before we loved Him. "We love Him because He first loved us" (**1 John 4:19**). The only way to be happy in this life and receive the gift of the Holy Spirit is to love God and do all of His commandments. "For this is the love of God, that we keep His commandments. And His commandments are not burdensome" (**1 John 5:3**).

Psalm 19:7–11 provides the **seven** answers to our questions in this section. The Bible, which contains God's law, is important because:

1. "The law of the LORD is perfect, converting the soul" (**Psalm 19:7**). The Bible converts the soul. God's law is so all-encompassing, so multifaceted, and so perfect that it changes (for the better) the soul. Criminals have been changed by God's Word. They have been transformed and set free, spiritually and emotionally, while still within prison walls. Broken marriages that were far gone have been put back together and brought to a place of total harmony, simply by studying God's Word and obeying it. I have seen addiction broken, depression lifted, people healed, and families restored by the Word of God, the Holy Bible.

2. "The testimony of the LORD is sure, making wise the simple" (**Psalm 19:7**). The phrase "testimony of the Lord" means bearing witness of the things God has done for you in your life. You may not realize it, but God has done many wonderful things in your life. *Have you ever recovered from an illness? Have you or someone you know*

ever overcome an obstacle that you thought was insurmountable? Have you ever landed a great job that you did not think you would even qualify for? These are all "testimonies of the Lord," which are things that God has done for you. The fact that you are alive is a testimony of the Lord. Another testimony is that God sent His only begotten Son to this earth to die for everyone's sins, so that you and I could someday live again as spirit beings. *Are you thankful to God for all of these things?* The testimonies of the Lord are so sure, so reliable that they can make simple people wise and skilled at daily living.

A simple person is not very smart in the eyes of this world, but to God, a simple person is a humble person, yielding his whole life to God. The Bible says that God promises to make the simple people wise. *And where do you get wisdom?* You receive wisdom from God when you respect and honor Him.

"The fear of the lord is the beginning of wisdom; A good understanding have all those who do His commandments. His praise endures forever" (**Psalm 111:10**). "The fear of the lord is the beginning of knowledge, but fools despise wisdom and instruction" (**Proverbs 1:7**). "The fear of the lord is the beginning of wisdom, and the knowledge of the Holy One is understanding" (**Proverbs 9:10**). The word fear can also be translated as "having respect for." Respecting God is the beginning of wisdom. Again, the Holy Bible makes simple people wise in the things of God. *Is God allowing you to understand His words today?*

3. "The statutes of the Lord are right, rejoicing the heart" (**Psalm 19:8**). The phrase "statutes of the Lord" are God's rulings or His principles for daily living, and God says, "They are right." You know, there is a certain joy that comes to a human heart when it rightly understands what the Holy Bible says.

Now look at what **Jeremiah 15:16** says about God's Word and your happiness: "Your words were found, and I ate them [meaning to fully understand and apply God's Word], and Your word was to me the joy and rejoicing of my heart; For I am called by Your name, O LORD God of hosts." To eat God's words means to apply and make them part of your life. That's what Jeremiah was inspired to write. Applying God's words should make you joyful.

4. "The commandment of the LORD is pure, enlightening the eyes" (**Psalm 19:8**). Sad but true, the world we live in is very dark. All around us difficult, perplexing, painful things happen to people, and most people have no idea why it happens. They are in the dark. People in the dark are those who value what is worthless and disdain what is priceless. These are people who wink at perversity and wince at morality. Those who embrace foolishness and reject true wisdom are the "wise of the world." If you ask them why there is so much suffering in the world, they will undoubtedly blame God for it. Or they may say, "If there was a God, He would stop all the suffering." The real reason why this world is in such a mess is simply because the wise of the world never consulted the Holy Bible for true answers. They have forgotten their God and the enlightened words from His Bible. They have essentially kicked God out of their schools, homes, and lives in such a way that a person cannot even pray in a public place.

God and His Holy Word is what dispels darkness and confusion and gives light to our paths. The phrase "the commandment of the Lord is pure" means that His commandments are so radiant, so absent from any impurities that they bring brightness into every human heart and into this dark world as a whole. "Your word is a lamp to my feet and a light to my path" (**Psalm 119:105**). Just think: if just the Ten Commandments (not the "ten suggestions") were dutifully kept by everyone, how much a better place would this world be to live in. No lying, no murder, no stealing, no killing, no adultery. This world would most definitely be a better place to live.

5. "The judgments of the LORD are true and righteous altogether" (**Psalm 19:9**). The Bible is true and righteous, through and through. "Sanctify them [set your people apart] by Your truth. Your word is truth" (**John 17:17**). God cannot lie, and what He says is the truth. "For this reason we also thank God without ceasing, because when you received the word of God which you heard from us, you welcomed it not as the word of men, but as it is in truth, the word of God, which also effectively works in you who believe" (**1 Thessalonians 2:13**). "Then He who sat on the throne said, 'Behold, I make all things new.' And He said to me, 'Write, for these words are true and faithful'" (**Revelation 21:5**). And God Himself is righteous. "Your righteousness is like the great mountains; Your judgments are a great deep; o lord, You preserve man and beast" (**Psalm 36:6**). "Let the heavens declare His righteousness, for God Himself is Judge. Selah" (**Psalm 50:6**). Both God and His judgments are true and righteous. So says your Bible!

6. "More to be desired are they then gold, Yea, than much fine gold; Sweeter also than honey and the honeycomb" (**Psalm 19:10**). The Bible is more precious than fine gold. "How sweet are Your words to my taste, Sweeter than honey to my mouth!" (**Psalm 119:103**). This means that God's Word will satisfy you much more than any earthly things that you might be tempted with. *How happy are most Hollywood stars? Are most stars happy and satisfied with their luxurious lives?* Just look at their divorce rate. I say no! Without God's Word, a person cannot be truly happy.

7. "Moreover, by them Your servant is warned, and in keeping them there is great reward" (**Psalm 19:11**). God's Word warns us of the dangers of lying, stealing, and committing adultery in this life. But observing God's commandments is rewarding now and in the hereafter. "Rejoice and be exceedingly glad, for great is your reward in heaven, for so they persecuted the prophets who were before you" (**Matthew 5:12**). If we read and do as the Bible instructs, not

only will we be happier people on this earth, but we also will happily enter into God's kingdom as immortal spirit beings. What a reward God has in store for each of us, if only we obey His holy Word, the Bible. "Beloved, now we are children of God; and it has not yet been revealed what we shall be [future tense], but we know that when He is revealed, we shall be like Him, for we shall see Him as He is" (**1 John 3:2**). "Then the seventh angel sounded: And there were loud voices in heaven, saying, 'The kingdoms of this world have become the kingdoms of our Lord and of His Christ, and He shall reign forever and ever!'" (**Revelation 11:15**). Finally, "And behold, I am coming quickly, and My reward is with Me, to give to everyone according to his work" (**Revelation 22:12**).

The Bible should be important to you, but it also is essential in building a relationship with God. In truth, the Bible is good for all humanity, if people would just believe and do what it says. As the old saying goes, "You can't buy happiness," but the Bible freely gives it to you, if you take what it says to heart. "In this you greatly rejoice, though now for a little while, if need be, you have been grieved by various trials, that the genuineness of your faith, being much more precious than gold that perishes, though it is tested by fire, may be found to praise, honor, and glory at the revelation of Jesus Christ, whom having not seen you love. Though now you do not see Him, yet believing, you rejoice with joy inexpressible and full of glory" (**1 Peter 1:6–8**). Truly, understanding and observing the whole Word of God brings happiness and great rewards. This is another piece of the giant jigsaw puzzle we just put in place.

Chapter 2
GOD'S TRUTH ABOUT GOD

2.1 UNDERSTANDING THE ONENESS OF GOD

Most people have their own opinions about God and how many beings there are in the Godhead. They assume their opinions are correct because of the teachings from their parents, teachers, faiths, ministers, priests, and friends. Some people only go with what's popular in beliefs these days. Others seem to be indifferent to know about God and have become willingly ignorant of this most important piece of the giant "jigsaw puzzle." Still others say, "God just doesn't seem real to me." In general, God seems to be a mystery.

What about you? What do you know about God? Has God always existed? Does God consist of one, two, or three persons? Don't just assume; you must know the true answers to these important questions. True answers come directly from the Holy Bible, with no human interpretation. As we will soon discover, God does reveal Himself to us in His Word, the Bible. In this chapter, I hope to make God very real to you by using Scriptures from the Bible. You see, God wants you and me to know Him as He reveals Himself to us through Scripture.

The Bible makes it very plain that there is one Lord, and there is one God. "Jesus answered him, 'The first of all the commandments is: "Hear, O Israel, the LORD our God, the LORD is one"'" (**Mark 12:29**). Compare this to **Deuteronomy 6:4**. "Hear, O Israel: The LORD our God, the LORD is one!" It plainly tells us that the Lord is "One." Also, the apostle Paul clearly tells us that God is one. "Therefore, concerning the eating of things offered to idols, we know that an idol is nothing in the world, and that there is no other God but one" (**1 Corinthians 8:4**). And again in **1 Timothy 2:5**, the Bible clearly states, "For there is one God and one Mediator between God and men, the Man Christ Jesus."

But many people do not fully comprehend how the Bible uses the word "one." This very fact contributes to the confusion about God. *How should we understand the "oneness" of God?* There are **four** important examples on how the Bible uses the word "one." Again, this is what God's Word says.

1. The Bible refers to two human beings, male together with a female, as one flesh. Let's go back after the creation of Adam and Eve, where we see the institution of the marriage covenant. Covenant means an agreement between God and man. "Therefore, a man shall leave his father and mother and be joined to his wife, and they shall become one flesh" (**Genesis 2:24**). Notice that two separate human beings, a male together with a female, become "one flesh" in a marital sexual union. Separate DNA substances from a man and woman combine together at conception to produce a new, unique human being. Therefore, the Bible considers two separate people, a man and a woman, united in marriage, as one flesh.

2. The congregation of Israel was gathered together as one man. "So, all the children of Israel came out, from Dan to Beersheba, as well as from the land of Gilead, and the congregation gathered together as one man before the LORD at Mizpah. ... so, all the people arose as one man, saying, 'None of us will go to his tent, nor will any turn back to his house;'... so all the men of Israel were gathered against the city, united together as one man." (**Judges 20:1, 8, 11**). For once, the entire nation of Israel was wholly unified in purpose and goal to meet a serious problem. Of course, there still remained many individual citizens of the same nation, but they tackled the problem "as one man." The phrase "as one man" refers

to the entire nation of Israel, which was fully united in purpose and goal to combat the problem. The Bible, then, considers an entire nation united in goal and purpose "as one man." Many people make up a nation, but when united in purpose and goal, the people become one.

3. The Holy Bible refers to many members in a church as one church. Notice what the apostle Paul says to the church in Galatia: "There is neither Jew nor Greek, there is neither slave nor free, there is neither male nor female; for you are all one in Christ Jesus" (**Galatians 3:28**). Paul says that all the church members are all "one in Christ." Consider also how Paul compares the parts of a human body to the members in a church. "For by one Spirit we were all one body—whether Jews or Greeks, whether slaves or free—and have all been made to drink into one Spirit. For in fact the body is not one member but many ... But now indeed there are many members, yet one body. ... Now you are the body of Christ, and members individually" (**1 Corinthians 12:13–14, 20, 27**). The one true church of God is referred to as the "body of Christ," composed of many members yet one body. Thus, all church members joined together become one in purpose and goal.

4. The Holy Bible clearly states that there is one God but composed of two separate spirit beings, the Father and the Son. Since God is composed of the Father and the Son, this makes God a family. Just as a human family consists of a father and a son, so is the God family. Notice in **John 17:3**, where Christ prayed to the Father. "And this is eternal life, that they [people] may know You [the Father], the only true God, and Jesus Christ whom You have sent." This clearly shows that there is only one God family, composed of two separate and distinct God beings. Christ is separate and distinct from the Father, yet they are one in purpose and goal. Notice the awesome prayer that Christ prayed just before His crucifixion:

> I do not pray for these alone [people who believe], but also for those who will believe in Me through their word; that they all may be one, as You, Father, are in Me, and I in You; that they also may be one in Us, that the world may believe that You sent Me. And the glory which You gave Me I have given them, that they may be one just as We are one: I in them, and You in Me; that they may be made perfect in one, and that the world may know that You have sent Me, and have loved them as You have loved Me (**John 17:20-23**).

Just as the Father and Christ are "One" in goal and purpose, they want their family, the church, to be one also. "I and My Father are one" (**John 10:30**). We see then that the Father and Christ are one, in the same sense as members of the church are to be one—one in purpose, belief, direction, faith, spirit, and attitude, all joined together by the Holy Spirit. The Father and Christ, then, are two separate spirit beings but both members of the same divine family with the same goal and purpose. Their goal and purpose is to save humanity and build a spiritual family.

In all of the above examples, the Bible is very clear on the biblical meaning of oneness. We should strive to reflect the love and unity of the divine family—God the Father and His Son, Jesus—in our marriages, family relationships, and daily lives.

Understanding the oneness of God allows us to correctly place another important piece of the giant jigsaw puzzle found in your Bible.

2.2   IS GOD A TRINITY?

The belief that there is one God made up of three separate divine beings is one of the central doctrines in today's modern Christian religion. Most Christians—Protestants and Catholics alike—believe in the "Trinity." Since so many people believe in the concept of the Trinity, one would think that it is readily found in the pages of the

31

Holy Bible. Yet, neither the word Trinity nor the Trinity doctrine is found in the Bible. Even *The New Catholic Encyclopedia* (1967, Vol. XIV, 299) states, "The trinity is a doctrine from about the year 325 AD, based partly on pagan, older triune gods. It is not in the Bible unless you really, really stretch it to fit. 'The Father, the Word, and the Holy Ghost [Spirit]: and these three are one' has been expunged in the Revised Standard Version of 1952 and 1971 and in many other Bibles, as it was a gross error that had encroached on the Greek text according to the Doctors of Divinity of the Church."

As we have already seen and proved through the Bible, the personages of the Father and the Son are clearly expressed throughout Scripture. But the so-called "third person of the Trinity" is an extremely nebulous concept. We are clearly introduced to two personages in the God family: The Word God and God the Father: "In the beginning was the Word and the Word was with God, and the Word was God" (**John 1:1**). Here would have been the most logical place to introduce all three of the divine personages. Yet the apostle John did not mention the Holy Spirit as part of the God family, a Trinity, or a third person. It is just not there! Check it out for yourself.

If someone asked you for biblical evidence of the Trinity, would you have proof to support your belief? And what exactly is the Holy Spirit of God, if it is not a person? I want to provide you with **three** solid reasons as to why the Holy Spirit cannot be the third person of the God family.

1. The Bible clearly tells us that the Holy Spirit is an "it." The Holy Spirit is not a male or female but is gender-neutral. Turn to **Acts 2:2–3**, where the Holy Spirit is translated correctly as an "it." "And suddenly there came a sound from heaven, as of a rushing mighty wind and **it** [not he or she] filled the whole house where they were sitting. Then there appeared to them divided tongues, as of fire, and one [one of these tongues of fire] sat upon each of them and they were all filled with the Holy Spirit and began to speak in other tongues [languages] as the Spirit gave them utterance." In

the Scripture above, the Holy Spirit of God is clearly referred to as being like the wind or fire, which gave people power to speak various languages (not gibberish). The Holy Spirit is not masculine or feminine in gender but, like the words wind and fire, is gender-neutral and translated as "it."

However, in the book of John, specifically in chapters 14, 15, and 16, Jesus is recorded as referring to the Holy Spirit as the "comforter;" the "parakletos," in Greek. Parakletos is gender-neutral but was incorrectly translated as "he" in English: "he teaches," "he comforts," "he admonishes," instead of being translated as: "it teaches," "it comforts," and "it admonishes." In these instances, the Holy Spirit of God was personified as "he." To make the personification error clearer, I would like to give you **two** examples of translating a phrase from Italian (my native language) to English:

A. Nouns ending with the letter "o" in Italian are masculine; the article in Italian is "il" translated "the." "Il libro" should be correctly translated as "the book."

But a translator who is not fluent with translation rules could easily mistranslate "libro" as a masculine noun—because it ends with an "o"—when, in reality, "book" should be correctly translated as "it"—gender-neutral.

For example, if you want to say "It [the book] is beautiful," in Italian, you would translate it as "esso e bello." Again, because "esso" and "bello" end in "o," this phrase could easily be mistranslated to read, "He is beautiful"—in this case, "book" is erroneously personified as "he" instead of "it." *Is the book a "he?"* Of course not! The book is an "it" and gender-neutral. This is precisely what happened in the translation of the Holy Spirit. In Italian and many other romance languages, the Holy Spirit is translated as "spirito santo"—translated as "he" because the words end with an "o." As in the example of the word "book," the Holy Spirit should be correctly translated as an "'it."

B. Feminine nouns end in an "a" in Italian use the article "la" for the word "the." "La finestra" should be correctly translated as "the window."

But a translator who is not fluent with translation rules could easily mistranslate "finestra" as feminine because it ends with an "a," when in reality, "finestra" should be correctly translated as "it"—gender-neutral.

If you want to say, "It [the window] is small," in Italian, you would translate it as, "Essa e piccola." Because "essa" and "piccola" both end in "a," the window may seem feminine in gender to a translator. *Is the window a "she?"* Of course not! The window is an "it"—gender-neutral.

Scriptures referring to God's Holy Spirit in John 14, 15, and 16 all were erroneously personified as a "he." Translators are apt to make these mistakes, not Almighty God. But God has allowed the mistranslations to continue for some reason.

Personifications are also found elsewhere in the Bible. In **Proverbs 9:1**, the word "wisdom" is personified as feminine. "Wisdom has built her house, she has hewn out her seven pillars…" *Is wisdom female?* Of course not! Wisdom is an "it" and a gift from God.

The word "church" in the Bible also is personified as "she." **Revelation 12:14** states that the true church will flee into the wilderness, where "she will be nourished for a time, times and a half time." Here, the church is personified as a woman who will be nourished during a time of great trouble just ahead of us. This particular church will be Christ's bride, a chaste and pure "lady." View **Ephesians 5:27**, "that He might present her to Himself a glorious church, not having spot or wrinkle or any such thing, but that she should be holy and without blemish."

Revelation 17:3–4 speaks of a great false church, also personified as a woman, "sitting on a scarlet beast." Take a look at verses 3–4: "So he carried me away in the Spirit into the wilderness. And I saw a woman sitting on a scarlet beast which was full of names of blasphemy, having seven heads and ten horns. The woman was arrayed in purple and scarlet, and adorned with gold and precious stones and pearls, having in her hand a golden cup full of abominations and the filthiness of her fornication." *Is this great false church an actual woman?* Of course not! The word church in both instances was erroneously personified as a woman.

Even to this day, we personify things like cars ("She's a great ol' heap") or boats and cruise ships ("She crossed the Atlantic in only five days"). Of course, cars and boats are not feminine or masculine but gender-neutral. They are things.

Incidentally, John is the only writer in the New Testament who uses the Greek word "parakletos" for the Holy Spirit. Matthew, Mark, Luke and Paul use the Greek word "pneuma" for spirit, and it is gender-neutral, correctly translated as "it."

Interestingly enough, in the Old Testament, the Hebrew word for spirit is "rauch"—*and guess what?* It is feminine in gender and translated as "she." *Is the Holy Spirit a she?* Of course not! All of the foregoing results in the phrase "Holy Spirit" being translated as all three genders. *Which gender is it, and how could this have happened?* As with any translation, if the translator was not fluent in a language or did not know how to correctly apply all the rules of translating—or simply wanted to promote a false theory of the Trinity—that person could have the Holy Spirit mistranslated to read "he" or "she."

But the Holy Spirit of God is His "power" that He uses to make things happen. "For I will not dare to speak of any of those things which Christ has not accomplished through me, in word and deed, to make the Gentiles obedient—in mighty signs and wonders, by the power of the Spirit of God, so that from Jerusalem and round about to Illyricum I have fully preached the gospel of Christ" (**Romans 15:18–19**). And "concerning His Son Jesus Christ our Lord, who was born of the seed of David according to the flesh, and declared to be the Son of God with power according to the Spirit of holiness, by the resurrection from the dead. Through Him we have received grace and apostleship for obedience to the faith among all nations for His name" (**Romans 1:3–5**).

2. The Holy Spirit cannot be a person because if it were, we would find Christ praying to the wrong "god" throughout His entire

human life. Christ always prayed to the Father, never to the Holy Spirit. In **Matthew 1:20** Joseph finds out, "For that which is conceived in her [Mary] is of the Holy Spirit."

If Christ was conceived by the Holy Spirit, and the Holy Spirit was the third person of the Trinity, wouldn't that make the Holy Spirit Christ's true father? Shouldn't Christ have prayed to the third person, the Holy Spirit? Yet, we find Christ always praying to God the Father. *Was Christ praying to the wrong person throughout His whole life on earth?* No! Christ knew full well what He was doing in praying to God the Father. He knew that God the Father used His divine power to miraculously impregnate Mary so He could be conceived through her. The Holy Bible makes this plain. God the Father is Christ's true Father, not the third person of the so-called Trinity.

Sometimes, Christians cite **Matthew 28:19** to justify their theory of the Trinity; specifically, the third person. Here, Christ, speaking to the apostles, says, "Baptizing them in the name of the Father, and of the Son and of the Holy Spirit, teaching them to observe all things I have commanded you." The above Scripture does not say that the Holy Spirit is a person. It says that people are baptized "in the name" of the Father, Son and Holy Spirit. So, why are we baptized in the name of the Father?

We are baptized "in the name" of the Father because everything in heaven and earth is in the Father's name. "For this reason I bow my knees to the Father of our Lord Jesus Christ, from whom the whole family in heaven and earth is named" (**Ephesians 3:14–15**).

We are baptized in the Son's name because Christ died for all of us. "For I delivered to you first of all that which I also received: that Christ died for our sins according to the Scriptures" (**1 Corinthians 15:3**).

We are baptized in the name of the Holy Spirit because it too must have a name. It (Holy Spirit) allows us to become begotten sons of God. "The Spirit Himself [correctly translated, "Itself"] bears witness with our spirit that we are children of God, and if children, then heirs— heirs of God and joint heirs with Christ, if indeed we suffer with Him (Christ), that we may also be glorified together" (**Romans 8:16–17**).

3. The Holy Spirit cannot be a person because Paul, in all his letters to the various churches of God, does not greet the Holy Spirit as a person at all. Paul's standard greeting to God's churches is "Grace be unto you from God the Father and the Lord Jesus Christ." Read each one of Paul's greetings to the churches. You'll find that the Holy Spirit is consistently left out, which would be considered blasphemy. *Would Paul blaspheme the Holy Spirit?* Of course not! If he did, he would have committed the unpardonable sin. "Assuredly, I say to you, all sins will be forgiven the sons of men, and whatever blasphemies they may utter; but he who blasphemes against the Holy Spirit never has forgiveness, but is subject to eternal condemnation" (**Mark 3:28–29**).

The only place where Paul mentions the Holy Spirit is in **2 Corinthians 13:14** and only in connection with fellowship, not in the opening greetings to the churches. "The grace of the Lord Jesus Christ, and the love of God, and the communion of the Holy Spirit be with you all. Amen." True Christians should commune (come together) to worship God in spirit and in truth. True Christians also commune and fellowship with one another and God, using the divine power of His Holy Spirit. Remember the Holy Spirit is a special gift from God that is freely given to those who repent of their sins and are baptized. "Then Peter said to them, 'Repent, and let every one of you be baptized in the name of Jesus Christ for the remission of sins; and you shall receive the gift of the Holy Spirit'" (**Acts 2:38**).

2 Peter 1:2–3 tells us exactly what the Holy Spirit is: "Grace and peace be multiplied to you in the knowledge of God and of Jesus our Lord, as His divine power has given to us all that pertain to life and godliness, through the knowledge of Him who called us by glory and virtue." The divine power of God is His Holy Spirit, and it is an "it." It's not a he or she or any person.

In **Psalm 104:30**, David tells us that God uses His divine power to create and renew. "You send forth Your Spirit, they are created; And You renew the face of the earth." Remember Mary was impregnated by the power of God's Holy Spirit. Jesus became God the Father's Son by the use of God's power.

Out of sheer desperation, mainstream Christians turn to **1 John 5:7-8** to try to justify their Trinity theory. "For there are three that bear witness in heaven: the Father, the Word, and the Holy Spirit; and these three are one." At first glance, this Scripture seems to prove the Trinity theory, but the information in the margin of my Bible says, "omit the words from 'in heaven' **verse 7** through 'on earth' **verse 8**." In other words, **verse 7** should be totally omitted from the New Testament because it is not found in the original Greek. Further evidence shows **verse 7** is not found in the Phillips, Revised Standard Version, Williams, or Living Bible (paraphrased) translations. Obviously, someone wanted to promote the Trinity doctrine and handwrote **verse 7** in the margin of the 1688 Bible.

Verse 7, then, should be totally omitted, and **verse 8** should correctly read, "And there are three that bear witness on earth: the Spirit, the water, and the blood; and these three agree as one." The words Spirit, water, and blood are originally translated from the Greek. All three are gender-neutral, and all three should be translated as "it."

*But why do these **three** words: Spirit, water and blood "bear witness on earth?"* Let the Bible answer the question.

1. God's Holy Spirit bears witness with our human spirit, in that we are begotten sons of God. "The Spirit Himself [itself] bears witness with our spirit that we are children of God" (**Romans 8:16**).

2. The water bears witness of our baptism. "Or do you not know that as many of us as were baptized into Christ Jesus were baptized into His death? Therefore, we were buried with Him through baptism into death, that just as Christ was raised from the dead by the glory of the Father, even so we also should walk in newness of life" (**Romans 6:3–4**).

3. The blood bears witness of Christ's death. "But God demonstrates His own love toward us, in that while we were still sinners, Christ

died for us. Much more then, having now been justified by His blood, we shall be saved from wrath through Him" (**Romans 5:8–9**).

As we have thoroughly seen and proved, the third person cannot be a person in the Godhead at all. Therefore, the Trinity theory has no basis in biblical fact. The Holy Spirit is, in fact, God's divine power that He uses to: create, renew, conceive, beget, and commune. Besides all this evidence, the word "Trinity" is not found anywhere in the Holy Bible.

If one believes in the theory of the Trinity, then he shuts the door on God's real purpose for creating humanity, which is to bring many sons and daughters into His spirit family. "For it was fitting for Him, for whom are all things and by whom are all things, in bringing many sons to glory, to make the captain of their salvation perfect through sufferings" (**Hebrews 2:10**).

What you have just read provided three solid reasons as to why the Trinity does not exist in the Bible. But only the Father and His beloved Son are in a family called God, and they want us to be part of that God family, to live with them throughout eternity when we fully become in their image, after their likeness, as immortal spirit beings. Knowing that there is no such thing as a Trinity should shed much light as to the nature of God and should enhance clarity by adding yet another valuable piece of spiritual knowledge to that giant jigsaw puzzle.

2.3   Who Is the God of the Old Testament?

It is safe to say that many Christians believe in God. Most likely, they also believe in the divine personages of God the Father and His Beloved Son, Jesus the Christ. But let's separate the deity for a moment and take a close look at modern Christianity's belief about the two divine persons in the Godhead.

What beliefs do modern Christians have about God the Father? Don't most Christians believe that God the Father is the God of the Old Testament? Most Christians also believe that God the Father made "all things." They might also view the Father as conservative and a very strict lawgiver, severely punishing and even killing people for breaking the Ten Commandments.

What beliefs do modern Christians have about Jesus, the Son of God? Don't most Christians believe that God the Son is the God of the New Testament, who came down from heaven to this very earth, to die and save humankind from their sins? Don't they view the Son of God as being more generous and liberal, healing people when they are sick and forgiving them when they sin? After all, they ask, "Didn't Christ give humanity only two great commandments instead of God the Father's original Ten Commandments" found in **Exodus 20**?

What are these two great commandments that Jesus gave? "'Teacher, which is the great commandment in the law?' Jesus said to him, 'You shall love the LORD your God with all your heart, with all your soul, and with all your mind.' This is the first and great commandment, And the second is like it: 'You shall love your neighbor as yourself.' On these two commandments hang all the Law and the Prophets" (**Matthew 22:36–40**). Christ taught us to love God, which is the first great commandment, and second, to love our neighbors as ourselves.

Are the above statements relatively accurate on how the deity—God the Father and Jesus the Christ—are viewed by most Christians? Is God the Father the God of the Old Testament and Jesus the Christ the God of the New Testament? Are God the Father and Jesus at odds with one another? These are important questions that should concern you. You need to know about God the Father and God the Son so that you won't be deceived by other people.

Let's set the stage by going to the very beginning, back to the time when nothing physical existed—when there was no heaven, earth, or universe. *Who or what was alive before anything was created?* Most people believe that the beginning of the Bible is found in **Genesis 1:1** but, as we shall see, the actual beginning of the Bible is found in **John 1:1–3**, where nothing existed except God. Remember the Bible is unlike any other book because it is God-breathed. "In the beginning was the Word, and the Word was with God, and the Word was

God. He [the Word] was in the beginning with God. All things were made through Him, and without Him nothing was made that was made" (**John 1:1–3**).

If we study each phrase in context, they are easier to comprehend. The noun "Word" in the Greek is "Logos," and it means "one who speaks" or spokesman. It is interesting to note that in my Italian Bible, the words used for "the Word" are "il Verbo" and are literally translated as "the Verb," meaning "action by words." It means, "one who speaks and the task is accomplished." In the English language, verbs denote action. The "Word" is the One who speaks, and after He speaks, the action is accomplished. "And the Word became flesh and dwelt among us, and we beheld His glory, the glory as of the only begotten of the Father, full of grace and truth.… For the law was given through Moses, but grace and truth came through Jesus Christ" (**John 1:14, 17**). The "Word" (who was with God) divested Himself of His glory and came to earth as a flesh-and-blood human being, known to us by the name of Jesus.

The Bible makes it clear that only two spirit beings were alive in the very beginning: the Word God and God Himself.

This "Word" was with God, and He too was God. To better understand **John 1:1–3**, try to think of the word "God" as a person's last name, like Smith. For example, let's say the Smith family consists of two people: Steven (the son) and Smith himself (Steven's father). If their names were in **John 1:1–3**, it might read, "In the beginning was Steven (the son) and he was with Smith (the father), and Steven was also a Smith. Steven was in the beginning with Smith. All things were made through Steven and nothing was made that was made without Steven." This example shows there are two members in the Smith family. One is Steven, the son, and the other is Smith, the father. Yet, there is just one family.

From the example above, **John 1:1–3** should be clear: "In the beginning was the Word [God] and the Word was with God. The same Word God was in the beginning with God. All things were made through Him [the Word God] and without Him nothing was made that was made." Here, the apostle John, before anything existed, introduced the two God beings who belong to the God-kind. Just as there is human-kind, animal-kind, and plant-kind, there is also the God-kind or God family. There was the Word, and there was God, plain and simple. It was the Word God who divested Himself of His glory and came to earth as Jesus, the Messiah.

Do these two God beings have names or titles? We discovered from **John 1:17** that the Word God became known to us by the name of Jesus, the Christ. The apostle John saw and bore witness of Christ. "That which was from the beginning, which we have heard, which we have seen with our eyes, which we have looked upon, and our hands have handled, concerning the Word of Life—the Life was manifested, and we have seen, and bear witness, and declare to you that Eternal Life which was with the Father and was manifested to us" (**1 John 1:1–2**). Notice the "Word of Life" was with the Father.

The Father was manifested (made known) to us by the Word, who later became Christ. "No one has seen God [the Father] at any time. The only begotten Son, who is in the bosom [care] of the Father, He has declared Him" (**John 1:18**). Jesus, the Father's only begotten Son, has declared the Father to us.

By now, you should have two names or titles firmly fixed in your mind: God the Word and God the Father. Both of these personages belong to the God family. Therefore, when Jesus came to earth, He was both God and man simultaneously. "Who, being in very nature God, did not consider equality with God something to be used to his own advantage; rather, he made himself nothing by taking the very nature of a servant, being made in human likeness. And being found in appearance as a man, he humbled himself by becoming obedient to death—even death on a cross!" (**Philippians 2:6–8 NIV**).

Now we come to the **two** most important Scriptures that provide unmistakable proof in identifying the God of the Old Testament.

1. No person, no human has ever seen the Father, yet many people have seen the Word God. Reference **John 1:18** above. We would

have never known about God the Father if it weren't for His only begotten Son, Jesus, who declared or revealed Him to us. Christ declared or spoke to us about the Father! But the Word God was seen in **Genesis 32:23–28**, where we find Jacob wrestling with a "Man." *With whom did Jacob wrestle? If you wrestle with someone, wouldn't you see his face at some point during the wrestling match?* Let's take a look:

> He took them, sent them over the brook, and sent over what he had. Then Jacob was left alone; and a Man wrestled with him until the breaking of day. Now when He saw that He did not prevail against him, He touched the socket of his hip; and the socket of Jacob's hip was out of joint as He wrestled with him. And He said, "Let Me go, for the day breaks." But he said, "I will not let You go unless You bless me!" So, He said to him, "What is your name?" He said, "Jacob." And He said, "Your name shall no longer be called Jacob, but Israel; for you have struggled with God and with men, and have prevailed." (**Genesis 32:23–28**)

Notice that the nouns/pronouns Man, He, Me, and You are all capitalized because they refer to the Word God. It was the Word God who wrestled with Jacob! It was the Word God who manifested Himself as a Man and blessed Jacob by changing Jacob's name to Israel.

2. No human has ever heard the Father's voice, yet many people have heard the Word God's voice. "And the Father Himself, who sent Me, has testified of Me. You have neither heard His voice at any time, nor seen His form" (**John 5:37**). Since no one has ever heard the Father's voice or seen His form, it becomes crystal clear that the voice the people heard was the voice of the Word God, the Jesus of Nazareth.

Remember that the Word God is the One who speaks, and things are accomplished. We read about the Lord God speaking to Adam and Eve in the garden. "And they [Adam and Eve] heard the sound of the LORD God walking in the garden in the cool of the day, and Adam and his wife hid themselves from the presence of the LORD God among the trees of the garden. Then the LORD God called to Adam and said to him, 'Where are you?' So, he said, 'I heard Your voice in the garden, and I was afraid because I was naked; and I hid myself'" (**Genesis 3:8–10**). Not only did Adam and Eve hear the voice of the Lord God or Word God speaking to them, but they actually saw Him as He walked in the garden with them.

You might ask, "Who spoke out the Ten Commandments to Moses if it wasn't God the Father?" Since no one has ever heard God, the Father, it was the Word God, Jesus the Christ who thundered out the Ten Commandments! When Christ was asked about which is the greatest commandment, "Jesus answered him… 'And you shall love the Lord you God with all your heart, with all your soul, with all your mind and with all your strength. This is the first commandment. And the second, like it, is this: "You shall love your neighbor as yourself." (**Mark 12:31**). Christ merely summarized the original Ten Commandments into two great commandments.

Do these two great commandments differ from the original Ten Commandments? No! What most Christians fail to realize about the two great commandments is that the first four of the original ten deal with loving God; the last six deal with your loving your neighbor as yourself.

Christ certainly did not do away with any of the original Ten Commandments, nor did He nail them to the cross, nor is He at odds with God the Father. As previously explained, the Father and His Son are two separate spirit beings but "one" in goal and purpose. It was the Word God who spoke to Moses; it was not God the Father.

Christ lived by the Ten Commandments, and they are still in effect for us today. True Christians must observe all the commandments, just as Christ did. He did not break any of them. *Who else could the God of the Old Testament be?* There could be no other but the Word God.

Word God only speaks as He is directed by the Father. "For I have not spoken on My own authority; but the Father who sent Me gave Me a command, what I should say and what I should speak" (**John 12:49**). The Word God speaks to us today through His written Word, the Holy Bible.

From the above verses and the proof given herein, a person who truly seeks to know God's truth will clearly see that the Word co-existed with God the Father from the beginning. Later, the Word God was made flesh and dwelt among men. We know Him as Christ. All things were created through Christ, and nothing was created without Him. No person other than Christ has seen the Father or heard the His voice. When the Word became flesh, He was seen and heard by many people in both the Old and New Testaments. Therefore, the God of both the Old and New Testaments is the Word God, Jesus the Christ.

Understanding this vital knowledge helps us to correctly place another big piece in the Bible's giant jigsaw puzzle.

2.4 WHO WAS CHRIST, AND WHAT WAS HIS MISSION ON EARTH?

The Word God divested Himself of His glory, was begotten by God's power (the Holy Spirit), was born of the Virgin Mary, and is known to us today as Jesus the Christ. We also learned that Jesus was the only begotten Son of the Father, full of grace and truth. "And the Word became flesh and dwelt among us, and we beheld His glory, the glory as of the only begotten of the Father, full of grace and truth" (**John 1:14**).

Many people today have their own opinion about who Christ was. Some believe that Christ was just a charismatic religious leader and not really the Son of God. Others living in His day thought He was possessed by a demon. Still others thought He was an alcoholic. "The Son of Man came eating and drinking, and they say, 'Look, a glutton and a winebibber, a friend of tax collectors and sinners!' But wisdom is justified by her children" (**Matthew 11:19**).

Whatever your opinion is of Jesus the Christ, one thing is for certain: He electrified, stunned, and transformed the world. Over the centuries, His life and teachings have changed billions of lives. Hundreds of millions believe and worship Him every day. But despite His teachings, Christ was misunderstood, misjudged, mistreated, and eventually crucified. And almost no one, not even His own people, grasped what His mission was in life. "But when His own people [the Jews] heard about this, they went out to lay hold of Him, for they said, 'He is out of His mind'" (**Mark 3:21**). Even today, Christ is totally misunderstood by modern Christianity.

"When Jesus came into the region of Caesarea Philippi, He asked His disciples, saying, 'Who do men say that I am?'" (**Matthew 16:13**). Some disciples said, "Some people say You are John the Baptist, while others say You are Elijah, the prophet." For certain, the general populace in Christ's day was not sure who Christ was. "Then the Jews surrounded Him and said to Him, 'How long do keep us in doubt? If You are the Christ, tell us plainly'" (**John 10:24**). Also, "We know that God spoke to Moses; as for this fellow [Christ], we do not know where He is from" (**John 9:29**).

Further evidence of people's ignorance about Christ is found in **Luke 24:21**, where shortly after He was crucified, one of His followers stated, "But we were hoping that it was He who was going to redeem Israel. Indeed, besides all this, today is the third day since these things happened." People back then were looking and hoping for a powerful king with a huge army to save Israel, not a little baby born in Bethlehem to a poor family. Again, people in Christ's day were thoroughly confused about who Jesus was, even though His coming was prophesied in Scripture, millennia ago.

Nevertheless, today's Christians, clergy, theologians, and Bible scholars know full well who Christ is. Every Sunday, many clerics present sermons about who Christ was and what miracles He performed, but all fail miserably to tell their congregations what His all-important mission was. In other words, Christians can tell you all about Christ, the person, but they never tell you about the important message He came to preach. Because of this very fact, modern Christianity is deceived about Christ's mission.

Who was Christ before becoming human? **Three** important clues provide vital and valuable information about who Jesus was.

1. Christ was a member of the God family known as the Word. Notice again: "In the beginning was the Word, and the Word was with God, and the Word was God. He was in the beginning with God. All things were made through Him, and without Him nothing was made that was made.... And the Word became flesh and dwelt among us, and we beheld His glory, the glory as of the only begotten of the Father, full of grace and truth." (**John 1:1–3, 14**). Notice here that the Word God became a flesh-and-blood human. The Word divested Himself from glory and came down to earth as a real person, known to us as Jesus the Christ.

"John bore witness of Him and cried out, saying, 'This was He of whom I said, "He who comes after me is preferred before me, for He was before me"'" (**John 1:15**). "Preferred before me" means that Christ existed as the Word God before John the Baptist was born. Yet when it came to a physical birth, John was six months older than Christ. "And of His fullness we have all received, and grace for grace. For the law was given through Moses, but grace and truth came through Jesus Christ" (**John 1:16–17**).

2. Christ existed before Abraham was born. To the Jews, the problem was that Abraham lived about 1,500 years before Christ's birth, yet Christ said that He existed before Abraham. By making this claim, Christ revealed that He was the same being who was known to the Jews as the God of Abraham, Isaac, and Jacob. "Jesus said to them, 'Most assuredly, I say to you, before Abraham was, I AM'" (**John 8:58**).

Anciently, this same great Word God first revealed Himself to Moses in Exodus. While speaking to God, Moses asked Him what His name was. Notice the Word God's response: "And Moses said unto God, Behold, when I come unto the children of Israel, and shall say unto them, the God of your fathers hath sent me unto you; and they shall say to me, what is His name? What shall I say unto them? And God said unto Moses, I AM that I AM: and He said, Thus shalt thou say unto the children of Israel, I AM hath sent me unto you" (**Exodus 3:13–14 KJV**).

"I AM that I AM" is an awesome phrase relating to the personal name of the God in the Old Testament, the Hebrew name YHWH. It is commonly rendered as lord in our English Bibles, but it is translated as "Jehovah" in other Bibles. "I AM that I AM" means "the One who has always existed" or "the One who was, is, and always will be." No human can always exist, but the God family can.

Notice also: "I am Alpha and Omega, the beginning and the ending, saith the Lord, which is, and which was, and which is to come, the Almighty" (**Revelation 1:8 KJV**). Again, in **Revelation 22:13**, "I am Alpha and Omega, the beginning and the end, the first and the last." Even the prophet Isaiah states the same concept. "Thus, saith the LORD the King of Israel, and his redeemer the LORD of hosts; I am the first, and I am the last; and beside me there is no God" (**Isaiah 44:6 KJV**).

Keep in mind that the Hebrew noun for God is "Elohim" and is singular in form but consists of more than one person. In this case, the God family consists of the Father and the Son. They both belong to the God family, of which there is only one. The word "family" is similar to the word "God" because it is singular in form but composed of more than one member.

The distinction about always existing, like the first and the last, can only apply to the God family. The Jews in Christ's day knew exactly what He meant by the phrase "I AM that I AM" and immediately picked up stones to try to kill Him—they did not believe that He was God in the flesh and or that He existed before Abraham. "Then the Jews took up stones again to stone Him" (**John 10:31**). They erroneously thought that Christ was guilty of blasphemy, which, back then, carried the death penalty. By claiming the name "I AM," Jesus was saying that He was the God whom the Hebrews knew as YHWH.

3. Christ asked the Father to give back the glory that He once had before the earth was created. "And now, O Father, glorify Me together with Yourself, with the glory which I had with You before the world was" (**John 17:5**). These powerful words prove unmistakably that Christ was the Word God and had "glory" before coming to earth.

The Jews confronted Jesus on another occasion about His identity. Notice Christ's response. "Then the Jews surrounded Him and said to Him, 'How long do You keep us in doubt? If You are the Christ, tell us plainly.' Jesus answered them, 'I told you, and you do not believe. The works that I do in My Father's name, they bear witness of Me'" (**John 10:24–25**).

In other words, the many miracles that Christ performed should have made the Jews believe that He was God in the flesh, but the Jews refused to believe Him. The next statement, in **John 10:30**, infuriated the Jews so much that they desired to kill Him: "I and My Father are one." This statement means that even though the Father and Jesus are two separate, divine God-beings they are "one" in goal, purpose, character, and mission, having the same outlook and philosophy on life.

The apostle John makes it even clearer who Christ was before becoming human. "That which was from the beginning, which we have heard, which we have seen with our eyes, which we have looked upon, and our hands have handled, concerning the Word of life" (**1 John 1:1**).

There is overwhelming evidence, and there is no question that Jesus understood and presented Himself to be Jehovah, the YHWH, God of the Old Testament, the Word God.

Who was Christ while on earth? Was He really the Son of God in the flesh? Here are **four** important points to ponder on who Christ was while on earth.

1. God the Father called Christ His beloved Son. "And suddenly a voice came from heaven, saying, 'This is My beloved Son, in whom I am well pleased'" (**Matthew 3:17**). Since no one has ever heard the Father's voice, it becomes clear that an angel spoke the above words on the Father's behalf. Consider also: "And a cloud came and overshadowed them; and a voice came out of the cloud, saying, 'This is My beloved Son. Hear Him!'" (**Mark 9:7**).

2. Jesus called Himself the Son of God. "The Jews answered him, 'We have a law, and according to our law He ought to die, because He made Himself the Son of God'" (**John 19:7**). Christ told them that He was the Son of God, but they refused to believe Him; instead, they wanted to crucify Him. "Which none of the rulers of this age knew; for had they known, they would not have crucified the Lord of glory" (**1 Corinthians 2:8**). Again, in **John 10:35–36** "If He called them gods, to whom the word of God came (and the Scripture cannot be broken), do you say of Him whom the Father sanctified and sent into the world, 'You are blaspheming,' because I said, 'I am the Son of God?'"

3. The apostle Peter called Christ the Son of the living God. Christ asked Peter, "Who do you think I am?" "Simon Peter answered and said, 'You are the Christ, the Son of the living God'" (**Matthew 16:16**), The word "Christ," from the Greek, means the "anointed one," or in the Hebrew language, it is translated as "Messiah."

4. Even a Roman centurion admitted that Christ was the Son of God. "So, when the centurion, who stood opposite Him, saw that He cried out like this and breathed His last, he said, 'Truly this Man

was the Son of God!'" (**Mark 15:39**). Who was Christ while on earth? He was the only begotten Son of God the Father.

What was Christ's mission on earth? What were the real reasons Christ came to earth? You may be surprised by these **eleven** reasons as to why He came:

1. Christ came to this world to die for sinners so that they might be saved. "This is a faithful saying and worthy of all acceptance, that Christ Jesus came into the world to save sinners, of whom I am chief" (**1 Timothy 1:15**).

2. Christ came to do the will of the Father. "For I have come down from heaven, not to do My own will, but the will of Him who sent Me" (**John 6:38**). Remember that since the Father and the Son are One in purpose and goal, it is Their will to give us the gift of everlasting life, upon repentance and baptism. Notice also: "I can of Myself do nothing. As I hear, I judge; and My judgment is righteous, because I do not seek My own will but the will of the Father who sent Me" (**John 5:30**).

3. Christ came because God does not want you to perish. "For God so loved the world that He gave His only begotten Son, that whoever believes in Him should not perish but have everlasting life. For God did not send His Son into the world to condemn the world, but that the world through Him might be saved" (**John 3:16–17**). God wants to give you and me and all of humanity the gift of eternal life, but a price for our trespasses had to be paid. The penalty for breaking God's law is death. "For the wages of sin is death, but the gift of God is eternal life in Christ Jesus our Lord" (**Romans 6:23**).

4. Christ came as a light to the world. The world today is in total darkness, just as it was in Christ's day. "I have come as a light into the world, that whoever believes in Me should not abide in

darkness" (**John 12:46**). When a person sins, he lives in darkness, but Christ came into the world as a light to show the world its sins. When you shine a flashlight in a dark room, it dispels darkness and exposes everything in the room—the good, the bad, and the ugly. "Then Jesus spoke to them again, saying, 'I am the light of the world. He who follows Me shall not walk in darkness, but have the light of life'" (**John 8:12**).

5. Christ came to show people their sins. "If I had not come and spoken to them, they would have no sin, but now they have no excuse for their sin" (**John 15:22**). Without Christ and without God's law, we would not know what sin is. Christ came to earth to show everyone their sin. Upon His death and our heartfelt repentance, His blood would blot out our sins at baptism.

6. Christ came to show humanity their need for salvation. "For all have sinned and fall short of the glory of God" (**Romans 3:23**). Christ is the only person who never sinned and therefore is qualified to take all of our sins away to save us.

7. Christ came to die as a Lamb without blemish. "The next day John saw Jesus coming toward him, and said, 'Behold! The Lamb of God who takes away the sin of the world!'" (**John 1:29**). Without Christ's sacrifice, we would all carry the death penalty. But Christ's sinless life made it possible for us to be reconciled back to the Father. Christ's resurrection from the dead makes it possible for us to someday live again through a resurrection.

8. Christ came as the Lamb of God, who took away the sins of the world by shedding His precious blood and dying for everyone. "Knowing that you were not redeemed with corruptible things, like silver or gold, from your aimless conduct received by tradition from your fathers, but with the precious blood of Christ, as of a lamb without blemish and without spot. He indeed was

foreordained before the foundation of the world, but was manifest in these last times for you" (**1 Peter 1:18–20**).

9. Christ came to be wounded for our transgressions. "But He was wounded for our transgressions, He was bruised for our iniquities; The chastisement for our peace was upon Him, and by His stripes we are healed. All we like sheep have gone astray; We have turned, every one, to his own way; And the LORD has laid on Him the iniquity of us all" (**Isaiah 53:5–6**).

10. Christ came to earth to fulfill the law. But notice what Christ Himself said about His mission and the law: "Do not think that I came to destroy the Law or the Prophets. I did not come to destroy but to fulfill" (**Matthew 15:17**). To fulfill the law means that Christ kept it flawlessly and in its entirety. He epitomized the law. *Why would He do away with it? If we are to be followers of Christ, and He kept the law, shouldn't we also observe it?* Of course, we should.

11. Christ came to preach the good news of the coming kingdom of God. "And Jesus went about all Galilee, teaching in their synagogues, preaching the gospel, and healing all kinds of sickness and all kinds of disease among the people" (**Matthew 4:23**). Again, in Matthew, we find Christ preaching the will of His Father. "Then Jesus went about all the cities and villages, teaching in their synagogues, preaching the gospel of the kingdom, and healing every sickness and every disease among the people" (**Matthew 9:35**).

The above reasons are all valid and true as to Christ's mission on earth. In order to be saved, it is necessary to believe in Christ and His message about the coming kingdom of God to this earth.

What was Christ's message to this sick and dying world? Notice what Christ's clear message was to everyone. "Whatever city you enter, and they receive you, eat such things as are set before you. And heal the sick there, and say to them, 'The kingdom of God has come near to you'" (**Luke 10:8–9**). Christ's message or "gospel" to this sick world was to preach of a coming divine world government to this earth— not a flawed and patched-up human world government but a divine government, set up by Christ at His return. That coming world government is called the kingdom of God, wherein Christ (along with His saints) will rule as kings and priests. "And have made us kings and priests to our God; And we shall reign on the earth" (**Revelation 5:10**).

Yes, Jesus, the Messiah, went all over Galilee, teaching and preaching the message of the coming kingdom of God. Notice again in Matthew: "And Jesus went about all Galilee, teaching in their synagogues, preaching the gospel of the kingdom, and healing all kinds of sickness and all kinds of disease among the people" (**Matthew 4:23**).

Notice what Mark says: "The beginning of the gospel of Jesus Christ, the Son of God" (**Mark 1:1**). Gospel means "good news." *What is the good news?* The good news to all humanity, back then and now, is the coming kingdom of God to this earth.

Over and over, we see Christ's message—His gospel—being preached in all Judea. *How many ministers have you heard preach about the coming kingdom of God?* I suspect it's not very many. "Now after John was put in prison, Jesus came to Galilee, preaching the gospel of the kingdom of God and saying, 'The time is fulfilled, and the kingdom of God is at hand. Repent, and believe in the gospel'" (**Mark 1:14–15**). People are to repent and believe the good news of the coming kingdom of God.

Even after Christ rose from the dead, He spoke about the coming kingdom of God. Take a look at **Acts 1:3** "To whom He also presented Himself alive after His suffering by many infallible proofs, being seen by them during forty days and speaking of the things pertaining to the kingdom of God." Also, in **Mark 8:35** "For whoever desires to save his life will lose it, but whoever loses his life for My sake and the gospel's will save it."

Not only did Christ preach the gospel of the kingdom of God, but He commissioned His apostles to preach the same good news about a coming divine kingdom. "Then He called His twelve disciples together and gave them power and authority over all demons, and to cure diseases. He sent them to preach the kingdom of God and to heal the sick" (**Luke 9:1–2**).

Christ also appointed seventy other people to preach the good news of the coming kingdom of God. "After these things the Lord appointed seventy others also, and sent them two by two before His face into every city and place where He Himself was about to go. ... And heal the sick there, and say to them, 'The kingdom of God has come near to you'" (**Luke 10:1, 9**).

Can you see the significance of who Christ was; what His mission was while on earth; and why the gospel of the kingdom of God coming to this earth is so important? This message is not being proclaimed in any of the Christian churches today. Instead of preaching the gospel of the kingdom of God, modern-day clergy teach messages about Christ, the person, and the miracles He performed.

Finally, notice **Matthew 24:14** "And this gospel of the kingdom will be preached in all the world as a witness to all the nations, and then the end will come." When the gospel of the kingdom of God has been preached to the entire world as a witness, then the end of this age will come. Today, Christ's message of the coming kingdom of God to this earth has been made available to you as a witness.

2.5   WHY DOES GOD ALLOW SUFFERING?

Humans tend to be comfortable believing in God when everything is going their way—riches, grandeur, a lovely home, wonderfully obedient children. But when tragedy strikes, they can quickly begin to doubt the very existence of God. Perhaps they have lost a loved one through an untimely death, divorce, some type of illness, or old age. Maybe their children have gone astray, taking the broad path that leads to misery, pain, and suffering, instead of taking the godly, narrow way that leads to life, health, and happiness. Contemplate **Matthew 7:13** "Enter by the narrow gate; for wide is the gate and broad is the way that leads to destruction, and there are many who go in by it."

Besides tragedies, there are many appalling evils in this crime-ridden world. There are many rapes, murders, and violence of every sort occurring and escalating every day. We are cursed with injustices, sicknesses, and diseases. There are broken homes and broken people who live in illiteracy and poverty. We have had two devastating world wars that killed millions of people, and we hear rumors of world wars yet to come. We see an escalation of destruction and misery due to tornadoes, earthquakes, tsunamis, volcanic eruptions, floods, and droughts.

Why does a wonderful, loving, powerful, merciful God allow such suffering? People often ask, *"If God is all powerful and loving, why doesn't He immediately put an end to all this misery?"* Many people come to the conclusion that neither God nor religion offers answers to this world's problems. Others believe that God just does not care about us. But these same people do not understand the real reasons why God allows suffering.

I want to provide you with **three** important reasons why God allows suffering. We must fully understand that suffering is directly related to the word "freedom."

1. God allows suffering because God has given all humans the freedom to choose right or wrong. They can choose life or death. Most people believe that freedom means doing anything you want at any time you want, and it does not matter to them whether it hurts someone else. Fortunately for us, Almighty God does not agree with humanity's definition of freedom. True freedom from God means loving and having outgoing concern for others. It is having the freedom to always choose to obey God and to choose to help others so that they may live and not suffer. Let's take a close look at **Deuteronomy 30:19**, "I call heaven and earth as witnesses today against you, that I have set before you life and death, blessing and cursing; therefore, choose life, that both you and your descendants may live." God urges us—He begs us—to choose life and to choose the right way to live, which leads to happiness and eternal

life with Him. You should note that God will never force you to choose life; you must want it enough to choose it for yourself.

Other people may ask, *"Why didn't God just create us so that we would always choose the right way to live and never sin? Couldn't Almighty God have done this?"* The answer is yes. God could have done this. But then, God would have created robots. God does not want robots. Instead, God chose to make us in His own image, after His likeness, giving us the ability to choose, measure, analyze, and imagine, just as He does. The difference is that God knows the right way to live, and we honestly and sincerely do not. We must always rely on God to show us the right way to live. Our first parents, Adam and Eve, were also given the freedom to choose. As you know, they chose the wrong way. They chose to eat the fruit that God told them not to eat. By so choosing, they disobeyed God. This act of rebellion meant that they did not believe what God said. The penalty for disobeying God was death (reference **Romans 6:23**).

Since they did not believe what God said to them, they chose to decide for themselves, with the influence of Satan, what was good and what was evil. The end result of their choice and our choice is what we have today—the decadent world with its myriad problems, diseases, and utmost confusion in all aspects of living. Everybody does what is right in their own eyes. "In those days there was no king in Israel; everyone did what was right in his own eyes" (**Judges 21:25**). And in **Deuteronomy 12:8**, "You shall not at all do as we are doing here today—every man doing whatever is right in his own eyes."

Being the loving and just God that He is, He also gave the angels a choice, millions of years before creating humankind. Over one-third of them chose to rebel against God and followed a false god named Satan. So having the freedom to choose is only good if we choose God's way of living, which is the way of giving and outgoing concern for others. Otherwise, having the freedom to choose apart from what God intended will lead to unhappiness, misery, and—ultimately—spiritual death.

We must also realize that Satan exerts a tremendous and pervasive power over humans through suffering. Satan is the instigator of much of the human misery. He has the ability to influence the human mind in a very negative way. In short, he hates humans! Reference **2 Corinthians 4:4**, where it says that Satan is "the god of this world." In **Ephesians 2:2**, he is called the "prince of the power of the air who works in the sons of disobedience." **1 Peter 5:8** tells us that Satan is our "adversary." All these descriptions refer to Satan, the Devil, to whom God gave temporary rule over this world. But rest assured God will never relinquish His ultimate control over the affairs of man to Satan. Let us not forget that God is supreme ruler over the universe. Satan takes orders from God.

But God allows Satan and uses him to do certain things to accomplish His will. "And the LORD said to Satan, 'Behold, all that he has is in your power; only do not lay a hand on his person. So, Satan went out from the presence of the LORD'" (**Job 1:12**). And in **Job 2:6**, "And the LORD said to Satan, 'Behold, he is in your hand, but spare his life.'"

2. God allows suffering because God uses suffering to build godly character in us, using trials, difficulties, and tribulations. We must always be ready to say no to evil thoughts and deeds, thereby growing in godly attributes. *How else can we grow to be better people? If everything went well for us all the time, would we need God?* Probably not. God wants to have a relationship with us. He does not want us to forget Him. "For we are His workmanship, created in Christ Jesus for good works, which God prepared beforehand that we should walk in them" (**Ephesians 2:10**). According to the Bible, "walk in them" means people helping others by doing good works. "For it is God who works in you both to will and to do for His good pleasure" (**Philippians 2:13**). All the patriarchs, prophets, and apostles—and especially Christ—suffered tremendously while on earth. But each of them was never tested beyond what he could endure. "No temptation has overtaken you except such as is common to man; but God is faithful, who will not allow you

to be tempted beyond what you are able, but with the temptation will also make the way of escape, that you may be able to bear it" (**1 Corinthians 10:13**).

Let's take a look at **1 Peter 3:18**, "For Christ also suffered once for sins, the just for the unjust, that He might bring us to God, being put to death in the flesh but made alive by the Spirit." *Haven't we all suffered many times in this life?* Some people are suffering right now, but God is building godly character in them to be used later, when His kingdom comes to earth. Our trials, tribulations, and sufferings are not going to waste. The Bible states that we should be happy when we go through trials because it means that God is building righteous character in us. Righteous character means having the ability to choose the right way. "My brethren, count it all joy when you fall into various trials, knowing that the testing of your faith produces patience" (**James 1:2–3**).

3. God allows suffering because of time and chance. "I returned and saw under the sun that—The race is not to the swift, nor the battle to the strong, nor bread to the wise, nor riches to men of understanding, nor favor to men of skill; But time and chance happen to them all" (**Ecclesiastes 9:11**).

Many good and bad things happen to people, regardless of whether they are good or bad. They just happened to be at the wrong place at the wrong time. Christ clarified the concept of time and chance: "For those eighteen on whom the tower in Siloam fell and killed them, do you think that they were worse sinners than all other men who dwelt in Jerusalem? I tell you, no; but unless you repent you will all likewise perish" (**Luke 13:4–5**). Christ is telling His followers that the eighteen people did not die because they were worse sinners than others but because of time and chance. This, of course, is speaking of the spiritual death, because we must all die a physical death. "And as it is appointed for men to die once, but after this the judgment" (**Hebrews 9:27**). Many calamities happen to people because of time and chance.

You might ask, *"Why didn't God spare the eighteen people?"* You might believe that the eighteen people died and will never live again and that they went to either heaven or hell. That is simply not true because "no one has ascended into heaven except He who came down from heaven even Christ" (**John 3:13**). The Holy Bible reveals that the people of Siloam died, like all other humans who have died, will be resurrected back to physical life again in the great white throne judgment. (See **Hebrews 9:27**, above.)

Most people do not know about the great white throne judgment resurrection, where all humans who were not called to be in the first resurrection will live again in the flesh. God could have easily spared the eighteen people of Siloam, but God knew He would resurrect them in the future resurrection. The eighteen people were not lost forever, as some people think.

> Then I saw a great white throne and Him who sat on it, from whose face the earth and the heaven fled away. And there was found no place for them. And I saw the dead, small and great, standing before God, and books were opened. And another book was opened, which is the Book of Life. And the dead were judged according to their works, by the things which were written in the books. The sea gave up the dead who were in it, and death and Hades delivered up the dead who were in them. And they were judged, each one according to his works. Then death and Hades were cast into the lake of fire. This is the second death. (**Revelation 20:11–14**)

The above Scripture says that "the small and great will stand before God." This will occur at the great white throne judgment, after the one thousand year reign of Christ on earth.

Not to be confused with the great white throne judgment, the first resurrection occurs for a separate group of people whom God called during their lifetime and died. These include prophets and apostles, among others.

> And I saw thrones, and they sat on them, and judgment was committed to them. Then I saw the souls of those who had been beheaded for their witness to Jesus and for the word of God, who had not worshiped the beast or his image, and had not received his mark on their foreheads or on their hands. And they lived and reigned with Christ for a thousand years. But the rest of the dead did not live again until the thousand years were finished. This is the first resurrection. Blessed and holy is he who has part in the first resurrection. Over such the second death has no power, but they shall be priests of God and of Christ, and shall reign with Him a thousand years. **(Revelation 20:4–6)**

As true Christians, what are we supposed to do for people who suffer? Is there any help for them? The answer is yes! **First**, spiritually, we need to continually pray for them. **Second**, physically, we need to do good works; for example, a phone call, a short note, a card, an e-mail, or a short visit. **Third**, we need to show compassion for the sufferer. We should do these things even if the sufferer goes to another church.

Remember the second great commandment: "Love your neighbor as yourself." It says to love your neighbor, not just those who go to your church. Also, we are to show our light to the world, not just to the people in our church. Showing compassion means to feel their pain. Christ exemplified compassion for the people. "But when He saw the multitudes, He was moved with compassion for them, because they were weary and scattered, like sheep having no shepherd" (**Matthew 9:36**). Having compassion and helping others in need is what is meant by loving your neighbor as yourself.

In summary, God allows human suffering because humankind, in general, is unwilling to believe what God says and is unwilling to obey Him. Sometimes humans bring temptations and sufferings on themselves. Sometimes God allows Satan to bring calamities on people, ultimately to help them develop godly character. That's the bottom line. People today want freedom but want it their way. They want to make the choice for themselves and keep God out of the picture. But their choices usually end up in misery, pain, suffering, and—ultimately—spiritual death. Most people do not realize that God Himself is very eager to heal and to show mercy, love, and compassion on us all, but repentance, baptism, and obedience are His prerequisites. Here is another piece of the giant jigsaw puzzle put in place.

2.6   COMMON MYTHS ABOUT GOD

By many measures, Americans are strongly religious—so says Pew Forum's Religious Landscape Survey, dated February 2008. Sixty-three percent of those surveyed say their Scriptures are the Word of God; seventy-four percent believe in life after death; and a whopping ninety-two percent believe in God. But for many people in the United States, God is still a mystery. Some still struggle to answer the question of creation versus evolution. Then there are those who have ruled out evolution but still question God and their own beliefs about Him.

Many people have doubts and misconceptions about God. Dr. Michael Lindsay, a Rice University sociologist of religion, said, "The survey shows religion in America is, indeed, three thousand miles wide and only three inches deep"—meaning there is a wide variety of beliefs about God, but their understanding is rather shallow. "My people are destroyed for lack of knowledge. Because you have rejected knowledge, I also will reject you from being priest for Me; Because you have forgotten the law of your God, I also will forget your children" (**Hosea 4:6**).

I would like to explore **eight** fundamental myths about God.

1. There is really no way to please God. After all, people reason, "I am an imperfect human being trying to please a perfect God." Some feel that pleasing God is an *"impossible task, so why waste time trying to please Him?"* They further say that "It is impossible for us to keep the Ten Commandments and besides, Christ nailed them to the cross." The end result of such reasoning is that people tend to forget God.

But is there a way, humanly speaking, to please God and make God happy? What does the Holy Bible say about pleasing God? The Bible describes at least **three** ways to please God:

A. One way to please God is found in **Hebrews 11:6**, "But without faith it is impossible to please him: for he [a person] that cometh to God must believe that He is, and that He [God] is a rewarder of them that diligently seek him." This Scripture clearly tells us that one way to please God is to have faith in Him, to believe in Him, and to also believe what He says.

What exactly is faith? The Bible tells us, "Now faith is the substance of things hoped for" (**Hebrews 11:1**). *What is this substance we hope for?* Our hope should be that we and our loved ones obtain everlasting life through a resurrection. *Can we see everlasting life?* No! But it is something we hope for. Having hope is similar to having faith. Faith, therefore, is a very important attribute to have in order to please God.

Hebrews 11:1 continues, "The evidence of things not seen." *Can God be seen?* No, but we know God exists because of all the things He created. We see the sun, moon, stars, planets, plants, animals, and humans. Because we can see God's wonderful creation, we have faith that He exists. That is an example of faith. Remember that faith is also the substance hoped for.

B. A second way to please God is found **1 John 5:2–3**. "By this we know that we love the children of God, when we love God, and keep his commandments. For this is the love of God, that we keep His commandments. And His commandments are not burdensome." All humans are God's children, and God wants us to love Him, love our neighbor, and keep His commandments. God's commandments were not nailed to the cross, as some people think. God wants us to keep or observe them all as His Son did, while on earth. In **Hebrews 11**, we read that Abel, Noah, Enoch, Abraham, and many others pleased God. *Weren't they all human?* Yes, of course they were! Yet all of them pleased God. They pleased Him by observing all of His Ten Commandments. They did not observe them perfectly, but God looks on the human heart. "But the LORD said to Samuel, 'Do not look at his appearance or at his physical stature, because I have refused him. For the LORD does not see as man sees; for man looks at the outward appearance, but the LORD looks at the heart'" (**1 Samuel 16:7**). Today, we must continue to please God in the ways mentioned above. Only Christ, the Messiah, the one we claim to worship, observed all of God's commandments perfectly and lived a sinless life.

As for the belief that the Ten Commandments were nailed to the cross, look at what God says in **Malachi 4:6** "For I am the lord, I do not change." And in **Hebrews 13:8**, it clearly states, "Jesus Christ is the same yesterday, today and forever." These Scriptures say that God does not change and neither do His Ten Commandments. They are still valid and in effect today. In **Exodus 20**, the Bible tells us that all of His commandments are binding on us today. You will find the phrase "throughout your generations" sprinkled throughout the entire Bible. But notice a few examples: "Speak also to the children of Israel, saying: 'Surely My Sabbaths you shall keep, for it is a sign between Me and you throughout your generations, that you may know that I am the LORD who sanctifies you'" (**Exodus 31:13**). "You shall do no manner of work; it shall be a statute forever throughout your generations in all your dwellings" (**Leviticus 23:31**). "This shall be a perpetual statute

throughout your generations in all your dwellings: you shall eat neither fat nor blood" (**Leviticus 3:17**). All of God's servants keep all of
God's commandments, including the fourth.

    C. A third way to please God is found in **1 Peter 5:6–7**. "Therefore,
humble yourselves under the mighty hand of God, that He
may exalt you in due time, casting all your care upon Him,
for He cares for you." God cares and loves His creation very
much, but He especially loves a person who has a humble and
contrite heart. A person who is humble and contrite is meek
and does not think more highly of himself than he ought to
do. Conversely, God dislikes a proud look. Notice **Proverbs
21:4**—"A haughty look, a proud heart, and the plowing of the
wicked are sin."

2. God is too far away. *Does **Hebrews 13:5** say that God is far away?*
"Let your conduct be without covetousness; be content with such
things as you have. For He Himself has said, 'I will never leave you
nor forsake you.'" *Does that sound like God is too far away? How
about **Jeremiah 23:23–24**?* "'Am I a God near at hand,' says the
LORD, 'And not a God afar off? Can anyone hide himself in secret
places, so I shall not see him?' says the LORD; 'Do I not fill heaven
and earth?' says the LORD.'" The Bible says that God is very near to
us and is very concerned about us and our welfare. Scripture tells
us that God is not far away.

One of the things that I clearly remember when my wife and I
came out of Catholicism and were first called into God's church in
1977 in Dayton, Ohio, was that the brethren talked about God as
if He was a very, very close friend of theirs. They used phrases like
"Well, I will pray to God for you tonight"; "I will keep you on my
prayer list"; and "I am waiting for God to answer my prayer." They
said, "God will find you a job," or "God will take care of that for you."
Since we never had heard such words in the Catholic Church, we

did not know what to make of them. The words were foreign to us but comforting.

"So that we may boldly say, the Lord is my helper, and I will not fear what man shall do unto me" (**Hebrews 13:6**). God, through the author of Hebrews, says that He is a helper. *How can a helper be too far away? If someone does not forsake you, does not that mean he'll be close by to help you, especially in time of trouble?*

"Behold, I am with you and will keep you wherever you go, and will bring you back to this land; for I will not leave you until I have done what I have spoken to you" (**Genesis 28:15**). Many times, in His holy Word, God tells us that He will not leave us. *Do we believe Him?* God does not and cannot lie. He means what He says and says what He means. God is definitely much closer to us than we think.

"Teaching them [the people] to observe all things that I have commanded you; and lo, I am with you always, even to the end of the age. Amen" (**Matthew 28:20**). God promises us that He is always with us, never leaving us, even to the end of this age. What a promise that is, and we have it in writing! *Do you believe what God says?*

3. God does not seem to care about us. People say, "Look at all the suffering, hatred, and injustice going on in the world—all the wars, disasters, disease epidemics, and crimes. *Why doesn't God do something? Why doesn't He help us?*" They tend to blame God for all the suffering in the world today because they think God is ruling this world right now. But Christ tells us that His kingdom is not of this world. "Jesus answered, 'My kingdom is not of this world. If My kingdom were of this world, My servants would fight, so that I should not be delivered to the Jews; but now My kingdom is not from here'" (**John 18:36**). Christ's kingdom is not here yet.

Now look at who the real god of this world is. The Holy Bible tells us that Satan is the "god of this age." Notice "whose minds the god of this age has blinded, who do not believe, lest the light of the gospel of the glory of Christ, who is the image of God, should shine on them"

(**2 Corinthians 4:4**). Most people tend to forget that Satan blinds the human mind in such a way as to bring calamities upon them by their not believing what God tells them and by breaking God's physical and spiritual laws. We have, in essence, kicked God out of our schools, homes, offices, and, essentially, our lives. The truth is that we turned against God by not believing and obeying Him. We have tuned into Satan's wavelength, the one who has deceived and blinded the whole world.

God is allowing Satan and his demons to rule this world temporarily. God is allowing Satan to deceive the people who have forgotten the true God. "So, the great dragon was cast out, that serpent of old, called the Devil and Satan, who deceives the whole world; he was cast to the earth, and his angels were cast out with him" (**Revelation 12:9**). God cast Satan and his demons from heaven to earth. With the influence of Satan, men rule over other men to their own hurt. **Ecclesiastes 8:9** tells us, "One man rules another to his own hurt." God is allowing these things to happen to show humankind that most people cannot live in peace without Him. *Does humankind, in general, believe God, and have people learned their lesson?* Probably not! This is a big lesson that God wants us to learn.

But God cares for us so much. "For God so loved the world [the people in the world] that He gave His only begotten Son, that whoever believes in Him should not perish but have everlasting life" (**John 3:16**). *Does this sound like God does not care for us? Or is it that the vast majority of people do not care for God?*

Not only does God care for and love us, but He has big plans for each one of us, if we would only believe and obey Him. "'For I know the plans I have for you,' declares the lord, 'plans to prosper you and not to harm you, plans to give you hope and a future. Then you will call upon me and come and pray to me, and I will listen to you'" (**Jeremiah 29:11–12 NIV**). *How many priests, ministers, bishops, reverends, or pastors quote this Scripture? Have you read that in your Bible lately?* God has a master plan for each one of us to participate in, if we would only listen to Him and do as He asks. "He who does not love, does not know God, for God is love" (**1 John 4:8**).

4. God is unreliable. People say, "He is not there when they need Him, or that God doesn't answer their prayers on time." Others say, "I asked God to help me find a job, and He didn't. I asked God to heal me, and He didn't. I asked God to help me with this problem, and He didn't." *Sound familiar?*

Let us allow the Bible to answer such statements.

> "For My thoughts are not your thoughts, nor are your ways My ways," says the LORD. For as the heavens are higher than the earth, so are My ways higher than your ways, and My thoughts than your thoughts. For as the rain comes down, and the snow from heaven, and do not return there, but water the earth, and make it bring forth and bud, that it may give seed to the sower and bread to the eater, so shall My word be that goes forth from My mouth; It shall not return to Me void, but it shall accomplish what I please, and it shall prosper in the thing for which I sent it. For you shall go out with joy, and be led out with peace; The mountains and the hills shall break forth into singing before you, and all the trees of the field shall clap their hands. Instead of the thorn shall come up the cypress tree, and instead of the brier shall come up the myrtle tree; And it shall be to the LORD for a name, for an everlasting sign that shall not be cut off. (**Isaiah 55:8–13**)

God and His words are so reliable that He likens them to rain and snow falling on the earth to nourish plants and, in turn, nourish us. There is never a time when the rain falls to the earth and does not nourish the plants, animals, and us. So are God and His Word.

Notice also, "Declaring the end from the beginning, and from ancient times things that are not yet done, Saying, 'My counsel shall stand, and I will do all My pleasure,' Calling a bird of prey from the east, the man who executes My counsel, from a far country. Indeed, I have spoken it; I will also bring it to pass. I have purposed it; I will also do it" (**Isaiah 46:10–11**).

Is God unreliable? "The Lord is not slack concerning His promise, as some count slackness, but is longsuffering toward us, not willing that any should perish but that all should come to repentance" (**2 Peter 3:9**).

These are powerful words from an all-powerful, reliable, and loving creator God. God said, through the apostle Peter, that, He is not slack but waits patiently. *What is God waiting for?* He's waiting for us to repent from our sins. *Do you believe what God says about Himself?*

5. God does not know what He is doing. People may say He is experimenting with us. "Behold, I stand at the door, and knock: if any man hears my voice, and open the door, I will come in to him, and will sup with him, and he with me. To him that overcomes will I grant to sit with me in my throne, even as I also overcame, and am set down with my Father in his throne. He that hath an ear, let him hear what the Spirit says unto the churches" (**Revelation 3:20–22**). God has a rock-solid plan for saving humanity, and He definitely knows what He's doing, more so than all of human knowledge put together.

6. God acts wickedly and unjustly. **Job 24:10** answers this myth. "Therefore, listen to me, you men of understanding: Far be it from God to do wickedness, and from the Almighty to commit iniquity." God never acts unjustly. Some people might say that God killed all the people in Noah's day with a huge flood. *Isn't that doing wicked things?* God killed all the people, except Noah and his family, because the vast majority of people turned to all kinds of wickedness, so God put them to death. By allowing them to die, He showed great mercy and compassion because God promised that all those people would be raised from the dead in the great white throne judgment and be given a second chance as physical humans. The people in Noah's day are not lost forever. They will live again! (See sections 2.5 and 5.1 to learn more about the great white throne judgment.)

7. You cannot trust God. Notice how **Psalm 9:10** answers this myth: "And those who know Your name will put their trust in You; For You, lord, have not forsaken those who seek You." Also, "And He said unto me, it is done. I am Alpha and Omega, the beginning and the end. I will give unto him that is athirst of the fountain of the water of life freely. He that overcomes shall inherit all things; and I will be his God, and he shall be my son" (**Revelation 21:6–7**). God's words are so trustworthy that no human words can compare to them. "God is not a man, that He should lie, nor a son of man, that He should repent. Has He said, and will He not do? Or has He spoken, and will He not make it good? Behold, I have received a command to bless; He has blessed, and I cannot reverse it" (**Numbers 23:19–20**). "As for God, His way is perfect; The word of the LORD is proven; He is a shield to all who trust in Him" (**2 Samuel 22:31**).

8. God is out to get us. "The instant I speak concerning a nation and concerning a kingdom, to pluck up, to pull down, and to destroy it, if that nation against whom I have spoken turns from its evil, I will relent of the disaster that I thought to bring upon it" (**Jeremiah 18:7–8**).

God only punishes us when we do evil in His sight, but if we wholeheartedly repent and do not willingly break His laws anymore, God will forgive and bless us. God loves us all and wants us all to be in His kingdom, but we must repent and obey His commandments. Obtaining this clear picture is yet another piece of the giant jigsaw puzzle that hardly anyone preaches about.

Let us, as men and women of God, continue to be focused on our benevolent God, who wants us to know that there are ways to please Him; that He not only exists but is close by and has not forsaken us; and that He not only cares for us but loves us very much and has big plans for us all. And finally, God reminds us that He is totally reliable and accurate in all things. Let's hold fast and remember these wonderful truths about our loving God, now and forever.

Chapter 3
GOD'S TRUTH ABOUT ANGELS

3.1   BASIC QUESTIONS AND ANSWERS ABOUT ANGELS

The Bible has a lot to say on the topic of angels. The Old Testament speaks of them over one hundred times. The New Testament speaks of angels over 175 times. Angels are mentioned in thirty-four of the sixty-six books found in the Holy Bible. With hundreds of such references on angels, the topic of angels clearly is an important one—and one on which we should be well informed. *Why be informed?* So, others won't be able to deceive you.

There are many varying and preconceived ideas about angels in the world of modern Christianity. *For example, what do angels look like?* Some people think of angels as cute, tiny, innocent boys or girls with halos on their heads and having two small wings; they fly around, bouncing from cloud to cloud, and hold tiny harps in their hands. Others view angels as full-grown people, going from place to place, appearing and then disappearing, helping or rescuing other people on earth, just in the nick of time, from disaster. People also have preconceived ideas about demons. Devils or demons are usually pictured as clothed in red and having a long, pointed tail and horns on their heads, and they usually hold a pitchfork in their hands.

Do all these various ideas come from the Holy Bible, or are they man-made depictions of angels? How can we find the truth about angels? The one and only source for truth about many topics in life, including angels, are readily found in the pages of your Holy Bible. You may be surprised to find some interesting truths that you may not have known. Before we begin the study on angels, be sure to ask God in earnest prayer to open your mind to His truth.

Let us begin by asking some basic questions about angels, the answers to which are not my opinions but are found in the Holy Bible.

What is an angel? The word "angel" comes from the Latin word "angelus," and it literally means "messenger." So, in one sense, angels are messengers from God. There are many examples of angels delivering messages from God to humans on earth. A prime example is when an angel informed Zacharias that he and his wife, Elizabeth, would have a son in their old age. "Then an angel of the Lord appeared to him [Zacharias], standing on the right side of the altar of incense. And when Zacharias saw him [the angel], he was troubled, and fear fell upon him" (**Luke 1:11–12**).

As a messenger, an angel appeared to Mary, the future mother of our Messiah, and announced to her that she would bear a son as a virgin and that she would name Him Immanuel. Notice that in this example, God lets us know the angel by name. "Now in the sixth month the angel Gabriel was sent by God to a city of Galilee named Nazareth, to a virgin betrothed to a man whose name was Joseph, of the house of David. The virgin's name was Mary. And having come in, the angel said to her, 'Rejoice, highly favored one, the Lord is with you; blessed are you among women!'" (**Luke 1:26–28**).

The word angel also means "to minister," serve, help, rescue, and save people who are chosen by God to inherit salvation. "But to which of the angels has He [God the Father] ever said: 'Sit at My right hand, till I make your enemies your footstool'? Are they [angels] not all ministering spirits sent forth to minister for those who will inherit salvation?" (**Hebrews 1:13–14**). People chosen by God have included Noah, Abraham, Isaac, Jacob, Daniel, all the apostles, and others who believed in God and did as God commanded them, despite adversity. Some people living today, who are trying to walk a godly life (like you and me), also may have been called by God.

A prime example of an angel ministering is found in the book of Daniel, where an angel shuts the mouths of lions, thus saving Daniel from a horrific death. Remember that Daniel was called by God to be a prophet, and God sent an angel to rescue him from death. Daniel was a brilliant, young Jewish lad, prophesying during the Babylonian captivity of the Jews. "Then Daniel said to the king, 'O king, live forever! My God sent His angel and shut the lions' mouths, so that they have not hurt me, because I was found innocent before Him; and also, O king, I have done no wrong before you'" (**Daniel 6:21–22**).

In another example, we find an angel rescuing Daniel's three friends—Shadrach, Meshach, and Abednego—from a fiery furnace. "Then King Nebuchadnezzar was astonished; and he rose in haste and spoke, saying to his counselors, 'Did we not cast three men bound into the midst of the fire?' They answered and said to the king, 'True, O king.' 'Look!' he answered, 'I see four men loose, walking in the midst of the fire; and they are not hurt, and the form of the fourth is like the Son of God'" (**Daniel 3:24–25**). One of the four men that the king saw was an angel. And this angel, given power from God on high, caused the three human men not to be hurt or burned by the fire. There are many other examples, but I believe these examples highlight the important point that angels are messengers and ministering helpers, sent by God to accomplish a mission and to help His people. There may be angels living among us humans after all.

Angels may be involved in one or more of the following:

1. Providing protection: "For He shall give His angels charge over you, to keep you in all your ways" (**Psalm 91:11**).

2. Giving guidance: "And while he lingered, the men took hold of his hand, his wife's hand, and the hands of his two daughters, the LORD being merciful to him, and they brought him out and set him outside the city. So it came to pass, when they had brought them outside, that he [the angel] said, 'Escape for your life! Do

not look behind you nor stay anywhere in the plain. Escape to the mountains, lest you be destroyed'" (**Genesis 19:16–17**).

3. Providing encouragement: "And the Angel of the LORD appeared to him [Gideon]), and said to him, "The LORD is with you, you mighty man of valor!" (**Judges 6:12**).

4. Providing deliverance in time of trouble: "Now behold, an angel of the Lord stood by him (Peter), and a light shone in the prison; and he struck Peter on the side and raised him up, saying, 'Arise quickly!' And his chains fell off his hands" (**Acts 12:7**).

5. Giving strength: "Then an angel appeared to Him [Christ] from heaven, strengthening Him" (**Luke 22:43**).

Sadly, the service of angels is rendered largely unseen and often unrecognized by most of humanity today. There may have been instances where humans have entertained angels and were not aware of it. "Do not forget to entertain strangers, for by so doing some have unwittingly entertained angels" (**Hebrews 13:2**). In **1 Chronicles 16:34**, it states that we should be watchful of such help and give thanks to God who sends His angels to our aid. "Oh, give thanks to the LORD, for He is good! For His mercy endures forever."

Can we see angels? In **Luke 1:12**, Zacharias, the priest, "saw him," the angel. In **Luke 1:28**, we read that the angel "having come in, the angel said to her." Certainly, Mary must have seen the angel "come in." In **Daniel 3:24**, King Nebuchadnezzar actually saw "four men" in the fiery furnace, one of which was an angel sent by God. So yes, angels can be seen by the human eye but only if they transform themselves into a physical human. God gives angels the power to transform themselves to be physical men, as the need arises.

But remember, that the primary composition of all angels (good or evil) is spirit. To be spirit means that they cannot be seen by the human eye. The only other way we can see angels is for us to become spirit beings, just like they are, which will happen at a resurrection. Once transformed, angels' resemblance to men can be so realistic that they can actually be taken to be human beings. Reference **Hebrews 13:2**, above, and look again at **Hebrews 1:14**, "Are they [the angels] not all ministering spirits sent forth to minister [help] for those who will inherit salvation?"

What do angels look like in their natural, created state? We know that angels can transform themselves into human beings. The Bible speaks of **three** types of angels, and all three look different, each having various roles and responsibilities. Let's take a look at the types of angels, beginning with the lowest in rank.

1. The "Seraphim" is **third** in rank among angels. The Hebrew word "seraphim" means "burning ones." This no doubt, refers to the seraphim's burning desire to serve their creator God. "In the year that King Uzziah died, I saw the Lord sitting on a throne, high and lifted up, and the train of His robe filled the temple. Above it stood seraphim; each one had six wings: with two he covered his face, with two he covered his feet, and with two he flew. And one cried to another and said: 'Holy, holy, holy is the LORD of hosts; The whole earth is full of His glory!'" (**Isaiah 6:1–3**). Notice that each seraphim has six wings and hovers over God's throne.

2. The "Cherubim" is **second** in rank among angels. These are powerful and majestic creatures that also surround God's throne. Notice what they look like.

> Also, from within it came the likeness of four living creatures. And this was their appearance: they had the likeness of a man. Each one had four faces, and each one had four wings. Their legs were straight, and the soles of their feet were like the soles of calves' feet. They sparkled like the color of burnished bronze. The hands of a man were under their wings on their four sides; and each of

the four had faces and wings. Their wings touched one another. The creatures did not turn when they went, but each one went straight forward. Unlike the seraphim, each cherubim has four wings and each one has four faces! As for the likeness of their faces, each had the face of a man; each of the four had the face of a lion on the right side, each of the four had the face of an ox on the left side, and each of the four had the face of an eagle. Thus were their faces. Their wings stretched upward; two wings of each one touched one another, and two covered their bodies. And each one went straight forward; they went wherever the spirit wanted to go, and they did not turn when they went. (**Ezekiel 1:5–12**)

In **Ezekiel 10:1**, we find these same creatures are explicitly called the "cherubim:" "And I looked, and there in the firmament that was above the head of the cherubim, there appeared something like a sapphire stone, having the appearance of the likeness of a throne." So far, neither the seraphim nor the cherubim look like tiny innocent children with halos on their heads. These are powerful and awesome looking creatures, made by God for His special purposes.

3. The "Archangel" **is first** in rank among angels. The word "archangel" implies the highest rank among angels. The Bible states that only Michael is designated an archangel, but there may be more. "Yet Michael the archangel, in contending with the devil, when he disputed about the body of Moses, dared not bring against him a reviling accusation, but said, 'The Lord rebuke you!'" (**Jude 9**). Also, "For the Lord Himself will descend from heaven with a shout, with the voice of an archangel, and with the trumpet of God. And the dead in Christ will rise first" (**1 Thessalonians 4:16**). This, of course, is speaking of a future resurrection, where God's called-out people will rise from the dead first with the voice of an archangel.

According to Daniel, Michael, the archangel, is the special guardian and protector of God's people (Israel). "At that time Michael shall stand up, the great prince who stands watch over the sons of your people; And there shall be a time of trouble, such as never was since there was a nation, even to that time. And at that time your people shall be delivered, everyone who is found written in the book" (**Daniel 12:1**). Also, Michael is called "one of the chief princes." There may be more than one chief prince. "But the prince of the kingdom of Persia [Satan] withstood me [Gabriel] twenty-one days; and behold, Michael, one of the chief princes, came to help me, for I had been left alone there with the kings of Persia" (**Daniel 10:13**). The kings of Persia are referred to elsewhere in the Bible as demons. The Bible does not state who the other "chief princes" are, but it does name **three** high-ranking angels by name:

1. "Lucifer" means "light bringer." He was the one who rebelled against God and is now Satan, the Devil (**Isaiah 14:12**).

2. "Gabriel" means "mighty one of God." He appeared to Zacharias (**Luke 1:19**); to Mary, the mother of Christ (**Luke 1:26**); and to Daniel on two separate occasions (**Daniel 8:16; 9:21**).

3. "Michael" means "who is like God," protector of God's people (Israel). It seems that all the angels have multiple wings and do not look like innocent little babies with halos. Fallen angels do not have pitchforks in their hands or horns on their heads, nor are they red in color.

If angels are composed of spirit, can they die? The Bible clearly tells us that angels cannot die. They were created spirit beings by God, and, according to the Bible, spirit cannot die. "Nor can they [God's people who will be changed to spirit in the first resurrection] die anymore, for they are equal to the angels and are sons of God, being sons of the resurrection" (**Luke 20:36**). Once God's chosen people die, they will be resurrected in the first resurrection as spirit beings, equal to angels in the sense that they cannot die. What wonderful news this is!

Can angels marry? The Bible clearly states that angels cannot marry. "For when they [God's people in the first resurrection] rise from the dead, they neither marry nor are given in marriage, but are like angels in heaven" (**Mark 12:25**). Notice that the primary habitat of angels is heaven, not earth. "And He said to him, 'Most assuredly, I say to you, hereafter you shall see heaven open, and the angels of God ascending and descending upon the Son of Man'" (**John 1:51**). Angels descend from heaven, accomplish their mission, and ascend back up to heaven. And since angels cannot and do not marry, it follows that they cannot reproduce or have baby angels. This, of course, means that angels in their natural state (spirit) are sexless. There are no male or female angels. The number of angels God created is a firm, fixed number that cannot increase or decrease by death or reproduction.

3.2 IN-DEPTH QUESTIONS AND ANSWERS ABOUT ANGELS

Where exactly did angels come from? Angels were created by God's spoken word and therefore came from Him. "Praise Him, all His angels; Praise Him, all His hosts! Praise Him, sun and moon; Praise Him, all you stars of light! Praise Him, you heavens of heavens, and you waters above the heavens! Let them praise the name of the LORD, For He commanded and they were created" (**Psalm 148:2–5**). God created angels and the sun, moon, and stars. He created them all! That's how awesome God is: He commanded, and all things were instantaneously created.

Since angels and all the hosts were created by God, we can understand that angels have not always existed. They were created at a certain point in time, but the Bible does not say when that point in time was. It could have been hundreds, thousands, millions, or billions of years ago. But we do know that before that point, nothing existed except God, wherein He commanded and the angels were created. Angels could not have been human prior to that time because God created angels as angels, the first time. The belief that angels were first created as human is not found in the Bible. But remember that angels have the power to transform themselves into human beings. Angels and the whole creation all had a beginning; they did not always exist. The God family is the only family that has always existed. The God family has no beginning or end; they always have been. "'I am the Alpha and the Omega, the Beginning and the End,' says the Lord, 'who is and who was and who is to come, the Almighty'" **(Revelation 1:8)**.

When were angels created? From the book of Job, we find that the angels were created before God created the heavens and the earth because they "shouted for joy" at God's newly created universe. *How long before?* The Bible does not say. But take a look at Job: "Where were you [God speaking to Job] when I laid the foundations of the earth? Tell Me, if you have understanding. Who determined its measurements? Surely you know! Or who stretched the line upon it? To what were its foundations fastened? Or who laid its cornerstone, When the morning stars [angels] sang together, and all the sons of God [angels] shouted for joy?" **(Job 38:4–7)**.

How do we know that "sons of God" refer to angels? "Now there was a day when the sons of God came to present themselves before the LORD, and Satan also came among them" **(Job 1:6)**. Lucifer (who later became Satan) is an angel who turned against God, and he, in this instance, was "among the sons of God." The only way a person can be among the sons of God is if he already is a son or becomes a son of God through a resurrection. Angels are created sons of God. Christ was the only begotten Son of God. We can become begotten sons of God if we obey God and receive the gift of God's Holy Spirit. No human can ever present himself before God, only angels and God's only begotten Son, Jesus the Christ, can do that, because they are spirit. Only through a resurrection can humans become spirit. Only then are we "born again." (See section 5.1 for more information on what the Bible says about being born again.)

Which of the two God beings created the angels? There are two God beings but only one God family: God the Father and God the Word (who later became Christ, His beloved Son). The Father and the Son make up the God family. The Bible tells that all things were created through the Word God. "In the beginning was the Word, and the Word was with God, and the Word was God. He was in the beginning with God. All things were made through Him [the Word], and without Him nothing was made that was made" (**John 1:1–3**). Notice that the Bible says "all things," which means everything, including the angels, were created by the Word God.

To confirm that angels were created by Christ, take a look at **Colossians 1:16**. "For by Him [Christ] all things were created that are in heaven and that are on earth, visible and invisible, whether thrones or dominions or principalities or powers. All things were created through Him and for Him." God the Father speaks to His Son, and His Son commands it into existence.

How many angels did the Word God create? The Bible does not specifically state the exact number of angels that God created. But it does say that a very large number of them were created. "But you have come to Mount Zion and to the city of the living God, the heavenly Jerusalem, to an innumerable company of angels" (**Hebrews 12:22**). Many, many angels were created. Again, **Revelation 5:11** tells us that ten thousand times ten thousand angels exist: "Then I looked, and I heard the voice of many angels around the throne, the living creatures, and the elders; and the number of them was ten thousand times ten thousand, and thousands of thousands."

Thus, an innumerable number of angels were created by Christ. We, as humans, cannot even count the number of angels. But God knows all of them by name, just as He knows the billions of planets and galaxies throughout the universe by name. "He counts the number of the stars; He calls them all by name" (**Psalm 147:4**).

Were all the angels good when God created them? All the angels in God's universe were created good and holy, just as God made and pronounced all His creation "very good." "Then God saw everything that He had made, and indeed it was very good. So, the evening and the morning were the sixth day" (**Genesis 1:31**). Notice that it says "everything that He had made" was very good, so God did not create evil angels; that would contradict the statement. In addition, creating evil angels would be totally inconsistent with God's holy character. **Jude 6** tells us that some angels rebelled against God and broke His laws: "And the angels who did not keep their proper domain, but left their own abode, He [God] has reserved in everlasting chains under darkness for the judgment of the great day." Angels who "did not keep their proper domain" refers to those angels who went along with their leader, Satan, the Devil. For them, God has reserved everlasting chains under darkness.

Did God create a devil? One of the most important questions might be the origin of a devil. *Where did he come from?* An associated question is whether there really is an evil force in the world today. Human reasoning might assume that if God created all things, then God created evil and a devil too. *But did God really create evil and a devil? What exactly does the Bible say about the devil? Did God create him to harass humanity forever?* These are very important questions that deserve true Bible answers; only God's answers will suffice.

Science, religion, and higher education do not truly know the answers to these questions. *Why?* It is because all three institutions have rejected revealed biblical knowledge coming from their creator God through His Word, the Holy Bible. Science does not believe in God. Religion does not believe what God says in the Bible. Higher education has chosen to kick God and the Bible out of their classrooms in favor of evolution and the big bang theory. As a result, humanity finds itself in the present sad state of affairs. Remember that for every effect there is a cause.

Let us turn to **Genesis 1:1-2**, where there seems to be a disparity. "In the beginning God created the heavens and the earth" (**Genesis 1:1**). We must remember that when God creates, He creates things that are wonderful, beautiful, and in complete harmony with everything else He created. But then we find a startling statement that is contrary to a beautiful creation. "The earth was without form, and void; and darkness was on the face of the deep. And the Spirit of God was hovering over the face of the waters" (**Genesis 1:2**).

Most people might miss the clear meaning in this verse. The English words "without form and void" are translated from the Hebrew words "tohu" and "bohu." These two words, used together in Scripture, indicate an uninhabitable wasteland—a condition of desolation and destruction. *Why would God create an uninhabitable planet?* The answer is that God did not and does not create in that manner. As we have already read, all of creation was "very good." *So, what happened between **verses 1 and 2 of Genesis 1**?* Something must have happened to change God's original, beautiful, and otherwise "very good" creation of the earth for it to become "void and empty."

Hebrew scholars are quick to point out that the Hebrew word "Hayah" found in **Genesis 1:2** was incorrectly translated as "was." But, as we will see in **Genesis 19:26**, Hayah was correctly translated as "became." The earth became empty and void. It was not originally created by God in that state of emptiness. "But his [Lot's] wife looked back behind him, and she became a pillar of salt" (**Genesis 19:26**). Lot certainly did not marry "a pillar of salt!" She was not always a pillar of salt. But because she disobeyed God's instructions (the cause) and looked back at the city that was burning, she became a pillar of salt (the effect).

People still ask, *"What caused the earth to become void and empty?"* Usually, the cause has to do with disobeying God in some way. In Lucifer's case, he rebelled against Almighty God, His law, His government, and His way of life. In essence, Lucifer wanted to kick God off His throne and be God himself. The effect of Lucifer's rebellion was that the earth became void and empty. And that is precisely how evil entered the universe and how Lucifer, through his own choice, became Satan, the adversary. Because of Satan's rebellion, he was thrown out of heaven and onto earth. As the late Paul Harvey would say, "Now you know the rest of the story." God had to renew the face of the earth for humans to live. With this knowledge, a true Christian can understand why earth's surface had to be renewed.

"How you are fallen from heaven, O Day Star, son of Dawn! How you are cut down to the ground, you who laid the nations low! For you [Lucifer] have said in your heart: 'I will ascend into heaven, I will exalt my throne above the stars of God; I will also sit on the mount of the congregation on the farthest sides of the north; I will ascend above the heights of the clouds, I will be like the Most High" (**Isaiah 14:12–14**).

What led Lucifer to rebel against God? I'd like to provide **five** important character changes that happened within Lucifer that led him to rebel against His maker.

1. Even though God gave Lucifer great authority, Lucifer wanted to be God. "Son of man, say to the prince of Tyre, 'Thus says the Lord GOD: "Because your heart is lifted up, and you say, 'I am a god, I sit in the seat of gods, in the midst of the seas,' yet you are a man, and not a god, though you set your heart as the heart of a god" (**Ezekiel 28:2**).

Who is this prince of Tyre? Notice that this "prince" was perfect in the day he was created. No human is in any way perfect. Also, take note that this prince was an anointed cherub, a type of angel. Lucifer was the anointed cherub. This prince was in the Holy Mountain (or government) of God and walked back and forth among the fiery stones. *Can any human walk on fiery stones?* Absolutely not! Lastly, the prince was also in the Garden of Eden. This prince is none other than Satan, the Devil. "Son of man, take up a lamentation for the king [prince] of Tyre, and say to him, 'Thus says the Lord GOD: "You were the seal of perfection, full of wisdom and perfect in beauty. You were in Eden, the garden of God; every precious stone was your covering: The sardius, topaz, and diamond, Beryl, onyx, and jasper, Sapphire, turquoise, and emerald with gold. The workmanship of your timbrels and pipes was prepared for you on the day you were created" (**Ezekiel 28:12–13**).

Notice also, "For you [Lucifer] have said in your heart: 'I will ascend into heaven, I will exalt my throne above the stars of God; I will also sit on the mount of the congregation on the farthest sides of the north; I will ascend above the heights of the clouds, I will be like the Most High" (**Isaiah 14:13–14**). Notice Satan's attitude—he wanted to be exalted and worshipped, just like God was. Satan became jealous of God and thought only of himself. No love existed within Satan.

2. Even though God created Lucifer with great wisdom, Lucifer's heart became proud and boastful because of his riches. "With your [Lucifer's] wisdom and your understanding you have gained riches for yourself, and gathered gold and silver into your treasuries; By your great wisdom in trade you have increased your riches, and your heart is lifted up because of your riches" (**Ezekiel 28:4–6**).

3. Even though God created Lucifer with perfect beauty, iniquity (or lawlessness) was found in him. "Son of man, take up a lamentation for the king of Tyre, and say to him, 'Thus says the Lord GOD: "You were the seal of perfection, full of wisdom and perfect in beauty... You [Lucifer] were perfect in your ways from the day you were created, till iniquity was found in you.... Your heart was lifted up because of your beauty; you corrupted your wisdom for the sake of your splendor; I cast you to the ground, I laid you before kings, that they might gaze at you" (**Ezekiel 28:12, 15, 17**).

4. Even though God gave Lucifer wealth, he became violent, and he sinned. "By the abundance of your trading you became filled with violence within, and you sinned" (**Ezekiel 28:16**). "So, the great dragon was cast out, that serpent of old, called the Devil and Satan, who deceives the whole world; he was cast to the earth, and his angels (called demons) were cast out with him" (**Revelation 12:9**). Satan still rules and deceives this world today, causing wars, hatred, envy, jealousy, sicknesses, and confusion among nations

and people. Just as Satan deceived Adam and Eve, so he deceives all of humanity today.

5. Even though God allowed Lucifer to be in His government, Lucifer was cast out of it because of his many sins. "You were the anointed cherub who covers; I established you; you were on the holy mountain of God; you walked back and forth in the midst of fiery stones. You were perfect in your ways from the day you were created, till iniquity [lawlessness] was found in you" (**Ezekiel 28:14–15**). "Your heart was lifted up because of your beauty; you corrupted your wisdom for the sake of your splendor; I cast you to the ground, I laid you before kings, that they might gaze at you" (**Ezekiel 28:17**).

Let it be known that our great God neither created evil nor a devil. Evil was brought into the universe by Lucifer's rebellion and jealousy against God, after which he became known as Satan, the Devil. His rebel rule was not a government based on God's principle of out-flowing love, giving, and concern for others but was based on self-centeredness, jealousy, vanity, lust, greed, envy, hatred, and destruction. Instead of bringing light, as his name suggests, Lucifer brought darkness, desolation, and deception. Lucifer also introduced the first lie to our first parents, Adam and Eve. The lie was that they would not die if they ate of the forbidden fruit. People today continue to believe that same lie. They believe that they will not die but will go to heaven or hell and live forever. (Reference sections 4.7 and 4.9 on dying.)

Do demons try to hurt humans? You bet they do! Consider the following Scripture: "Be sober, be vigilant; because your adversary the devil walks about like a roaring lion, seeking whom he may devour" (**1 Peter 5:8**). Our adversary on this earth is not another human being but Satan, the Devil, and his demons, who seek to devour and destroy each one of us, because at our resurrection, we will be higher in authority than all the angels. "Put on the whole armor of God that you may be able to stand against the wiles of the devil. For we do not wrestle against flesh and blood, but against principalities, against powers, against the rulers of the darkness of this age, against spiritual hosts of wickedness in the heavenly places" (**Ephesians 6:11–12**).

Satan always tempts people to lie, cheat, steal, commit adultery, and make wrong choices or do other wrong things. He tempted Christ many times while on earth. While Satan tempts us to do wrong all the time, God tests us to make the right decisions. That is the big difference.

Satan has the power to deceive the human heart with lies, hatred, envy, and greed, if we let him. He constantly accuses us of wrongdoing before God, trying to destroy us. "Then I heard a loud voice saying in heaven, now salvation, and strength, and the kingdom of our God, and the power of His Christ have come, for the accuser of our brethren, who accused them before our God day and night, has been cast down" (**Revelation 12:10**). Satan and his followers constantly accuse and slander our brothers and sisters in Christ, who keep God's laws and do His commandments.

In Daniel, Satan and his demons also try to detain holy angels from accomplishing their God-given mission to help us. "Then he [Gabriel] said to me, 'Do not fear, Daniel, for from the first day that you set your heart to understand, and to humble yourself before your God, your words were heard; and I have come because of your words. But the prince of the kingdom of Persia withstood me twenty-one days; and behold, Michael, one of the chief princes, came to help me, for I had been left alone there with the kings of Persia'" (**Daniel 10:12–13**). Satan and his demons always try to hurt, deceive, or destroy God's people and detain holy angels from accomplishing their godly mission.

What can we do to protect ourselves against evil angels? As Christian soldiers, we must ask God, in prayer, for protection and constantly be on guard against these evil spirit beings. We must be firmly girded with God's truth. "And take the helmet of salvation, and the sword of the Spirit, which is the word of God; praying always with all prayer and supplication in the Spirit, being watchful to this end with all perseverance and supplication for all the saints" (**Ephesians 6:17–18**). It is true that God knows our every need, but He also wants to hear from us in prayer.

We must also put on the whole armor of God so we can withstand evil. "Therefore, take up the whole armor of God, that you may be able to withstand in the evil day, and having done all, to stand" (**Ephesians 6:13**). The phrase "whole armor of God" means to be truthful, peaceful, and always have faith in God.

"Stand therefore, having girded your waist with truth, having put on the breastplate of righteousness, and having shod your feet with the preparation of the gospel of peace; above all, taking the shield of faith with which you will be able to quench all the fiery darts of the wicked one" (**Ephesians 6:14–16**).

1 Peter 5:8 admonishes us, "Be sober, be vigilant; because your adversary the devil walks about like a roaring lion, seeking whom he may devour."

3.3   WHO IS THE "RULER" OF THIS WORLD?

Who really rules this world, and how does he deceive humans? While on earth, Christ said that his kingdom was not of this world. "Jesus answered, 'My kingdom is not of this world. If My kingdom were of this world, My servants would fight, so that I should not be delivered to the Jews; but now My kingdom is not from here'" (**John 18:36**). Even when Christ came to earth the first time, He said that His kingdom was not on earth. Remember, that because of rebellion, Satan and his demons were cast out of heaven to this earth. This earth is where Satan temporarily rules today. "Now is the judgment of this world; now the ruler of this world will be cast out" (**John 12:31**). Also, "I will no longer talk much with you because the ruler of this world Satan is coming and he has nothing much on me" (**John 12:30**).

Being sneaky and vicious, Satan works subtly, invisibly, affecting the attitudes and minds of unknowing and unbelieving humans. In **2 Corinthians 4:4**, Paul refers to Satan as the "god of this age"—"Whose minds the god of this age has blinded, who do not believe, lest the light of the gospel of the glory of Christ, who is the image of God, should shine on them."

Just like Satan "blinded" the minds of Adam and Eve, he has successfully blinded all humanity throughout the ages, and because Satan is invisible, most people do not know the true cause of their problems. All they see are the effects.

Paul also refers to Satan as "the prince of the power of the air." Take a look: "In which you once walked according to the course of this world, according to the prince of the power of the air, the spirit who now works in the sons of disobedience" (**Ephesians 2:2**).

Some readers may think that Satan cannot influence the human mind, but I ask you to carefully consider the following questions: *Didn't Satan influence the minds of Adam and Eve in the garden of Eden? Didn't Satan influence Herod's mind, the Roman ruler over Israel, who caused the killing of all innocent infants under the age of two? Didn't Satan tempt Christ three times while in the desert?* The answer to all these questions and many similar ones is, yes, Satan can and does powerfully influence human minds. But people do not know or believe that he can. Satan is today the invisible power that sways the entire world into the dark and evil realm of war, poverty, murder, and rape. And the disbelieving humanity unknowingly allows him to do just that because most do not believe what is stated in the Bible. To complicate the matter further, the Bible tells us that humans, in general, do not want "to retain God in their knowledge." They do not want knowledge from God, and they do not want to believe what God says. Take a look at **Romans 1:28**, which says, "And even as they did not like to retain God in their knowledge, God gave them over to a debased mind, to do those things which are not fitting."

The phrase "debased mind" indicates a foolish mind; a mind devoid of godly knowledge. A debased mind rejects the Bible and God's truth found therein. It is a mind that rejects revealed knowledge and accepts man-made theories like evolution and the big bang. "For since the creation of the world His invisible attributes are clearly seen, being understood by the things that are made, even His eternal power and

Godhead, so that they [the disobedient people] are without excuse, because, although they knew God, they did not glorify Him as God, nor were thankful, but became futile in their thoughts, and their foolish hearts were darkened. Professing to be wise, they became fools" (**Romans 1:20–22**). This is yet another vital and correctly placed piece of the giant jigsaw puzzle. Satan, today is the temporary ruler of this world.

3.4   QUESTIONS AND ANSWERS ON THE FATE OF SATAN AND HIS DEMONS

What's going to happen to Satan and his demons? Let us read **Jude 6–7**: "And the angels who did not keep their proper domain, but left their own abode, He [God] has reserved in everlasting chains under darkness for the judgment of the great day; as Sodom and Gomorrah, and the cities around them in a similar manner to these, having given themselves over to sexual immorality and gone after strange flesh, are set forth as an example, suffering the vengeance of eternal fire." Remember that Satan is composed of spirit and, according to the Bible, cannot die, but he and his demons will have a day of judgment, resulting in everlasting chains under darkness. Ultimately, Satan will be thrown into the lake of fire. "The devil, who deceived them, was cast into the lake of fire and brimstone where the beast and the false prophet are. And they will be tormented day and night forever and ever" (**Revelation 20:10**). Clearly, the fate of Satan and his demons is not a good one.

What does Satan look like today? Lucifer was created as the anointed cherub; therefore, he looks like the cherubim described in section 3.1. "You were in Eden, the garden of God; every precious stone was your covering: The sardius, topaz, and diamond, beryl, onyx, and jasper, sapphire, turquoise, and emerald with gold. The workmanship of your timbrels and pipes were prepared for you on the day you were created. You were the anointed cherub who covers; I established you; you were on the holy mountain of God; you walked back and forth in the midst of fiery stones" (**Ezekiel 28:13–14**).

Satan and his demons are not red in color, neither do they have horns or carry pitchforks. These ideas come from man's imagination and are not found anywhere in the Holy Bible. Lucifer looks the same as when God created him, but his name was changed to Satan after his rebellion against God. He still looks like the cherubim. He still looks beautiful; he is very smart and full of wisdom, although his wisdom became corrupted.

Does Satan know he's going to lose to God in the end? Satan thinks he can win a war against God. In thinking this thought, the mind of Satan and his followers has become warped; corrupted; filled with envy, pride, hatred, and jealousy; and is delusional. *Why is Satan's mind delusional?* Because he thinks he can become greater, smarter, and more powerful than his maker Imagine that! That's like the pot thinking that it's greater than the potter. It cannot happen, yet Satan thinks it can! That's why he is delusional and does not believe that he will lose in the end, even though the Bible clearly states he will be cast into the lake of fire and brimstone. (Reference **Revelation 20:10.**)

Why doesn't Satan get on God's side again? Because Satan and his followers are spirit beings, they cannot die, and their sins cannot be repented. God tested all the angels, as He tests all humans. Whatever decision each angel made at that fateful point in time, when God tested all of them, is irrevocable—their choice, good or bad, is binding forever. Two-thirds of the angels chose to remain loyal to their Creator. The sinning angels chose to rebel against God and corrupted themselves into thinking they could overthrow Him. Because humans die, they can wholeheartedly repent of their sins, using Christ's shed blood to wipe their sins away, and be given another chance to live God's way of life in a future resurrection.

As Paul states, those who are called to partake in the first resurrection will judge the angels. That's why Satan hates and wants to accuse and destroy humans in general but especially God's people. "Do you not know that the saints will judge the world? And if the world will be judged by you, are you unworthy to judge the smallest matters? Do you not know that we shall judge angels? How much more, things that pertain to this life?" (**1 Corinthians 6:2–3**).

How do humans compare with the angels? Both are finite and limited. Humans were created physical and are subject to decay, and all must die at least once. In the case of Lazarus who died in Christ's day, Jesus, the Christ, resurrected him to physical life, only to die physically again. "And as it is appointed for men to die once, but after this the judgment" (**Hebrews 9:27**). After humans die, they will be resurrected, either in the first resurrection as spirit beings at Christ's return or the great white throne judgment as physical beings, after Christ's one thousand year reign on earth. Notice the first resurrection mentioned: "Nor can they [God's people] die anymore, for they are equal to the angels and are sons of God, being sons of the resurrection" (**Luke 20:36**). "Then I saw a great white throne and Him who sat on it, from whose face the earth and the heaven fled away. And there was found no place for them" (**Revelation 20:11**). Angels are created as spirit beings and do not decay, neither can they die but are limited in what they can do. Just as humans cannot be at two places at once, neither can angels. (Reference **Daniel 10:13**.)

"You have made him a little lower than the angels; You have crowned him with glory and honor, and set him over the works of Your hands" (**Hebrews 2:7**). The Scripture points out that mortal man is made "a little lower" than the angels. But upon a resurrection, humans will be changed into spirit and will judge the angels. Again, that is why Satan and his demons are jealous and try to destroy humans. "What is man that You are mindful of him, and the son of man that You visit him? For You have made him a little lower than the angels. And You have crowned him with glory and honor. You have made him to have dominion over the works of Your hands; You have put all things under his feet" (**Psalm 8:4–6**).

Both angels and humans depend on God for continued existence and well-being. Both worship God. "Praise Him, all His angels; Praise Him, all His hosts!" (**Psalm 148:2**). Both are responsible and accountable to God. "And when He [Christ] has come, He will convict the world of sin, and of righteousness, and of judgment: of sin, because they do not believe in Me; of righteousness, because I go to My Father and you see Me no more; of judgment, because the ruler of this world [Satan] is judged" (**John 16:8–11**). Both angel and man will ultimately be judged by God, according to their works.

Other distinctions already mentioned include humans marry, have sex organs, have offspring, grow old, and die. Angels cannot marry, are sexless, cannot reproduce, are ageless, and do not die.

How do angels compare to God? There is no comparison. "For who in the heavens can be compared to the LORD? Who among the sons of the mighty can be likened to the LORD?" (**Psalm 89:6**). Even though angels are created powerful, beautiful, and intelligent spirit beings, God is infinitely greater than all the angels put together. He is the Creator; angels were created beings. Angels, like humans, have a beginning, in that they were created at a certain point. God has always existed. (Reference **Revelation 1:8; 22:13; Isaiah 45:5**.)

Angels cannot be everywhere at once. Scripture clearly tells us that angels fly from one place to another. "Yes, while I was speaking in prayer, the man Gabriel, whom I had seen in the vision at the beginning, being caused to fly swiftly, reached me about the time of the evening offering" (**Daniel 9:21**). Also, "But the prince of the kingdom of Persia withstood me twenty-one days; and behold, Michael, one of the chief princes, came to help me, for I had been left alone there with the kings of Persia" (**Daniel 10:13**).

God is omnipotent and omnipresent. He is Almighty and all powerful. God created everything from nothing. "When Abram was ninety-nine years old, the LORD appeared to Abram and said to him, 'I am Almighty God; walk before Me and be blameless'" (**Genesis 17:1**). "'I am the Alpha and the Omega, the Beginning and the End,' says the Lord, 'who is and who was and who is to come, the Almighty'" (**Revelation 1:8**).

God is omniscient. "Who has declared from the beginning, that we may know? And former times, that we may say, 'He is righteous'? Surely there is no one who shows, surely there is no one who declares, surely there is no one who hears your words" (**Isaiah 41:26**). Also consider, "Tell and bring forth your case; Yes, let them take counsel together. Who has declared this from ancient time? Who has told it from that time? Have not I, the LORD? And there is no other God besides Me, a just God and a Savior; there is none besides Me" (**Isaiah 45:21**).

Should humans worship angels? The Colossian church in Paul's day committed this very sin of worshipping angels. Look at what Paul said to the Colossian church: "Let no one cheat you of your reward, taking delight in false humility and worship of angels, intruding into those things which he has not seen, vainly puffed up by his fleshly mind" (**Colossians 2:18**).

Paul also warned the members of the church in Rome not to worship the creation instead of the Creator. Remember that God created angels, and they are not to be worshipped. "Therefore, God also gave them up to uncleanness, in the lusts of their hearts, to dishonor their bodies among themselves, who exchanged the truth of God for the lie, and worshiped and served the creature [Satan] rather than the Creator, who is blessed forever. Amen" (**Romans 1:24–25**).

Suffice it to say that only God the Father and Christ are worthy of worship and no one else—not ever! "You shall have no other gods before Me" (**Exodus 20:3**). "But the hour is coming, and now is, when the true worshipers will worship the Father in spirit and truth; for the Father is seeking such to worship Him" (**John 4:23**).

Christ specifically stated that we should pray to the Father in His name. "And whatever you ask in My name, that I will do, that the Father may be glorified in the Son" (**John 13:14**). "You did not choose Me, but I chose you and appointed you that you should go and bear fruit, and that your fruit should remain, that whatever you ask the Father in My name He may give you" (**John 15:16**). As stated in **Matthew 6:9**, Christ taught His disciples how to pray: "In this manner, therefore, pray: Our Father in heaven, Hallowed be Your name." It becomes crystal clear that Christ, our Savior and Lord, wants us to pray to God the Father in His name.

As followers of Christ, we should take great comfort in how God has set up His universe. He has ordained authority, including that of the entire angelic realm, for the optimum benefit of humanity. Remember, angels are ministering spirits, created to serve God and His creation, including humans. Remember also that holy angels never do their own thing but only do what the God family commands them to do.

I hope that this study on angels has helped you to see more of the giant jigsaw puzzle. God is still on His throne, still alive and well, and still cares for His creation very much. Satan and his demons, as rulers of this present evil world, only have a short time left before God dethrones them forever and begins to intervene in human affairs. Only with divine leadership will there be long-lasting peace, harmony, happiness, and true justice on this earth. Only then will there be no more war, no sickness, no poverty, no more sorrow, no more pain and suffering, and no more death. Notice the following powerful Scripture: "And God will wipe away every tear from their eyes; there shall be no more death, nor sorrow, nor crying. There shall be no more pain, for the former things have passed away" (**Revelation 21:4**).

I hope that God speeds that day!

Chapter 4
GOD'S TRUTH ABOUT MAN

4.1   THE ORIGIN OF MAN AND THE UNIVERSE

As we learned in the previous chapter, the invisible and powerful Satan, the Devil, is the real cause of human problems and suffering in this world. He works in and through the minds and attitudes of human beings, just as he did with our first parents, Adam and Eve. It is certainly not God who causes hardships because He made us and loves us. However, God does want us to love, worship, and obey Him. Take another look at **John 3:16**, which reads, "For God so loved the world that He gave His only begotten Son, that whoever believes in Him should not perish but have everlasting life." God loves us, but humanity as a whole, under the influence of Satan, does not know Him, nor does it believe what He says in His Holy Bible. And because most people do not believe what God says, they make their own individual decisions. Everyone is doing what is right in their own eyes, without consulting the Holy Bible. "You shall not at all do as we are doing here today—every man doing whatever is right in his own eyes" (**Deuteronomy 12:8**). The end result of everyone doing what they think is right is what we have today—endless chaos, wars, and widespread deadly disease epidemics.

In this chapter, we will focus our attention on the true origin of man and the universe and that relationship. You will discover **four** biblical truths that will stir your spirit and greatly enhance your Bible knowledge.

1. *Who made man and the universe? Did man just evolve, or was he created by intelligent life?* The Bible tells us plainly that "all things were created through the Word," and the Word God later became Jesus the Christ, the Son of God, our Savior. (Please refer to chapter 2 of this book to refresh your memory about the Word God.) "All things were made through Him [Word God], and without Him nothing was made that was made" (**John 1:3**). *Is it possible that the phrase "all things" would include the vast expanse of the universe?* Recall that "created" literally means to make something from nothing. As we will soon see, God sustains it all through the power of His Word.

   The book of Hebrews reaffirms what we just read in **John 1:3**. Take a look at **Hebrews 1:1–3**, which reads, "God, who at various times and in various ways spoke in time past to the fathers by the prophets, has in these last days spoken to us by His Son, whom He has appointed heir of 'all things,' through whom also He [the Word God] made the worlds; who being the brightness of His glory and the express image of His person, and upholding all things by the word of His power, when He had by Himself purged our sins, sat down at the right hand of the Majesty on high." Man and the universe were made through the Word God.

2. *What was the condition of "all things" when the Word God created them?* God said that His creation "was very good." "Then God saw everything that He had made, and indeed it was very good. So, the evening and the morning were the sixth day" (**Genesis 1:31**). Remember that when God creates, He creates in great beauty and in total harmony with everything else. But as we learned, after Satan's rebellion against God, the entire universe, including earth, became void, empty, decayed, and lifeless. Other than the God family and the angels, no life as we know it exists on any planet other than earth. With Satan's rebellion against God, sin entered the world.

But most scientists do not believe what the Bible says, nor do they believe in God. So, they continue their vain search to find some form of life on various planets, but as the Bible plainly says, the planets are lifeless, decayed, and empty. Now, take a look at what Paul states in the New Testament: "For the earnest expectation of the creation eagerly waits for the revealing of the sons of God. For the creation was subjected to futility [uselessness], not willingly, but because of Him who subjected it in hope; because the creation itself also will be delivered from the bondage of corruption [empty, wasted] into the glorious liberty of the children of God. For we know that the whole creation groans and labors with birth pangs together until now" (**Romans 8:19–22**).

In other words, the entire vast universe is waiting and "groaning" for God's children to set it free from being empty and useless, to someday becoming inhabited and useful. That's what "glorious liberty" means. God wants us, His children, to be part of that glorious, liberating process of the universe when it will finally become inhabited, useful, and vibrant with life.

3. *Of all the things that God created, to whom did He give "dominion" over all the physical creatures on earth?* To be given dominion simply means to be given authority over things. David was inspired to write that God gave authority over all things to physical man. This includes the entire physical earth, the atmosphere, and the rivers and oceans. Notice what David writes: "You have put all things under his [man's] feet, all sheep and oxen—Even the beasts of the field, the birds of the air, and the fish of the sea that pass through the paths of the seas. O LORD, our Lord, how excellent is Your name in all the earth!" (**Psalm 8:7–9**).

Genesis 1:26–28 reaffirms this God-given dominion to man when it states,

> Then God said, "Let Us make man in Our image, according to Our likeness; let them have dominion

> over the fish of the sea, over the birds of the air, and over the cattle, over all the earth and over every creeping thing that creeps on the earth." So, God created man in His own image; in the image of God He created him; male and female He created them. Then God blessed them, and God said to them, "Be fruitful and multiply; fill the earth and subdue it; have dominion over the fish of the sea, over the birds of the air, and over every living thing that moves on the earth."

It is important to know and understand that we humans are created in the image and likeness of God Himself. He gave us His image. We look like Him. We are not animals and certainly did not evolve from some slimy, lower life, as some of the most "educated" suggest. We did not evolve from monkeys or gorillas, as the theory of evolution suggests.

4. *Will God someday expand man's dominion over physical things on earth to include things in the spiritual realm, which cannot be seen at this time?* The dominion that man has right now, in this present age, is limited to earthly, physical things. But in the New Testament, written much later, far more is revealed about man's future and his awesome destiny. Not "all things" are put under man at this time, just physical things. "For in that He [God] put all [earthly things] in subjection under him [man], He [God] left nothing that is not put under him. But now we do not yet see all things put under him" (**Hebrews 2:8**).

In other words, God has not yet put unseen things under man's authority because we do not yet see all things. The only things humans cannot see are spiritual things, and God has not yet put spiritual things under man's authority. The writer in Hebrews is speaking of a very real spiritual world that humans cannot see at this time. According to the Bible, man's responsibility and authority will be expanded to include this unseen yet very real spiritual world. This expansion of authority will happen when the kingdom of God is established on earth, and we become spirit through a resurrection. (We will learn more about the kingdom of God later in this book.)

Are you beginning to see a clearer picture of what God has in store for people who love Him and do what He says? What you are reading is one of the most important pieces of that giant jigsaw puzzle. (We'll take a closer look at what God has planned for us in section 7.4 of this book.)

"For I know the thoughts that I think toward you, says the LORD, thoughts of peace and not of evil, to give you a future and a hope" (**Jeremiah 29:11**). God is offering us a ground-floor opportunity, a tremendous future in His coming kingdom, but for now, we must endure and obey God by keeping all of His commandments. "Let us hear the conclusion of the whole matter: Fear God and keep His commandments, for this is mans all. For God will bring every work into judgment, including every secret thing, whether good or evil" (**Ecclesiastes 12:13–14**).

4.2   WHAT IS MAN?

"And the LORD God formed man of the dust of the ground, and breathed into his nostrils the breath of life; and man became a living being" (**Genesis 2:7**). The King James Version of this Scripture reads, "And the LORD God formed man of the dust of the ground, and breathed into his nostrils the breath of life; and man became a living soul." Notice that when God breathed into man's nostrils, man became a living being or living soul. The Bible does not say that God breathed into the nostrils of anything else He created—only man! By God's breathing into the man's nostrils, He gave him the "spirit of man." That is why man can have a special relationship with God and vice versa. There is no mention that man has an immortal soul. To the contrary, **Ezekiel 18:4** clearly tells us that if a soul sins, it will die: "Behold, all souls are Mine; The soul of the father as well as the soul of the son is Mine; The soul who sins shall die." A soul is composed of a body, has blood flowing in the veins, and breathes air. All physical creatures are composed of these three elements.

Since we all have sinned, we all shall die a physical death at some point. (Reference **Romans 3:23**.) But the Bible also states that we will be resurrected someday. The only person who never sinned was Christ, and even He had to die. Therefore, **Ezekiel 18:4** is speaking about a spiritual death from which there is no resurrection.

Death is not a continuation of life under different circumstances, as some people believe. Life and death are two opposite states. "For the wages of sin is death, but the gift of God is eternal life in Christ Jesus our Lord" (**Romans 6:23**). *If eternal life is a gift of God and comes only through Christ, why do Christians assume they already possess eternal life through an immortal soul?* We just read in Ezekiel that the soul who sins shall die. The Jewish encyclopedia further explains, "The belief that the soul continues of the dissolution of the body is ... speculation ... nowhere expressly taught in Holy Scriptures" (*Immortality of the Soul*, Volume VI, 564, 566).

We have seen that the assumption of the "immortal soul" began in the Garden of Eden with Satan's lie to Eve. Satan told Adam and Eve that if they ate of the forbidden fruit, they would surely not die. The implication of not dying is the basis for the false doctrine of the immortality of the soul as taught by most Christian denominations. The idea of the immortality of the soul gained popularity in the Greek culture and was introduced into an apostate, "paganized" Christianity, nearly two centuries after Christ died. Remember that the immortal soul theory did not originate from God. The erroneous "immortal soul" is man's philosophy of what happens at death, and that philosophy continues to be taught, deceiving billions of people.

The apostle Paul warned about relying on man's own reasoning and not relying totally on the Holy Bible. "Beware lest anyone cheat you through philosophy and empty deceit, according to the tradition of men, according to the basic principles of the world, and not according to Christ" (**Colossians 2:8**).

What makes man so unique from animals? Man possesses **three** important attributes that animals do not have:

1. Man is made in the "image and likeness of God." No other creature on this earth looks like us. God gave us His form and shape. God has a head, eyes, feet, and hair, just like we do. "And to the angel of the church in Thyatira write, 'These things,' says the Son of God, who has eyes like a flame of fire, and His feet like fine brass" (**Revelation 2:18**). "His head and hair were white like wool, as white as snow, and His eyes like a flame of fire; His feet were like fine brass, as if refined in a furnace, and His voice as the sound of many waters; He had in His right hand seven stars, out of His mouth went a sharp two-edged sword, and His countenance was like the sun shining in its strength" (**Revelation 1:14–16**).

2. God gave man "the spirit of man" which imparts his intellect, when He breathed into man's nostrils. "But there is a spirit in man, and the breath of the Almighty gives him understanding" (**Job 32:8**). "The burden of the word of the Lord against Israel. Thus says the Lord, who stretches out the heavens, lays the foundation of the earth and forms the spirit of man within him" (**Zechariah 12:1**). Notice that God forms the spirit of man within a human being. The spirit of man is absent in animals. Instead, God gave animals instinct.

But what exactly is the spirit of man? Since the spirit of man is a spiritual essence, it cannot be seen, measured, weighed, or even destroyed by humans. Humans rely on the spirit of man given by God at birth to reason, measure, write, compose music, paint, or go to the moon and back. The Bible also refers to these awesome abilities of man as "the things of man" and includes physical knowledge. "For what man knows the things of a man except the spirit of the man which is in him?" (**1 Corinthians 2:11**).

Remember, that God breathed the spirit of man into the living soul, and it cannot be destroyed by man. The body of a person is physical and deteriorates. Once a person dies, the breath of life departs, and that person is no longer a living soul. The soul is dead and goes to the grave, but the spirit of man, since it is a spiritual essence, goes back to God at death. "Then the dust will return to the earth as it was, and the spirit will return to God who gave it" (**Ecclesiastes 12:7**).

It is well to note that God can and will reactivate the spirit of man once a person's human body is resurrected. The spirit of man captures every nuance of life, thought, personality, looks, voice, and character that made the person exactly as he or she was when alive. In other words, once resurrected, we will be able to recognize each other.

Christ plainly taught that the physical body can be destroyed, but the spirit of man within his soul cannot be destroyed by man. Only God can destroy both. "And do not fear those who kill the body but cannot kill the soul [the spirit in man]. But rather fear Him who is able to destroy both soul [the spiritual death] and body in hell [grave]." (**Matthew 10:28**).

3. An additional spiritual gift was given to man that further distinguishes us from animals. It is only given by God at baptism to people whom He calls. It is called the Holy Spirit or Spirit of God. Just as the spirit of man gives humans physical knowledge, the Holy Spirit gives humans spiritual knowledge, which the Bible calls "the things of God." "But God has revealed them to us through His Spirit. For the Spirit searches all things, yes, the deep things of God. For what man knows the things of a man except the spirit of the man which is in him? Even so no one knows the things of God except the Spirit of God. Now we have received, not the spirit of the world, but the Spirit which is from God, that we might know the things that have been freely given to us by God" (**1 Corinthians 2:10–12**).

Sadly, the spirit of man has been notoriously mislabeled by Christians as being the immortal soul. But as we have seen, the soul who sins dies, and therefore, the soul cannot be immortal. However, the spirit of man and God's Holy Spirit return to God, while the soul goes to the grave.

We have clearly seen that the Bible does not teach the immortality of the soul. Rather, it teaches that the soul who sins shall die. Also, eternal life is a special gift from God and can only be given by God. In no case is it something that man already possesses. Understanding the difference between humans and animals sheds much light on God's giant jigsaw puzzle. These three attributes give man the opportunity to have a deep, personal relationship with God, and vice versa.

4.3   WHY WAS I BORN?

Have you ever asked yourself why you were born? Most people have pondered the meaning of their lives but have found no true answer for it. Most figure that their goal in life is to find a good job, make lots of money, get married, raise a family, be happy, die, and go to heaven. They firmly believe that these are the reasons for living. *But are these the real reasons why God put us on this earth? What does the Bible say is our purpose for living?* Few people know the true answer.

The true answer is not found in science, education, technology, or even in most of the world's religions. Only the Holy Bible has answers for your existence. And the creator God made certain we would have this vital knowledge. "The fear [respect] of the LORD is the beginning of wisdom; a good understanding have all those who do His commandments. His praise endures forever" (**Psalm 111:10**). It's not enough just to know that God exists and to know His commandments by heart. You must do His commandments. "For not the hearers of the law are just in the sight of God, but the doers of the law will be justified" (**Romans 2:13**).

You may be quite surprised to find that the so-called old, outdated book you own is very up to date and as modern as any book written today. It contains the very true answer to the question of *"Why was I born?"*

The first two chapters of Genesis clearly and emphatically tell us that humans are not animals. The Bible also does not tell us that we evolved from some lower life-form, like monkeys or gorillas, as we learned in school. *Which do you believe?* I hope you choose to believe the Holy Bible. It is the only source of God-given revealed knowledge.

The main problem with the theory of evolution is that scientists cannot seem to find skeletons of any in-between "man-apes." They have found skeletons of humans and apes but nothing in between. There is absolutely no physical evidence of any progression from ape to man. *If there ever was a progression from ape to man, why don't we see that progression continuing today?* Now, there are mutations of sorts, like a cat having six toes or a man being born with two thumbs, but never one creature turning totally into another, like a gorilla mutating into a human. Man is so far superior in skills and abilities that it is simply ridiculous to even think that we somehow evolved from animals. Yet that's the very lie that we have been taught by higher education. Evolution is just another lie initiated by Satan that most humans believe.

Is your mind ready to grasp the real truth about yourself from God's own instruction manual, the Holy Bible? I hope and pray that God opens your mind to see His true answers as to why you were born.

Read **Genesis 1:1** and study what it states: "In the beginning God created the heavens and the earth." Notice here that there are no theories, just a positive statement about the existence of God and that He created the heavens and the earth. "So, God created great sea creatures and every living thing that moves, with which the waters abounded, according to their kind, and every winged bird according to its kind. And God saw that it was good" (**Genesis 1:21**). Notice that God creates living things according to their kind. "And God made the beast of the earth according to its kind, cattle according to its kind, and everything that creeps on the earth according to its kind. And God saw that it was good. Then God said, 'Let Us make man in Our image, according to Our likeness; let them have dominion over the fish of the sea, over the birds of the air, and over the cattle, over all the earth and over every creeping thing that creeps on the earth'" (**Genesis 1:25–26**).

Humans are the only created physical beings who have a special relationship with their creator God. As we learned, God gave man the spirit of man, which empowers him to accumulate physical knowledge. No other species can come close to the empowerment that God has given humankind.

But what was/is God's purpose for making us into His image and likeness? The vast majority of people on earth fail to understand that very purpose. I want to provide you with four solid reasons as to why you were born and placed on this earth. These are not my opinions but actual reasons found in the Bible. Take a close look, study, and meditate on each of the **four** reasons as to why God put you and me on this earth.

1. You were born so that you can come to know God and believe what He tells you in the Holy Bible. In **Genesis 3:1–5**, God told both Adam and his wife, Eve, that they could eat of the fruit of any tree in the Garden of Eden, except the Tree of Knowledge of Good and Evil that was in the middle of the garden. *Did they believe what God told them?* No, they did not believe God; instead, they believed what the serpent told them. "So, when the woman saw that the tree was good for food, that it was pleasant to the eyes, and a tree desirable to make one wise, she took of its fruit and ate. She also gave to her husband with her, and he ate. Then the eyes of both of them were opened, and they knew that they were naked; and they sewed fig leaves together and made themselves coverings" (**Genesis 3:6–7**).

The serpent referred to here is none other than Satan, the father of lies. Notice **John 8:44**, where Jesus was speaking to the scribes and Pharisees: "You are of your father the devil [Satan], and the desires of your father you want to do. He [Satan] was a murderer from the beginning, and does not stand in the truth, because there is no truth in him. When he speaks a lie, he speaks from his own resources, for he [Satan] is a liar and the father of it."

It becomes painfully clear that Adam and Eve rejected God and determined for themselves what was good and what was evil. And ever since that time, humanity in general has relied on itself, with the influence of Satan, to determine what is good and evil and not rely on God. It is well to note here again that God cannot lie. **Titus 1:2** makes this very clear: "In hope of eternal life which God, who cannot lie, promised before time began." God always tells the truth, even if it hurts.

By tuning into Satan's wavelength, humans, in general, have produced all the problems and appalling evils found in this sick, wicked, and upside-down world. All the murders, rapes, broken homes, sicknesses, diseases of all sorts, and infidelity are the effects of not believing and doing what God says. *Are you going to believe what God says, or are you going to decide for yourself what's good or evil?* I hope and pray that you will believe God.

2. You were born so you can learn to always obey and trust God. Most people believe "in" God, but they don't believe what He says! If we believe God and obey Him, then we will be blessed by Him. Obedience brings blessings from God. "If you walk in My statutes and keep My commandments, and perform them, then I will give you rain in its season, the land shall yield its produce, and the trees of the field shall yield their fruit.... I will give peace in the land, and you shall lie down, and none will make you afraid; I will rid the land of evil beasts, and the sword will not go through your land.... I will walk among you and be your God, and you shall be My people" (**Leviticus 26:3, 6, 12**). Please take time to carefully read all of **Leviticus 26**.

Disobedience brings curses from God. "But it shall come to pass, if you do not obey the voice of the LORD your God, to observe carefully all His commandments and His statutes which I command you today, that all these curses will come upon you and overtake you: Cursed shall you be in the city, and cursed shall you be in the country. Cursed shall be your basket and your kneading bowl. Cursed shall be the fruit of your body and the produce of your land, the increase of your cattle and the offspring of your flocks" (**Deuteronomy 28:15–18**). Also please take time to carefully read all of **Deuteronomy 28**.

Christ obeyed God the Father to the point of death. "Though He was a Son, yet He learned obedience by the things which He suffered. And having been perfected, He became the author of eternal salvation to all who obey Him" (**Hebrews 5:8–9**). Remember, that it is one thing to believe in God, but it is quite another to believe and do what He says. *Will you believe and do what God says today?*

3. You were born so that you can learn to love God and other fellow humans. While Jesus lived on this earth, a young lawyer came to Him and asked Him what the greatest commandment was. He was hoping to trick Christ into saying which was the most important so the Jews could find fault in Him and ultimately kill Him.

Take a look at the account in **Matthew 22:35–40**, which says, "Then one of them, a lawyer, asked Him a question, testing Him, and saying, 'Teacher, which is the great commandment in the law?' Jesus said to him, 'You shall love the LORD your God with all your heart, with all your soul, and with all your mind. This is the first and great commandment. And the second is like it: You shall love your neighbor as yourself. On these two commandments hang all the Law and the Prophets.'"

Christ clearly stated that if you do these two great commandments, then you are fulfilling God's law and the purpose of why you were born. By the way, these two great commandments are not new, as most people believe. They were never meant to replace the Ten Commandments found in **Exodus 20**. The first four commandments expound on loving God; the last six expound on loving your fellow man. Christ did not do away with the original Ten Commandments.

He merely summarized them into two main commandments. Also, God's Ten Commandments were never nailed to the cross or done away with, as some people suggest. (Please refer to chapter 6 of this book to read more about God's Law.) Those who truly worship Jesus the Christ observe all of the commandments, even as He did.

4. You were born so that someday you can be resurrected as a spirit-being and be part of God's coming kingdom. Sometimes in the Bible, converted Christians, in whom God has given His Holy Spirit, are called heirs of God and joint heirs with Christ. *What are they heirs of?* When we are resurrected, we become joint heirs with Christ to inherit the kingdom of God. "The Spirit Himself [itself] bears witness with our spirit that we are children of God, and if children, then heirs—heirs of God and joint heirs with Christ, if indeed we suffer with Him, that we may also be glorified together" (**Romans 8:16–17**). To be glorified means to become spirit, and that happens in a resurrection.

"And He [God the Father] put all things under His [Christ's] feet, and gave Him to be head over all things to the church" (**Ephesians 1:22**). *Could this mean that we are appointed heirs with Christ and share authority with Him as spirit beings when He returns?* That is mind-boggling, yet it is true! "And if you are Christ's, then you are Abraham's seed, and heirs according to the promise" (**Galatians 3:29**). *What promise?* The promise of being heirs of God's kingdom as spirit beings, as Christ is! "Therefore, you are no longer a slave but a son, and if a son, then an heir of God through Christ" (**Galatians 4:7**). We are sons and daughters and heirs of God's kingdom through Christ.

These Scriptures clearly tell us that after we die (as Christ died), we will be resurrected (as Christ was) and live again (as Christ is living today) to rule with Him in God's kingdom. "Beloved, now we are children of God; and it has not yet been revealed what we shall be, but we know that when He [Christ] is revealed, we shall be like Him, for we shall see Him as He is" (**1 John 3:2**). As humans, we cannot see Christ as He is because He is spirit. We have to become spirit beings, through a resurrection, in order for us to see Him as He is. The good news is that the day of a resurrection may be upon us soon.

Do you see God's awesome purpose as to why you were born? Ultimately, you were born to live forever as a spirit being and be in God's literal, divine kingdom. But first you must live a physical life, die, and then be resurrected into a spirit. "And I [John] saw thrones, and they sat on them, and judgment was committed to them. Then I saw the souls of those who had been beheaded for their witness to Jesus and for the word of God, who had not worshiped the beast or his image, and had not received his mark on their foreheads or on their hands. And they lived and reigned with Christ for a thousand years" (**Revelation 20:4**). After the one thousand year reign of Christ, there will be a new beginning. "Now I saw a new heaven and a new earth, for the first heaven and the first earth had passed away. Also, there was no more sea. Then I, John, saw the holy city, New Jerusalem, coming down out of heaven from God, prepared as a bride adorned for her husband. And I heard a loud voice from heaven saying, 'Behold, the tabernacle of God is with men, and He will dwell with them, and they shall be His people. God Himself will be with them and be their God'" (**Revelation 21:1–3**).

Once you understand and believe the awesome purpose for your life, your mind will be filled with joy and happiness. Knowing this wonderful plan gives real purpose, meaning, and hope in this life. It is a purpose so wonderful that you will never totally comprehend the full height, breadth, weight, and splendor of it in this present physical life. "But as it is written: eye has not seen, nor ear heard, nor have entered into the heart of man the things which God has prepared for those who love Him" (**1 Corinthians 2:9**).

Know that God has plans for you—big plans. He wants you to live forever with Him as a spirit-being. Contemplate the words in **Jeremiah 29:11–12**, which say, "For I know the thoughts that I think toward you, says the LORD, thoughts of peace and not of evil, to give you a future and a hope. Then you will call upon Me and go and pray to Me, and I will listen to you."

This is yet another important piece of that giant jigsaw puzzle that God has so generously shown us. Ask God in prayer to open your mind to His divine truth. Again, your awesome destiny and the reason you were born is so you can live forever and be in God's kingdom.

4.4 WHAT EXACTLY IS REPENTANCE?

This section will focus on the deep, spiritual meaning of repentance. This very important topic demands your attention to obtain the true answers, which are found only in the Holy Bible.

What is repentance? Webster's Dictionary defines repentance as a "remorse for past conduct; a change of mind; a deep regret for past sins; being sorrowful for what has already occurred." Keep in mind that we have all sinned and come short of the glory of God. "For all have sinned and fall short of the glory of God" (**Romans 3:23**). We have all broken God's commandments, whether intentionally or unintentionally. By now, we should also know that the penalty for breaking God's Law is death. (Reference **Romans 6:23**.) Christ came down from the third heaven to save us from spiritual death. But before our sins can be forgiven by using Christ's shed blood, we must repent of them. God must know that we are truly sorry for breaking His Law. He wants us to commit our lives to living His way of life, which is the way of love, giving, and outgoing concern for others. Since we have all sinned, we all must repent.

In **Mark 1:15**, Christ commanded everyone, "Repent and believe the gospel." As already discussed, the word "gospel" means good news, and it refers to the establishment of the kingdom of God on this earth. People back then and those living today were/are commanded to repent and believe the good news of the coming kingdom of God. Peter also exhorted the very same message in **Acts 2:38**, when he said, "Repent, and let every one of you be baptized in the name of Jesus Christ for the remission [forgiveness] of sins; and you shall receive the gift of the Holy Spirit." Both of these Scriptures and many others in the Bible declare repentance.

Very few Christian denominations teach about repentance. Rather, their main focus is for you to "come as you are" and give money to their churches. Other churches talk about "planting your seed" so that God can bless you. "Planting your seed" means nothing more than giving your money to them. Other evangelicals call it "giving a love offering" or pledging a certain amount of money each month. I'm sorry to say that almost all denominations have turned Christianity into a money-making machine. They totally ignore the fact that God wants you to repent of your sins.

There are **five** important points to note about repentance:

1. Repentance is a deep, heartfelt sorrow for sins you have committed against God. Genuine repentance is not based on sentiment or emotion that is artificially stirred up at an altar call. It is not a temporary sorrow for getting caught doing something wrong. That is worldly sorrow; it is not godly sorrow! Repentance is a permanent, personal, deep, heartfelt sorrow for any thoughts, actions, or deeds that are not in harmony with God's word. Notice what **1 John 3:4** tells us: "Sin is the transgression [or breaking] of the law." Look at **Romans 5:12**, which says: "Therefore, just as through one man sin entered the world, and death through sin, and thus death spread to all men, because all sinned." The Scriptures you have just read define what sin is. Breaking His Ten Commandments is sin. *Have you broken any of God's commandments lately?* Notice the biblical answer to that question. "For all have sinned and fall short of the glory of God" (**Romans 3:23**). Even Abraham, Isaac, Jacob, Moses, Job, David, and many others God has called have broken God's Law. Yes, whether you admit it or not, you and I have broken God's commandments too. *Are you deeply sorrowful for breaking them?*

2. You must request repentance from God through prayer. This act of requesting repentance does not come easily or naturally to us. But God looks at the heart of a person. "But the LORD said to Samuel,

'Do not look at his appearance or at his physical stature, because I have refused him. For the LORD does not see as man sees; for man looks at the outward appearance, but the LORD looks at the heart'" (**1 Samuel 16:7**). God looks into your heart to see if you are truly sorry for sinning.

Repentance is the beginning of a deep, personal relationship between you and your maker. Genuine repentance means being wholeheartedly sorry for past sins you have committed. It also means you are sorry for hurting God. This is precisely why Christ came and died for us all. But we must request repentance from God. Notice **Psalm 51:1**, where David requested repentance from God: "Have mercy upon me, O God, according to Your loving kindness; According to the multitude of Your tender mercies, blot out my transgressions." David wholeheartedly requested that his sins be blotted out. He was very sorry for transgressing God's laws. So, God granted David's request. For some people, repentance might also include fasting, crying, and mourning. "'Now, therefore,' says the LORD, 'Turn to Me with all your heart, with fasting, with weeping, and with mourning'" (**Joel 2:12**). Repentance includes godly sorrow, which leads us to salvation. "For godly sorrow produces repentance leading to salvation, not to be regretted; but the sorrow of the world produces death" (**2 Corinthians 7:10**).

3. Only God can grant repentance. "Him God has exalted to His right hand to be Prince and Savior, to give repentance to Israel and forgiveness of sins" (**Acts 5:31**). "And a servant of the Lord must not quarrel but be gentle to all, able to teach, patient, in humility correcting those who are in opposition, if God perhaps will grant them repentance, so that they may know the truth, and that they may come to their senses and escape the snare of the devil, having been taken captive by him to do his will" (**2 Timothy 2:24–26**). If and when you come to your senses and repent, then you can escape the trap of being held captive by the Devil.

4. Repentance is a gift from God and may be granted to Jews and Gentiles alike. Gentiles are people who are not direct descendants of Israel. Some Greeks, Italians, Russians, Chinese, or Japanese may be Gentiles. "If, therefore, God gave them the same gift as He gave us when we believed on the Lord Jesus Christ, who was I that I could withstand God? When they heard these things they became silent; and they glorified God, saying, 'Then God has also granted to the Gentiles repentance to life'" (**Acts 11:17–18**). Consider also, "Testifying to Jews, and also to Greeks, repentance toward God and faith toward our Lord Jesus Christ" (**Acts 20:21**).

5. Once granted, repentance leads to baptism. "Then Peter said to them, 'Repent, and let every one of you be baptized in the name of Jesus Christ for the remission of sins; and you shall receive the gift of the Holy Spirit'" (**Acts 2:38**). Notice that repentance precedes baptism. Once God grants repentance, and we are truly sorry for past sins, then the next step is to have these sins removed. The act of blotting out our sins is known as baptism. Christ took our penalty of death upon Himself by dying on the tree stake for us, so that we could someday gain eternal life through a resurrection. "For the wages of sin is death, but the gift of God is eternal life in Christ Jesus our Lord" (**Romans 6:23**).

4.5   WHAT EXACTLY IS BAPTISM?

Baptism is a basic yet necessary and very important outward sign of being a true Christian. As in most other points of doctrine, modern Christian churches are at odds and confused on the topic of baptism. Most clergy say that it does not really matter which method is used for baptism as long as a person is baptized. Others say there is only one way to be baptized. *What's the correct way of being baptized, according to the Bible?* Remember that God is not the author of confusion. Notice what **1 Corinthians 14:33** says: "For God is not the author of confusion but of peace, as in all the churches of the saints." As humans, we tend to forget things from time to time; as such, we must refresh our memories about many things, including the important topic of baptism.

We must realize that in today's Christian world there are **three** basic methods of baptism:

1. The "sprinkling method," used by some Protestant churches, applies to people of all ages. The minister, priest, or reverend simply sprinkles water on people as he walks down an aisle of the church, and people become baptized.

2. The Catholic Church baptizes by "pouring" a small amount of water on an infant's forehead. The infant being baptized is usually less than a year old and has no concept of what is happening or what it means to be baptized. In a Catholic baptism, a godfather and godmother are used to baptize an infant. The godfather and godmother also act as guardian of the child in case something happens to the infant's mother and father. My mother told me that I was first baptized in the Catholic Church when I was about a month old. Of course, at that age, I knew nothing about sin, repentance, or baptism.

3. The third method of baptism is total "submersion" in water. Let us take a close look at the word "baptism," which comes from the Greek word "baptizo," meaning to be totally submerged in water. Baptizo constitutes a type of burial in a watery grave, so to speak. The body is totally submerged in water for just a second or two, to picture a type of death and burial from an old way of living. Afterward, as you rise up out of the water, baptism pictures a type of resurrection and life thereafter.

The Greek word for sprinkle is "rantiazo." The word for pouring is "cheo." Neither are found in the New Testament. God's holy Word only contains the word "baptizo." Therefore, sprinkling and pouring do not constitute a type of burial, so, biblically speaking, total submersion is the only proper way to be baptized.

Let us examine **three** examples of baptism that show total submersion as the proper way of being baptized:

1. We find John, the Baptist [Baptizer, he was not a Baptist] baptizing where there was much water. "Now John also was baptizing in Aenon near Salim, because there was much water there. And they came and were baptized" (**John 3:23**). This Scripture tells us that baptism requires "much water," as in a pool, river, lake, pond, or ocean. *Why would you need much water?* So, a person could be totally submerged as in a watery grave. John would have only needed a cupful of water to sprinkle or pour; instead, he baptized where there was much water.

2. In **Acts 8**, we find a eunuch who wanted to be baptized by the apostle Philip. Here, both the eunuch and Philip went "into the water." "So, he [Philip] commanded the chariot to stand still. And both Philip and the eunuch went down into the water, and he [Philip] baptized him. Now when they came up out of the water, the Spirit of the Lord caught Philip away, so that the eunuch saw him no more; and he went on his way rejoicing" (**Acts 8:38–39**). Notice that both men went down "into the water," and both came up out of the water. *Is it possible to come up out of the water from a sprinkling or a pouring?* Of course not!

3. We find that Jesus Himself was totally submerged in water at His baptism.

    > Then Jesus came from Galilee to John at the Jordan to be baptized by him. And John tried to prevent Him, saying, "I need to be baptized by You, and are You coming to me?" But Jesus answered and said to him,

115

"Permit it to be so now, for thus it is fitting for us to fulfill all righteousness." Then he allowed Him. When He had been baptized, Jesus came up immediately from the water; and behold, the heavens were opened to Him, and He saw the Spirit of God descending like a dove and alighting upon Him. And suddenly a voice came from heaven, saying, "This is My beloved Son, in whom I am well pleased." (**Matthew 3:13–17**)

At His baptism, Christ "came up immediately from the water." Biblically speaking and following Christ's example, total submersion in water is the only proper way of being baptized. Total submersion in water at baptism represents both a "type" of death and a "type" of resurrection.

After I learned about repentance, baptism, and the gift of the Holy Spirit by fervently studying the Bible, I realized the deep meaning of being baptized correctly. In a deep heartfelt prayer, I asked God to grant me repentance. It was then that I realized the deep meaning of life and God's plan to save humanity. I realized that I had been wrong about many things in life and wanted to repent and have all my sins forgiven. I wanted to make things right between me and God. I was baptized a few months later at the age of thirty-one.

Once you have requested and have been granted repentance by God and are deeply sorrowful for breaking God's Law, the next step is to be baptized and have your past sins blotted out by Christ's blood. "Have mercy upon me, O God, according to Your loving kindness; According to the multitude of Your tender mercies, blot out my transgressions" (**Psalm 51:1**). "Hide Your face from my sins, and blot out all my iniquities" (**Psalm 51:9**).

Baptism involves a symbolic burial of your old self and your old way of living by being totally submersed in a watery grave. Baptism is a "type" of death. "Or do you not know that as many of us as were baptized into Christ Jesus were baptized into His death? Therefore, we were buried with Him through baptism into death, that just as Christ was raised from the dead by the glory of the Father, even so we also should walk in newness of life" (**Romans 6:3–4**). All of the foregoing requires a person who is contemplating baptism to be a mature adult. Christ was about thirty years old when He was baptized. Little children and teenagers should not be baptized because most do not understand what sin is or the deep meaning of baptism.

The Bible refers to the old self or old way of living as "the old man." The old man includes lying, stealing, thinking evil thoughts, and generally breaking the Ten Commandments. "To walk in newness of life" is not "being saved," as some Christian denominations call it. (See chapter 5 for more information on what the Bible says about being saved.) Walking in newness of life means to live physically keeping all of God's commandments, laws, and statutes with zeal. This new way of living is what the Bible calls "conversion." "And [Christ]said, 'Assuredly, I say to you, unless you are converted and become as little children, you will by no means enter the kingdom of heaven'" (**Matthew 18:3**).

What is conversion? Conversion has to do with having a renewed mind. This means to have a new outlook on the way you live by placing God first in your life. Take a look at **Ephesians 4:20–24**, where Paul states, "But you have not so learned Christ, if indeed you have heard Him and have been taught by Him, as the truth is in Jesus: that you put off, concerning your former conduct, the old man which grows corrupt according to the deceitful lusts, and be renewed in the spirit of your mind, and that you put on the new man which was created according to God, in true righteousness and holiness." Also, look at **Romans 12:2**, which tell us, "And do not be conformed to this world, but be transformed by the renewing of your mind, that you may prove what is that good and acceptable and perfect will of God."

The renewing of our minds is directly related to the gift of God's Holy Spirit, which is given to us and dwells within us after we are baptized. **Acts 2:38** emphatically states that we should be baptized and receive the Holy Spirit: "Then Peter said to them, 'Repent, and let every one of you be baptized in the name of Jesus Christ for the remission [taking away] of sins; and you shall receive the gift of the

Holy Spirit.'" The Holy Spirit is God's power and gift to you at baptism to help you make it through life's journey. (Refer to section 2.2 to learn more about the power of the Holy Spirit.)

The apostle Paul also refers to the renewing of your mind as being spiritually minded. "For to be carnally minded is death, but to be spiritually minded is life and peace" (**Romans 8:6**). After baptism and upon conversion, true Christians should be more concerned with spiritual matters. That means putting God and His laws first in your new life, and that is precisely what leads you to receive the gift of eternal life, peace, and happiness. With a renewed mind, you can now devote your whole life to the spiritual things of God, instead of the carnal or material things of this world.

What are the spiritual things of God, and what can the Holy Spirit do for you? The Bible tells us exactly what the Holy Spirit does for us. "But the fruit of the Spirit is love, joy, peace, longsuffering, kindness, goodness, faithfulness, gentleness, self-control. Against such there is no law" (**Galatians 5:22–23**). The essence of God's Holy Spirit gives you peace of mind in that you will finally be at peace with God, knowing that your past sins are totally forgiven and that you are now trying to live God's way of life. Christ did not come to save us from a physical death. We all must die once, according to the Bible. Christ came to earth to save us from the second death (a spiritual death), from which there is no resurrection. **Revelation 21:8** clearly tells us about the second death: "But the cowardly, unbelieving, abominable, murderers, sexually immoral, sorcerers, idolaters, and all liars shall have their part in the lake which burns with fire and brimstone, which is the second death."

In summary, baptism is an outward physical sign, showing God that you are truly sorry for past sins (repentance) and for breaking His laws, His commandments, and His way of life, and now you want to make a "U-turn" in your life. With God's help, you decide that you want your past sins to be totally forgiven by using Christ's shed blood and to participate in the yearly Passover. (Reference **Leviticus 23** for a listing of God's annual feasts.) You now desire to be converted and have a renewed mind, which only comes with the in-dwelling of the Holy Spirit given to you at baptism by the laying on of hands.

A person contemplating baptism should become deeply aware of what the Savior has personally done for him or her. Jesus sacrificed His perfect life to pay the death penalty for all of our sins, once they are repented of. This is the importance of baptism and what it's all about. Every true Christian, trying to follow Christ's example, must be correctly baptized for the very real reasons provided. This is yet another important piece of the giant jigsaw puzzle that has been placed correctly.

4.6   IS THERE MORE THAN ONE HEAVEN?

Have you ever been told by Christians that when you die you will go to heaven if you've been good or hell if you've been bad? I was taught this concept in Catholic school. I am quite certain that the vast majority of Christian churches teach this same doctrine.

Let us take an honest look at what the Bible states about heaven— actually, it plainly mentions **three** separate heavens, yet no clergy ever speaks of them.

1. The atmosphere is the **first** heaven. Although the phrase "first heaven" is not in the Bible, for the purpose of clarity I'll call the atmosphere the first heaven. "Then God said, 'Let the waters abound with an abundance of living creatures, and let birds fly above the earth across the face of the firmament of the heavens'" (**Genesis 1:20**). The Holy Bible plainly says "heavens"—plural. **Genesis 1:1** also should correctly read "heavens."

For additional proof on the first heaven being our atmosphere, turn to **Genesis 27:29**, which reads: "Then Isaac his father answered and said to him: 'Behold, your dwelling shall be of the fatness of the earth, And of the dew of heaven from above.'" The dew and rain fall from heaven, our atmosphere, to water the earth. Notice also, "Rain down, you heavens, from above, and let the skies pour down righteousness; Let the earth open, let them bring forth salvation, and let righteousness spring up together. I, the LORD, have created it" (**Isaiah 45:8**). These Scriptures speak plainly of where the fowls fly and from where rain falls as heaven. So, according to the Bible, the first heaven is clearly the earth's atmosphere.

2. Outer space is the **second** heaven. According to your Bible, it's where the sun, moon, and stars are located. "And let them [sun, moon and stars] be for lights in the firmament of the heavens to give light on the earth; and it was so" (**Genesis 1:15**). *Aren't the sun, moon, and stars located in outer space?* In **Psalm 8:3**. David was inspired to write, "When I consider Your heavens, the work of Your fingers, the moon and the stars, which You have ordained." Notice that the word "heavens" is again plural.

3. God's throne is located is the **third** heaven. "Now this is the main point of the things we are saying: We have such a High Priest, who is seated at the right hand of the throne of the Majesty in the heavens, a Minister of the sanctuary and of the true tabernacle which the Lord erected, and not man" (**Hebrews 8:1–2**). Notice again that "heavens" is plural. The phrase "throne of the Majesty in the heavens" refers to God's throne. God's throne is located well beyond our atmosphere and even beyond outer space. No human can enter or even find God's throne because it is so far beyond our reach in every sense of the word.

4.7   DO GOOD PEOPLE GO TO HEAVEN WHEN THEY DIE?

Let's study **two** famous Bible personalities to see if they went to heaven upon death.

1. The **first** personality is King David. "And when He had removed him, He raised up for them David as king, to whom also He gave testimony and said, 'I have found David the son of Jesse, a man after My own heart, who will do all My will'" (**Acts 13:22**). Did King David, a man after God's own heart, go to heaven? Consider **Acts 2:29**, which tells us: "Men and brethren, let me speak freely to you of the patriarch David that he is both dead and buried, and his tomb is with us to this day." This is some startling truth!

   The Bible plainly states that David is dead and buried, and his tomb was still there during apostolic times. It is also there today. There is no mention of David's going to heaven. As a matter of fact, the Bible clearly states that David absolutely did not go to heaven. "For David did not ascend into the heavens, but he says himself: 'The LORD said to my Lord, "Sit at My right hand"'" (**Acts 2:34**). Again, the Bible clearly states that David did not ascend to heaven. But the Bible also makes plain the fact that David will be someday raised from the dead. "'For it shall come to pass in that day,' says the LORD of hosts, 'That I will break his yoke from your neck, and will burst your bonds; Foreigners shall no more enslave them. But they shall serve the LORD their God, and David their king, whom I will raise up for them'" (**Jeremiah 30:8–9**). Notice that the phrases "they shall serve" and "whom I will raise up" are both written in the future tense. David will be resurrected back to life and be Israel's king, sometime in the future!

2. Our **second** personality is Abraham. *Did he go to heaven upon death?* "Then the Jews said to Him, 'Now we know that You have a demon! Abraham is dead, and the prophets; and You say, "If anyone keeps My word, he shall never taste death"'" (**John 8:52**). The scribes and Pharisees knew that Abraham was dead and, in the grave, and did not go to heaven, but they did not grasp what Christ was saying to them. The phrase "never taste death" refers to a spiritual or everlasting death, not a physical death. Again, the Bible calls this everlasting death the "second" death, from which there is

no resurrection. Christ was telling the scribes and Pharisees that Abraham will never taste that second or everlasting death. "Then Death and Hades were cast into the lake of fire. This is the second death" (**Revelation 20:14**). The religious people, in Christ's day, erroneously thought that Christ was referring to a physical death. Remember we must all die a physical death, but afterward, there will be a resurrection. After that resurrection, God's people will never taste death again because they will be spirit beings.

As David will be resurrected, so will Abraham and others who obeyed the voice of their creator God during their lifetimes. Be sure to read **Hebrews 11** because it expounds on all of God's people who died and did not received the promise. The promise, of course, is everlasting life. No human has ever received everlasting life, only Christ (**John 3:13**).

4.8 DID THE PROPHET ELIJAH SKIP DEATH AND GO TO HEAVEN?

Some people think that Elijah, the prophet, skipped death and went directly to heaven. They believe that Elijah's account is proof that they and their loved ones will go to heaven when they die. Yet over nine hundred years after Elijah was taken up by a whirlwind, Jesus clearly said, "No man has ascended to heaven, but He that came down from heaven, even the Son of man" (**John 3:13**). *Is this a Bible contradiction? Did Elijah really go to heaven, even though Christ said that no man ever did?*

Let's take a close look at **four** Bible personalities who were living during the days of Elijah, and see what the Bible reveals about each of them. By doing so, we will set the stage for one of the most interesting and fascinating biblical events that few people fully understand. It will also answer the question of whether Elijah skipped death and went to heaven.

1. **First** Personality: Elijah was God's prophet for about forty-six years. He was sent to the kingdom of Israel and prophesied from about 898 to 852 BC. Fix the year 852 BC firmly in your memory because that year will come up again later. Elijah performed his duties well and was the leader of the "sons of the prophets." The phrase "sons of the prophets" does not mean that these people were descendants of prophets but were actually a group of prophets living as contemporaries. But in 852 BC, we find Elijah aging, and God wanted Elisha, a younger prophet, to continue His work. In 852 BC, Elijah was walking and talking with Elisha, when he was taken up to heaven by a whirlwind.

2. **Second** Personality: Elisha was a young friend and an understudy of Elijah. In the account, we will find Elisha picking up Elijah's mantle as Elijah was taken up to heaven by a whirlwind in 852 BC. The sons of the prophets told Elisha that his master or teacher (Elijah) was to be taken from him.

3. **Third** Personality: Joram (also known as Jehoram) was king over the ten northern tribes of Israel, ruling over a span of about twelve years from 852 to 841 BC. You can read that in **2 Kings 8:25** ("In the twelfth year of Joram the son of Ahab, king of Israel"). Jacob, later renamed Israel by God, had twelve sons, and each son through time became a separate tribe or nation. These ten tribes were called Israel and were located northwest of Jerusalem. The other remaining tribes, also called Israel, were located south of Jerusalem and consisted of Judah/Levi and Benjamin. Judah also had a king whose name was Jehoram. For the purpose of this section, Joram will be Israel's king (northern tribes), and Jehoram will be Judah's king (southern tribes).

It is important to note that the beginning of Joram's reign (852 BC) was also the beginning of young Elisha's prophetic reign but was the end of Elijah's reign. The fifth year of Israel's Joram's reign as king (848

BC) was the beginning year of Judah's king. "Now in the fifth year of Joram the son of Ahab, king of Israel, Jehoshaphat having been king of Judah, Jehoram the son of Jehoshaphat began to reign as king of Judah. He was thirty-two years old when he became king, and he reigned eight years in Jerusalem. And he walked in the way of the kings of Israel, just as the house of Ahab had done, for the daughter of Ahab was his wife; and he did evil in the sight of the LORD" (2 Kings 8:16–18). So, the son of Ahab married his first cousin. Incest is an evil thing in the sight of Almighty God. Notice the second half of 2 Kings 8:25, where it reads, "Ahaziah the son of Jehoram, king of Judah, began to reign."

4. **Fourth** Personality: Jehoram, king of Judah, was king for eight years, from 848 to 840 BC. Jehoram also was wicked and did evil in the eyes of God.

With this knowledge of these four personalities, we can begin reading the account in 2 Kings:

> And it came to pass, when the LORD was about to take up Elijah into heaven by a whirlwind, that Elijah went with Elisha from Gilgal…. Now the sons of the prophets who were at Bethel came out to Elisha, and said to him, "Do you know that the LORD will take away your master from over you today?" [This phrase is repeated in verse 5.] And he [Elisha] said, "Yes, I know; keep silent!" … "Then it happened, as they [Elisha and Elijah] continued on and talked, that suddenly a chariot of fire appeared with horses of fire, and separated the two of them; and Elijah went up by a whirlwind into heaven. And Elisha saw it, and he cried out, "My father, my father, the chariot of Israel and its horsemen!" So, he saw him no more. And he took hold of his own clothes and tore them into two pieces. He also

took up the mantle of Elijah that had fallen from him, and went back and stood by the bank of the Jordan. Then he took the mantle of Elijah that had fallen from him, and struck the water, and said, "Where is the LORD God of Elijah?" And when he also had struck the water, it was divided this way and that; and Elisha crossed over." (**2 Kings 2:1, 3, 11–14**)

God wanted to relieve Elijah from his duties as prophet and give that responsibility to his understudy, Elisha, so God decided to take Elijah out of Bethel by creating a special whirlwind and lifting Elijah up and away from that place. "Now when the sons of the prophets who were from Jericho saw him, they said, 'The spirit of Elijah rests on Elisha.' And they came to meet him, and bowed to the ground before him" (**2 Kings 2:15**).

The Holy Bible clearly states in **2 Kings 2:11** that Elijah went to heaven via a whirlwind. *But to which heaven did Elijah go?* Remember that the Bible speaks of three separate heavens, not just one, as most Christians believe. The three heavens remain a mystery to most mainstream Christians.

Elijah certainly was not and could not have been taken up to the third heaven because that is where God's throne is. No human knows where God's throne is located, as it is well beyond our reach. Also, consider this very important point: if Elijah never died and went directly into the third heaven, where God's throne is, then he would have preeminence over our Savior and Lord, and that just cannot be! Christ was the only One who went to the Father's throne in the third heaven after death.

Elijah could not have been taken to the second heaven because no human could live in outer space, and there could not have been a whirlwind there. There only remains the first heaven, where the birds and fowl fly and where rain falls—our atmosphere. It is the only place where a "whirlwind" could take place. Elijah was taken miraculously by a whirlwind into our atmosphere.

Some people believe that Elijah never died and that somehow, he escaped death and went directly into heaven. *Could this be true?* The Bible says that it is appointed for "all" men to die once. "And as it is appointed for men to die once, but after this the judgment" (**Hebrews 9:27**). This means that all men, including Elijah, have to die once. Elijah did not and could not have escaped death, Even God's only begotten Son, Jesus, had to die a physical death.

Some Christians believe that Elijah died at that time. But God's inspired Word does not say that Elijah died at that particular time; it says Elijah was taken up to the (first) heaven by a whirlwind. If Elijah had died right at that time, then there would have been no problem with Elisha assuming Elijah's duties. But Elijah was taken up from Bethel, alive, to the first heaven by a miraculous whirlwind. *Why?* Because God, being just and fair, removed Elijah alive so that Elisha could fulfill the responsibilities for that office, as prophet in that area.

2 Kings tells us something else of extreme importance: "Then they [sons of the prophets] said to him [Elisha], 'Look now, there are fifty strong men with your servants. Please let them go and search for your master, lest perhaps the Spirit of the LORD has taken him up and cast him upon some mountain or into some valley'" (**2 Kings 2:16**). *Who was Elisha's master?* It was Elijah.

The above Scripture clearly states that "fifty strong men" went out looking for Elijah, who was transported by a special whirlwind created by God's Holy Spirit, on some mountain or valley on earth. *But how do we know for certain that Elijah was still alive?* **2 Chronicles 21:12–15** tells of a letter written by Elijah to Judah's king, Jehoram, in the sixth year of his rule. Judah's Jehoram began his rule at age thirty-two in 848 BC. Six years later (842 BC), Jehoram, at age thirty-eight, received a handwritten letter from Elijah. Remember that Elijah was taken up in 852 BC. Therefore, a total of ten years had elapsed after Elijah was taken up by the whirlwind and before Elijah's handwritten letter to Judah's king, Jehoram.

Elijah's letter has been preserved by God for our learning.

And a letter came to him [Judah's Jehoram] from Elijah the prophet, saying, "Thus says the LORD God of your father David: Because you have not walked in the ways of Jehoshaphat your father, or in the ways of Asa king of Judah, but have walked in the way of the kings of Israel, and have made Judah and the inhabitants of Jerusalem to play the harlot like the harlotry of the house of Ahab, and also have killed your brothers, those of your father's household, who were better than yourself, behold, the LORD will strike your people with a serious affliction—your children, your wives, and all your possessions; and you will become very sick with a disease of your intestines, until your intestines come out by reason of the sickness, day by day." **(2 Chronicles 21:12–15)**

You might think that Jehoram would have been surprised to receive a handwritten letter from Elijah, who supposedly skipped death and went to heaven. But Jehoram was not surprised at all because he knew that Elijah did not die, nor did he go to the third heaven. Jehoram knew that Elijah was still alive, living on some mountain or valley on earth, because he'd just received Elijah's handwritten letter. This letter presents positive proof that Elijah was still alive and well on earth, some ten years after he miraculously was transported by a whirlwind to the first heaven onto a mountain or valley. Finally, it proves that Elijah was "not" made immortal, did "not" skip death, and did "not" go to the second or third heaven. Elijah had to suffer death at some point in his life, just as every human must.

This proves, beyond a shadow of a doubt, that both Elijah and Elisha died once—and everyone else must die at least once. No human can skip death—all of our ancestors have died, and all people who have ever lived and died are waiting for a resurrection from the dead. No one has ascended into heaven, except our Savior, Christ, as stated in **John 3:13**. As Christ died, we must also die, and as Christ was resurrected, so too we will be resurrected. "For since by man came death, by Man also came the resurrection of the dead. For as in Adam all die, even so in Christ all shall be made alive. But each one in his own order: Christ the firstfruits, afterward those who are Christ's at His coming" (**1 Corinthians 15:21–23**).

So far in human history, only Christ, the Son of God, has been resurrected from the dead, been made spirit, and has gone to the third heaven. All of our forefathers await a future resurrection. Lazarus, whom Christ raised from the dead, lived again, died a second time and is now awaiting another resurrection. As Christ is alive today, we also will be made alive someday but each in his or her order.

4.9   DO WICKED PEOPLE GO TO HELL WHEN THEY DIE?

Christianity's teaching on the subject of hell has been inconsistent through the centuries. Beliefs about hell have varied widely, depending on which theologian or religion you believe.

Generally speaking, however, the most popular belief of hell is that it is a place where wicked people go to be tortured, upon death, by an ever-burning fire. This is the hellfire and brimstone that many ministers teach about on Sunday. *But is that doctrine biblical?*

Some believe in a more modern interpretation of hell, which rejects the idea of physical torture and asserts that the torture of hell is mental anguish, caused by separation from God. A religious survey revealed that 53 percent of Americans embrace this idea. (*US News and World Report*, Jan. 31, 2000, 47). Still others believe that everyone will be saved in the end.

Certainly, all three beliefs of hell cannot be correct, so what exactly did Christ teach? Would a loving and merciful God torture people forever and ever? The confusion with regard to the teaching of hell is primarily because man's concept of hell is a mixture of a few Bible verses taken out of context, combined with some pagan ideas and human imagination—these are man's ideas of what hell is. It is not what God says.

The most comprehensive description of hell as a place of torture is not found in the Holy Bible but rather in the fourteenth-century work of the Italian poet Dante Alighieri, titled *The Divine Comedy*. In his play, Dante described an imaginary journey through hell, filled with fiery sufferings. From this play emerged the most popular Christian belief about hell. It is the belief that hell is located inside the earth, in a vast subterranean chamber filled with demons and evil human beings who are being tortured by an everlasting fire.

A prime example of this popular view of hell is found in a sermon excerpt given by the prominent Puritan minister Jonathan Edwards in 1741. Notice the words of his sermon: "Oh, sinner! Consider the fearful danger you are in: it is a great furnace of wrath, a wide and bottomless pit, full of the fire of wrath that you are held over in the hand of God... You hang by a slender thread, with the flames of divine wrath flashing about it and ready every moment to singe it and burn it asunder" (Karen Armstrong, *A History of God*, 1993, 284).

This human concept of hell was so terrible that the prospect of such a fate caused great anguish, fear, and anxiety among many Puritans. The Puritans were not the only ones tormented by the fear of hell. Many people today are frightened into obedience by Christian ministers and teachers using approaches similar to that of Jonathan Edwards. The idea that God sentences people to eternal punishment is so repulsive that some people totally turn away from belief in God and Christianity as a religion.

Does this human concept of hell describe the God of the Bible? Does God vengefully punish His sinners for all eternity or hold them over flames of fire by a thin thread? The biblical God that you and I know is a God of love, not hate. "In this is love, not that we loved God, but that He loved us and sent His Son to be the propitiation for our sins" (**John 4:10**). God loves us and wants only the best for us, but as any loving parent, He wants us to believe and obey Him. *Our obedience to Him is for our own good anyway, so why not obey God?* Notice also, "He who has My commandments and keeps them, it is he who loves Me. And he who loves Me will be loved by My Father, and I will love him and manifest Myself to him" (**John 14:21**).

The biblical God that we know does not want anyone to perish but only come to repentance. "The Lord is not slack concerning His promise, as some count slackness, but is longsuffering toward us, not willing that any should perish but that all should come to repentance" (**2 Peter 3:9**).

Again, God loves everyone. We are all His children. But everyone must learn to believe in and obey Him. And like any parent who loves his child, a fitting punishment is administered in love for wrongdoing but never lasting eternally. "For God so loved the world that He gave His only begotten Son, that whoever believes in Him should not perish but have everlasting life" (**John 3:16**). "But I say to you, love your enemies, bless those who curse you, do good to those who hate you, and pray for those who spitefully use you and persecute you, that you may be sons of your Father in heaven; for He makes His sun rise on the evil and on the good, and sends rain on the just and on the unjust" (**Matthew 5:44–45**). Many other Scriptures attest to the fact that we worship a loving, just, and merciful God, not one who is spiteful, hateful, or eternally vengeful.

But what does the Bible say about hell? Remember, the Bible is God's written Word. It tells the truth, even if it hurts or proves you wrong. *Is hell a place where wicked people burn eternally or are in mental torment? Do people really dangle by a string, waiting for an angry God to let go?*

These are very important questions, and you need to know the truth about hell from God Himself through His Holy Bible. You may be thoroughly surprised to learn that the Bible uses **three** distinct words that are all translated as "hell" in English, yet all three words have different meanings. Understanding the meanings of these words will help us in our honest quest to learn the truth about hell. Let's take a close look at each word.

1. The Hebrew word "sheol" used in the Old Testament has the exact same meaning as "hades" in the New Testament Greek. Both

words are translated as "hell," and both refer to the grave. The grave is simply a place where dead people are placed. Christ died and was placed in a tomb or grave. One passage in Psalms and another in Acts tell us that Christ's flesh did not decay in the grave because God the Father resurrected Him. "For You will not leave my soul in Sheol, nor will You allow Your Holy One to see corruption" (**Psalm 16:10**). "For You will not leave my soul in Hades, nor will You allow Your Holy One to see corruption" (**Acts 2:27**). All people who have ever lived and died are in the grave (sheol/hades). For the sailors who died at sea, the sea would be their grave. The Bible clearly states that all men will die at least once, but after death comes a resurrection. "And as it is appointed for men to die once, but after this the judgment, so Christ was offered once to bear the sins of many. To those who eagerly wait for Him, He will appear a second time, apart from sin, for salvation" (**Hebrews 9:27–28**). Some people God has called, such as Abraham, Isaac, and Jacob, will be resurrected as spirit beings in the first resurrection. This happens at the second coming of Christ. Others will be resurrected as flesh-and-blood human beings by God after the one thousand year reign of Christ on earth. "But the rest of the dead did not live again until the thousand years were finished. This is the first resurrection" (**Revelation 20:5**).

2. The Greek word "tartaroo" is translated as "hell" and is only used once in the Bible. "For if God did not spare the angels who sinned, but cast them down to hell [tartaroo] and delivered them into chains of darkness, to be reserved for judgment" (**2 Peter 2:4**). Tartaroo refers to the place where fallen angels or demons are restrained, awaiting God's judgment. Tartaroo applies only to demons, not humans. Nowhere in the Bible does it refer to a fiery hell where people are punished forever and ever after death.

3. Another Greek word used in the Bible and translated "hell" is "Gehenna." Gehenna does refer to a fiery punishment for the

wicked, but it is "not" as portrayed by man's imagination—dangling over a fiery furnace in perpetual torment. The word "Gehenna" is derived from the Hebrew word "ge-hinnon," which we might describe today as a city dump, where garbage, trash, and refuse is thrown and consumed in a constantly burning fire. In biblical times, carcasses of dead animals and bodies of despised criminals were burned in Gehenna—the criminals were already dead when their bodies were thrown in Gehenna. They were "not" living people being tormented by a burning fire.

Jesus simply used the city dump of His day—Gehenna—to illustrate the place and ultimate fate of wicked people. Scripture refers to the city dump site as the "the lake of fire." Just as the trash in the city dump was consumed by maggots and a constantly burning fire, so will the terribly wicked people be totally burned up by a future Gehenna fire. They will not be eternally tortured. The Gehenna fire will occur after the one thousand year reign of Christ on earth.

> And I saw the dead, small and great, standing before God, and books were opened. And another book was opened, which is the Book of Life. And the dead were judged according to their works, by the things which were written in the books. The sea gave up the dead who were in it, and Death and Hades delivered up the dead who were in them. And they were judged, each one according to his works. Then Death and Hades were cast into the lake of fire. This is the second death. And anyone not found written in the Book of Life was cast into the lake of fire." (**Revelation 20:12–15**)

The implication here is that the surface of the earth will become a molten mass, obliterating any evidence of human wickedness. The terribly wicked people who will not repent or obey God will be quickly burned up in the lake of fire. They will not be tormented night and day, forever and ever; they will be put out of their misery. But when God destroys a person in Gehenna, the resulting death is eternal. That person will simply cease to exist.

We are told in the Bible that God is a God of mercy and love. "Oh, give thanks to the LORD, for He is good! For His mercy endures forever" (**Psalm 118:29**). "But God, who is rich in mercy, because of His great love with which He loved us" (**Ephesians 2:4**). But those who willfully and willingly reject God's way of life, characterized by disobedience to His law of love, will be instantaneously consumed by fire and totally forgotten. God will not grant His priceless gift of eternal life to those who persist in rebelling against Him, but they will not be tortured for all eternity.

So, even the second death of the terribly wicked in a lake of fire is an act of justice and mercy on God's part. If these people will not love God and will not obey His laws of love, it will be better for them not to live anymore, according to God. Since God creates life, only He can take it away. The encouraging truth of the Bible shows that God is indeed a being of love, great mercy, wisdom, and righteous judgment. "The fear of the LORD is clean, enduring forever; The judgments of the LORD are true and righteous altogether" (**Psalm 19:9**). "The fear [respect] of the LORD is the beginning of wisdom; A good understanding have all those who do His commandments. His praise endures forever" (**Psalm 111:10**).

4.10 HOW DID HUMANITY GET TO THIS PRESENT CHAOTIC STATE?

Some of the world's highly educated people, such as scientists, philosophers, statesmen, and world leaders, do not believe that there is a God, let alone believe what He says in His Holy Bible. They would rather embrace the theory of evolution as to the origin of man and the big bang theory as to the origin of the universe. People who believe the aforementioned theories (and they are only theories) have become blind to the fact that there is a God who created all things, including man and the universe. God says exactly the same thing in Romans: "And even as they did not like to retain God in their knowledge, God gave them over to a debased mind, to do those things which are not fitting" (**Romans 1:28**). But to those willing to believe in God and do what He says, He gives His wisdom and truth. "The law of the LORD is perfect, converting the soul; The testimony of the LORD is sure, making wise the simple" (**Psalm 19:7**). By believing in God and doing what He says in the Bible, God says He makes simple people wise.

With that thought, how did humanity get to the present chaotic state in which we find ourselves today? How did we stray so far away from God and His way of life? There are **five** primary reasons why humanity is in such a chaotic state:

1. Most people reject biblical truth. *What exactly is truth?* Let's allow the Bible to answer this question. At His trial some two thousand years ago, Pilate asked Christ that very same question. "Pilate said to Him [Christ], 'What is truth?' And when he had said this, he went out again to the Jews, and said to them, 'I find no fault in Him at all'" (**John 18:38**). Pilate and many other people did not know or understand what the truth of God really was. Many people today do not know or care to know what truth is. One reason Christ came to earth was to tell the truth to everyone. "But because I tell the truth, you do not believe Me" (**John 8:45**). The Holy Bible is God's truth. "Sanctify them by Your truth. Your word is truth" (**John 17:17**).

Let's go back to the beginning of humanity in **Genesis 2**. Here, we see that our first parents rejected God's truth, just as most people reject it today by not keeping God's commandments and feast days. Adam and Eve were told by God Himself in the garden of Eden, "but of the tree of the knowledge of good and evil you shall not eat, for in the day that you eat of it you shall surely die" (**Genesis 2:17**). Then the serpent (Satan) approached Eve and lied to her. "For God knows that in the day you eat of it your eyes will be opened, and you will be like

God, knowing good and evil" (**Genesis 3:5**). Adam and Eve rejected God's truth and accepted Satan's lie.

We find the same rejection of truth today. *God tells us to observe His Ten Commandments, but how many billions of people have pictures or statues of Jesus and Mary in their homes, breaking the second commandment ("Thou shalt not make unto thee any graven image")? How many billions of people worship God on Sunday, while God tells us clearly to observe His seventh day (Sabbath)? How many people murder and rape?* As a result, humanity, as a whole, finds itself in a very desperate state.

2. Most people unknowingly reject God. In the Garden of Eden, Satan called God a liar by contradicting what God said. (Reference **Genesis 3:5**.) Adam went along with his wife, Eve, and also ate of the forbidden fruit, believing Satan and rejecting God. Both Adam and Eve were thrown out of the garden, cutting off their access to God, and eventually died, just as God had told them.

From that day forward, Satan has deceived the vast majority of people who reject biblical truth and God. "So, the great dragon was cast out, that serpent of old, called the Devil and Satan, who deceives the whole world; he was cast to the earth, and his angels were cast out with him" (**Revelation 12:9**).

In another example, we find ancient Israel rejecting God from being king over them. Instead, they wanted an earthly king to rule over them, like other nations living around them. "And the LORD told him: 'Listen to all that the people are saying to you; it is not you they have rejected, but they have rejected me as their king'" (**1 Samuel 8:7**). This is yet another powerful reason why we are in our present chaotic state. By not observing and honoring God's commandments and feast days, we reject God.

3. Most people do not fear God. Since most people reject the Bible and God, they do not fear or have respect for Him. "There is no

fear of God before their eyes" (**Romans 3:18**). "The fear of the LORD is the beginning of knowledge, but fools despise wisdom and instruction" (**Proverbs 1:7**).

4. Humanity has decided for itself what is good and what is evil. Each person has his/her own opinion about what is good or evil. Humans, however, do not know what is good or evil, nor do they know the way to lasting peace, happiness, prosperity, and health. Because of their unbelief and rejection, they have become totally unaware of what their awesome destiny is and what God has prepared for them. Most people believe that the difference between good and evil is relative to a person's situation. "The way of peace they have not known, and there is no justice in their ways; They have made themselves crooked paths; Whoever takes that way shall not know peace" (**Isaiah 59:8**). What powerful words these are! Let us not be like the vast majority of the people in the world today. Let us always rely on God to tell us, through His Word, what is good and what is evil. God knows what is best for His creation, and it is all found in the Holy Bible.

5. God gave the "wise of the world" over to a "debased" mind. The wise of this world today, without God and His revealed knowledge, still debate the existence of God, even though there is ample proof. Because most of humanity has rejected God and refused to believe what He says in the Bible, God has allowed their foolish minds to become debased. As stated earlier, a debased mind is a mind devoid of spiritual knowledge. Without spiritual knowledge, which is found only in God's Word, people become foolish. "And even as they did not like to retain God in their knowledge, God gave them over to a debased mind, to do those things which are not fitting" (**Romans 1:28**).

As the Bible says, people who profess to be wise are really fools, "because, although they knew God, they did not glorify Him as God, nor were thankful, but became futile in their thoughts, and their foolish hearts were darkened. Professing to be wise, they became fools, and changed the glory of the incorruptible God into an image made like corruptible man—and birds and four-footed animals and creeping things" (**Romans 1:21–23**).

The end result of not believing God or doing what He says is complete chaos in government, schools, science, and, yes, even in modern Christianity. We have a disbelieving humanity that continues to stumble along on its way, piling up mountains of human woes, discontent, unhappiness, sorrow, pain, suffering, and, ultimately, death, just as God said from the very beginning in the Bible. This is the terrible state of chaos we find ourselves in today. Practically all of humanity has followed our first parents' example. If only humans would believe their creator God, how much better this world would be! But the eternal God, nevertheless, has made this vital knowledge and truth available to you this day. *Will you believe God's truth, or will decide for yourself what is good or evil?* The choice is yours. Another piece of the giant jigsaw puzzle is now in your hands.

Chapter 5
GOD'S TRUTH ABOUT SALVATION AND RESURRECTIONS

5.1   WHAT EXACTLY IS SALVATION / BORN AGAIN?

It is common for today's Christians to quote only part of a Scripture on a particular subject and think they have the entire answer to the question at hand. By doing so, they read false meanings into Scriptures, teach half-truths, and lead other sincere and well-meaning Christians into spiritual blindness and deception.

Rarely do we find all there is to know about a subject in just one Scripture. **Isaiah 28:10** tells us how God's truths are revealed: "For precept must be upon precept, precept upon precept, line upon line, line upon line, here a little, there a little." This is precisely why the Bible is like a giant jigsaw puzzle—pieces of truth are scattered throughout its entirety and must be placed correctly. In addition, we must be diligent and search the Scriptures daily, asking God for guidance on the subject. "These were more fair-minded than those in Thessalonica, in that they received the word with all readiness, and searched the Scriptures daily to find out whether these things were so" (**Acts 17:11**).

Salvation is an important and complex topic that should concern all Christians because their eternal life depends on it. If a person does not know what salvation is or is not, he or she could be deceived. The Bible describes what salvation is.

The word "salvation" means the "act of saving." When used in a biblical sense, "to save" means to rescue someone from the consequences of sin, which is, spiritual death. "For the wages of sin is death, but the gift of God is eternal life in Christ Jesus our Lord" (**Romans 6:23**). This chapter will focus on a spiritual saving, not a physical saving. We all must die a physical death at our appointed time. "And as it is appointed for men to die once, but after this the judgment" (**Hebrews 9:27**) and "for all have sinned and fall short of the glory of God" (**Romans 3:23**). After a person dies physically, a resurrection and a judgment will take place. God Himself will resurrect and judge us. That is what the Bible teaches. We do not go to heaven or hell at death; we are simply dead and, in the grave, awaiting a resurrection and a judgment. The eternal consequence for breaking God's laws (sin) is a spiritual death, from which there is no resurrection. But God the Father sent His son, Christ, to save everyone from that spiritual death, upon repentance and baptism. God has a master plan for saving humanity from this spiritual death.

As far as salvation, the Bible speaks of **two** separate and distinct resurrections in which people are saved.

1. The **first** resurrection happens instantaneously as Christ returns to earth at the seventh trumpet. "Then the seventh angel sounded: And there were loud voices in heaven, saying, 'The kingdoms of this world have become the kingdoms of our Lord and of His Christ, and He shall reign forever and ever!'" (**Revelation 11:15**). The first resurrection has to do with people God has called through the millennia. Some of God's chosen people died long ago, such as Abraham, Isaac, and Jacob, but He has chosen other people in this present age who are still alive when Christ returns. "For if we believe that Jesus died and rose again, even so God will bring with Him those who sleep in Jesus. For this we say to you by the word of the Lord, that we who are alive and remain until the coming of the Lord will by no means precede those who are asleep. For the Lord Himself will descend from heaven with a shout, with the

voice of an archangel, and with the trumpet of God. And the dead in Christ will rise first" (**1 Thessalonians 4:14–16**).

The people in the first resurrection will be made kings and priests and will rule with Christ on earth for one thousand years. "And have made us kings and priests to our God; And we shall reign on the earth" (**Revelation 5:10**).

"Now this I say, brethren, that flesh and blood cannot inherit the kingdom of God; nor does corruption inherit incorruption. Behold, I tell you a mystery: We shall not all sleep, but we shall all be changed—in a moment, in the twinkling of an eye, at the last trumpet. For the trumpet will sound, and the dead will be raised incorruptible, and we shall be changed. For this corruptible must put on incorruption, and this mortal must put on immortality. So, when this corruptible has put on incorruption, and this mortal has put on immortality, then shall be brought to pass the saying that is written: "Death is swallowed up in victory" (**1 Corinthians 15:50–54**). The phrase "death is swallowed up" means that when God's people are resurrected and/or changed into spirit composition in the first resurrection, they cannot die anymore. They are saved, and death has no more power over them.

Contrary to what most Christians believe, salvation cannot and does not happen while a person is still alive physically. A person must die a physical death, be resurrected, and be changed into spirit composition; then he or she is saved. This is what happened to Christ, and that's what must happen to us. No one is saved today. Notice where Paul speaks of salvation as a future event: "Much more then, having now been justified by His blood, we shall be saved from wrath through Him. For if when we were enemies, we were reconciled to God through the death of His Son, much more, having been reconciled, we shall be saved by His life" (**Romans 5:9–10**). "We shall be saved" refers to a future resurrection. And in **1 Corinthians 15:50**, we read, "Now this I say, brethren, that flesh and blood cannot inherit the kingdom of God; nor does corruption inherit incorruption."

2. The Bible calls the **second** resurrection "the great white throne judgment," and it takes place immediately after the one thousand year reign of Christ on earth. The Bible refers to this large group of people as the "rest of the dead." "But the rest of the dead did not live again until the thousand years were finished..." (**Revelation 20:5**). The great white throne judgment will include all the billions upon billions of people who have ever lived, died, and never had a chance to know the true God, His name, or His truth because they were somehow deceived. It will be their opportunity to be resurrected. After the one thousand years, this vast number of people (the rest of the dead) will be resurrected be resurrected as flesh and blood human beings. All of these people, great and small, will live again physically on earth a second time. What a wonderful truth this is! God includes everyone in His plan of salvation! Some readers might be totally surprised by this resurrection, but that is exactly what the Bible teaches.

"And I saw the dead, small and great, standing before God, and books were opened. And another book was opened, which is the Book of Life. And the dead were judged according to their works, by the things which were written in the books" (**Revelation 20:12**). During their second physical life, this huge group of people will be provided their opportunity to live God's way of life, which leads them to become spirit beings, living forever in God's kingdom. The Bible does not reveal how long this group of people will live physically. But they will be taught God's way of life by spirit beings who were in the first resurrection.

But what happens to the people who are in the great white throne judgment resurrection but refuse to obey God? What happens to them? "But the cowardly, unbelieving, abominable, murderers, sexually immoral, sorcerers, idolaters, and all liars shall have their part in the lake which burns with fire and brimstone, which is the second death" (**Revelation 21:8**).

The people who are terribly wicked and do not want to be part of God's family or live His way of life will be cast into the lake of fire and will become ashes beneath the righteous' feet. This will be their second death, which is spiritual. This death will be an everlasting death without any resurrection. These people will simply cease to exist. They will "not" be tormented forever and ever in hell, as most Christians believe. "'You shall trample the wicked, for they shall be ashes under the soles of your feet on the day that I do this,' says the LORD of hosts" (**Malachi 4:3**). Also consider, "Then Death and Hades were cast into the lake of fire. This is the second death. And anyone not found written in the Book of Life was cast into the lake of fire" (**Revelation 20:14–15**).

It is important to note that Christ is the author of salvation, which is eternal. "And having been perfected, He became the author of eternal salvation to all who obey Him, called by God as High Priest according to the order of Melchizedek" (**Hebrews 5:9–10**). All those who obey God will receive eternal salvation. *How do we obey God?* By observing and living His laws daily, which are summed up in the Ten Commandments.

Remember that salvation belongs to God. We cannot save ourselves! No minister, rabbi, priest, reverend, pope, or any religious denomination or any church can save us; only God can. "And crying out with a loud voice, saying, 'Salvation belongs to our God who sits on the throne, and to the Lamb!'" (**Revelation 7:10**). "The Lamb" refers to Jesus, the Christ, as He was the Passover Lamb of God who was sacrificed for everyone.

What does the Bible say about being "born again?" Notice what Jesus told Nicodemus: "Jesus answered and said to him, 'Most assuredly, I say to you, unless one is born again, he cannot see the kingdom of God.' Nicodemus said to Him, 'How can a man be born when he is old? Can he enter a second time into his mother's womb and be born?' Jesus answered, 'Most assuredly, I say to you, unless one is born of water and the Spirit, he cannot enter the kingdom of God'" (**John 3:3–5**). In other words, unless a person is baptized (of water) and receives the gift of the Holy Spirit (God's power) he or she cannot enter the kingdom of God. So, when a person enters the kingdom of God as a spirit being, then he or she is "born again."

142

What did Christ mean by "born of water and of the Spirit?" To be born of water means to be totally submersed in water at baptism. To be born of the Spirit means to receive God's gift of the Holy Spirit at baptism by the laying on of hands. (See section 4.5 for more information on baptism.) "That which is born of the flesh is flesh, and that which is born of the Spirit is spirit" (**John 3:6**). "Born again" does "not" mean "giving your heart to the Lord," as mainstream Christianity teaches, or answering an altar call. No! To be born again means to become spirit through a resurrection.

Today, in this physical life, we are born of the flesh. In a future resurrection, we will be born of spirit. That is when salvation takes place. Once salvation takes place, that spirit being cannot die or sin anymore. "Whoever has been born of God does not sin, for His seed remains in him; and he cannot sin, because he has been born of God" (**1 John 3:9**).

"He who has the Son has life; he who does not have the Son of God does not have life" (**1 John 5:12**). The phrase "does not have life" refers to not having "everlasting" life. Only through living as Christ lived can a person receive everlasting life. Notice Christ's words: "Jesus said to him, 'I am the way, the truth, and the life. No one comes to the Father except through Me'" (**John 14:6**). Jesus also said, "I am the door. If anyone enters by Me, he will be saved" (**John 10:9**). Salvation is a gift that only God can give. "For the wages of sin is death, but the gift of God is eternal life in Christ Jesus our Lord" (**Romans 6:23**).

These meanings of being "saved" and "born again" come straight from your Bible. You have read God's master plan of saving His human creation from eternal death through one of two resurrections. This vital knowledge about salvation and born again, sheds much light on the giant jigsaw puzzle and God's love for His creation.

5.2   WHAT STEPS ARE NEEDED FOR SALVATION?

This chapter will present **eight** important steps that must take place in a person's life before salvation can occur. This is a very deep subject that demands your utmost attention, so be prepared to spend some time on it.

Everyone needs salvation because as the Bible tells us, "All have sinned and fall short of the glory of God" (**Romans 3:23**). And in **Romans 6:23**, the Bible tells us, "The wages of sin is death." Since all people have sinned, their punishment, according to the Bible, is spiritual, or everlasting death. Being made physical, all humans must die a physical death from which there is no escape. Spiritual death is what the Bible calls the "second death" from which there is no resurrection. God, from the very beginning of time, set His salvation plan in motion to save humanity from this spiritual death penalty. "He [Christ] indeed was foreordained before the foundation of the world, but was manifest in these last times for you" (**1 Peter 1:20**). Remember that Christ came to save us from the spiritual death by dying for us.

What does a person need to do to be saved? **Eight** sequential steps are required:

1. Acknowledge the fact that you have sinned and, according to God, deserve the spiritual death penalty. (Reference **Romans 3:23**, above.) It is very difficult for humans to admit that they have done wrong or sinned, but God requires this step in order for a person to be saved. God loves us and does not want anyone to die a spiritual death. Look at **2 Peter 3:9**, where we find that God is "not willing that any should perish [spiritual death] but that all should come to repentance." Just as any loving parent admonishes and punishes his child for wrongdoing, so God chastens us. "As many as I love, I rebuke and chasten. Therefore, be zealous and repent" (**Revelation 3:19**).

2. Repent of your sins. The apostle Peter states, "Repent, and let every one of you be baptized in the name of Jesus Christ for the remission of sins" (**Acts 2:38**). Repentance means to be wholeheartedly sorry for breaking God's laws. This means that you have become sick and tired of living the wrong way of life and now desire to change and begin living the right way of life—God's way. God's

way is the way of giving, the way of showing love toward God by obeying Him, and showing outgoing love and concern toward others. Satan's way is the way of get, self-centeredness, strife, and competition. "Repent, therefore and be converted that your sins may be blotted out, so that times of refreshing may come from the presence of the Lord" (**Acts 3:19**).

3. Be "converted." This means to change from Satan's way of living, to God's way of living—the way of love, which comes through repentance. (See section 4.4 for more information on repentance.) "And [Christ] said, 'Assuredly, I say to you, unless you are converted and become as little children, you will by no means enter the kingdom of heaven'" (**Matthew 18:3**). The Bible calls this life-transforming change of heart—to become like little children, "conversion." Most little children are eager to learn new things and to do what is right. They put their trust in their parents. We must become like little children, always trusting and obeying God. If you are truly converted, you are on your way to learning God's way of life. If you do your part of loving God and loving your neighbor, God will do His part in saving you.

Regrettably, many people assume that all they have to do is believe in God to be automatically saved. (See section 5.6 for more on believing.) Christianity, in general, fails to recognize and teach this second crucial step of deep personal repentance. They falsely believe that God will "accept you just as you are." The Bible never says to just come as you are. Instead, it tells us that before coming to God, we must make some drastic changes and turn our lives around by obeying all of God's commandments.

4. Ask God for the forgiveness of your sins. "In Him we have redemption through His blood, the forgiveness of sins, according to the riches of His grace" (**Ephesians 1:7**). Redemption means to free or buy back someone by paying a price. It is equivalent to

paying a ransom for a person who has been kidnapped in order to save that person's life. With His shed blood, Christ redeemed us to the Father. David provides us an example when he asks God to forgive him. "Have mercy upon me, O God, according to Your loving kindness; According to the multitude of Your tender mercies, blot out my transgressions" (**Psalm 51:1**). (A closer look at redemption is found in section 5.3.)

5. Be baptized. (Refer to section 4.5 for how to be correctly baptized.) Baptism is an outward sign that shows almighty God that you are putting to death (in a watery grave) your old self. God's way of living is not easy. Our journey on this earth does not end with baptism. We must fight and continue to resist sin and Satan. "Knowing this, that our old man was crucified with Him, that the body of sin might be done away with, that we should no longer be slaves of sin" (**Romans 6:6**).

6. God the Father removes your sins using Christ's shed blood to cleanse you. The apostle Paul writes of our salvation: "We have redemption through His blood, the forgiveness of sins" (**Colossians 1:14**). Jesus died an excruciatingly painful death by shedding His blood to redeem us from spiritual death. Christ's payment of the spiritual death penalty only becomes effective after all of the aforementioned steps are inculcated into a person's life. This is another reason why God the Father sent His beloved Son into this world. "God demonstrates His own love toward us, in that while we were still sinners, Christ died for us" (**Romans 5:8**).

7. Receive the free gift of God's Holy Spirit by the laying on of hands at baptism. At this point, we are sanctified or set apart for a special purpose. "And you shall receive the gift of the Holy Spirit" (**Acts 2:38**). The Holy Spirit allows us to understand the spiritual things of God, which include understanding God's holy days, His plan of salvation to save humankind, and the ability to understand

prophecy. The Holy Spirit also helps us make godly decisions in everyday life and not willfully sin. As humans, we will probably sin again and again but not willfully.

> My little children, these things I write to you, so that you may not sin. And if any man sin, we have an advocate with the Father, Jesus Christ the righteous: And He is the propitiation [sacrifice] for our sins: and not for ours only, but also for the sins of the whole world. And hereby we do know that we know Him, if we keep His commandments. He that says, I know Him, and keeps not His commandments, is a liar, and the truth is not in him. But whoso keeps His word, in Him verily is the love of God perfected: hereby know we that we are in Him. He that says he abides in Him ought himself also so to walk, even as He [Christ] walked. (**1 John 2:1–6**)

The Bible also says, "Through the Holy Spirit, God seals us, His Spirit serving as a guarantee of or down payment on our salvation" (**2 Corinthians 1:22**). In other words, the sealing by the Holy Spirit provides proof that we belong to God the Father and to Christ. "Now if anyone does not have the Spirit of Christ, he is not His ... as many as are led by the Spirit of God, these are the sons of God" (**Romans 8:9, 14**). By receiving the gift of the Holy Spirit, we become begotten sons and daughters of God.

God's gift of the Holy Spirit cannot be bought with money or anything else. It is freely given by God to those He has called. When Simon Magus saw the apostles lay hands on the sick, and they were healed, he wanted to buy the Holy Spirit. "And when Simon saw that through the laying on of the apostles' hands the Holy Spirit was given, he offered them [the disciples] money, saying, 'Give me this power also, that anyone on whom I lay hands may receive the Holy Spirit'" (**Acts 8:18–19**). The Holy Spirit is a free gift from God, if we acknowledge our sins, repent, and are baptized.

8. Become justified or made right in the sight of God. Once the steps to salvation are complete, God deals with us as though we had never sinned. The spiritual death penalty has no hold on us. "And such were some of you. But you were washed, but you were sanctified, but you were justified in the name of the Lord Jesus and by the Spirit of our God" (**1 Corinthians 6:11**). "Much more then, having now been justified by His blood, we shall be saved from wrath through Him" (**Romans 5:9**). "Moreover, whom He predestined, these He also called; whom He called, these He also justified; and whom He justified, these He also glorified" (**Romans 8:30**). Once we are justified, then we can be glorified, as Christ was glorified when He was resurrected spirit. To be glorified means to be changed into spirit composition.

> Jesus spoke these words, lifted up His eyes to heaven, and said: "Father, the hour has come. Glorify Your Son, that Your Son also may glorify You, as You have given Him authority over all flesh, that He should give eternal life to as many as You have given Him. And this is eternal life, that they may know You, the only true God, and Jesus Christ whom You have sent. I have glorified You on the earth. I have finished the work which You have given Me to do. And now, O Father, glorify Me together with Yourself, with the glory which I had with You before the world was. ... I do not pray for these alone, but also for those who will believe in Me through their word; that they all may be one, as You, Father, are in Me, and I in You; that they also may be one in Us, that the world may believe that You sent Me. And the glory which You gave Me I have given them, that they may be one just as We are one: I in them, and You in Me; that they may be made perfect in one, and that the world may know that You have sent Me, and have loved them as You have loved Me." (**John 17: 1–5, 20–23**)

But as true Christians, we must faithfully endure, even unto the end of our lives. "And you will be hated by all for My name's sake. But he who endures to the end shall be saved" (**Mark 13:13**). "But he who endures to the end shall be saved" (**Matthew 24:13**). If a true Christian, at some time during his life, after committing to serve God, turns away and renounces Jesus and God's way of life in word or action, he may lose his inheritance of everlasting life (salvation)—unless, of course, he fervently repents of his sins before God on a daily basis.

Do you see the emergence of God's wonderful plan and picture of saving humankind? God sent His Son to die for us so that someday we may obtain everlasting life. What a wonderful plan this is! No human could have thought of or planned such an awesome future for humanity. But we must be willing to change our lives, be converted, turn our lives around, and become better persons by keeping all of God's commandments. We must be willing to change from our way of living to God's way by using these eight steps. This is yet another piece of the giant jigsaw puzzle that we have put in place.

5.3   A CLOSER LOOK AT REDEMPTION

The word "redemption" literally means "to buy back." It is closely related to the word "salvation." When I was a youngster back in the 1960s, my mother saved S&H Green Stamps—these were trading stamps that could be redeemed for products from the S&H Green Stamps catalog. Each time she bought groceries, she earned Green Stamps, based on the amount of money spent at the store, and she glued the stamps to the pages of a booklet. Over time, she managed to save enough stamps to fill many booklets, and she finally redeemed the booklets for a brand-new toaster.

We can apply this concept of redemption in the biblical sense. Since all humans have sinned, we have cut ourselves off from having access to God the Father. Christ's mission on earth was to redeem us to the Father by paying the spiritual death penalty for us. Christ exchanged His perfect life to give us an opportunity to live again as spirit beings. To buy back all of humanity meant the price He paid for our sins had to be greater than the sum total of all human life. Christ's perfect life was worth that much to the Father. "Those who trust in their wealth and boast in the multitude of their riches, none of them can by any means redeem his brother, nor give to God a ransom for him, for the redemption of their souls is costly, and it shall cease forever, that he should continue to live eternally, and not see the pit" (**Psalm 49:6–9**).

Notice what **Hebrews 4:15** tells us about Christ's life: "For we have not a high priest which cannot be touched with the feeling of our infirmities; but was in all points tempted like as we are, yet without sin." Compare this with **Hebrews 2:9–10**, which tells us, "But we see Jesus, who was made a little lower than the angels for the suffering of death, crowned with glory and honor; that He [Christ] by the grace of God should taste death for every man. For it became Him [Christ], for whom are all things, and by whom are all things, in bringing many sons unto glory, to make the captain of their salvation perfect through sufferings." This is why Christ's ultimate sacrifice was necessary and acceptable to God the Father.

This state of forgiveness is represented by God's first feast day. It is called the Passover and is a memorial of Christ's death. Once per year, God instructs true Christians to remember and observe His Passover (**Leviticus 23**). Christ kept the Passover. "So, His disciples went out, and came into the city, and found it just as He had said to them; and they prepared the Passover" (**Mark 14:16**). "And He took bread, gave thanks and broke it, and gave it to them, saying, 'This is My body which is given for you; do this in remembrance of Me'" (**Luke 22:19**).

If we are to be like Christ, we should also keep the Passover. The Passover is not only a yearly reminder of Christ's death, but it is also a time to reflect on the sins that we inadvertently committed during the past year. During the feast of the Passover, we ask God's to forgive our sins. "So, this day [the Passover] shall be to you a memorial; and you shall keep it as a feast to the LORD throughout your generations. You shall keep it as a feast by an everlasting ordinance" (**Exodus 12:14**). "These are the feasts of the LORD, holy convocations which you shall proclaim at their appointed times. On the fourteenth day of the first month at twilight is the LORD's Passover" (**Leviticus 23:4–5**).

How many modern Christians observe the yearly Passover? Not very many! Some people say "communion" is available every day of the week at their churches, but that is not what God says to do. God says to observe the Passover at the appointed time. The Passover, where bread and wine are used as symbols of Christ's body and blood, only happens once per year, on the fourteenth day of God's first month. That is when the Passover bread and wine should be taken, not every day, not every week, and not once a month. Some Orthodox Jews may observe the Passover, but God commands that we all observe it. Remember the Bible says the Passover is one of God's annual feasts. It is not a Jewish feast. (See **Leviticus 23** for a complete listing of God's feast days.)

It is true that Christ was the Passover and that He took the place of the unblemished lamb that ancient Israel sacrificed once per year. Because of this fact, sacrificial animal offerings have been done away with, but the Passover feast itself has not been done away with, as some people believe. Christ partook of that same feast while on earth and told the disciples—and is telling us today—to "do this [at the Passover] in remembrance of Me." True Christians are to observe the Passover on a yearly basis, just as you would remember an important day like an anniversary. *How often do you celebrate an anniversary?* Once per year. God's master plan of salvation for humanity is outlined in God's feast days. A key element of God's salvation plan has to do with Christ's death and resurrection. Christ had to die to pay for our sins in order to redeem us. He also had to be resurrected in order to show us that we too will someday be resurrected. How awesome are God's ways!

People sometimes ask when did Christ die? Was Christ really in the grave for three days and three nights? Did He really rise from the dead early Sunday morning?

5.4   THE BIBLICAL TRUTH ABOUT CHRIST'S DEATH

Most of us have been taught that Christ died on Good Friday around three o'clock in the afternoon and that He rose from the dead early on Easter Sunday. Even today, this is what Christianity teaches because Jesus said He would be raised on the third day. Christ prophesied His own death and resurrection in **Matthew 16:21**, which tells us, "From that time Jesus began to show to His disciples that He must go to Jerusalem, and suffer many things from the elders and chief priests and scribes, and be killed, and be raised the third day." There is no question that Christ died and was resurrected from the dead on the third day. *But how do you get three days and three nights from Good Friday to early Sunday morning? Did Christ really mean three full days and three full nights, or did He just say three days and three nights, figuratively?* Most people count figuratively, counting Friday as one day, Saturday as the second day, and Sunday as the third day. But from Friday afternoon to early Sunday morning does not equal three days and three nights. Yet, that is precisely what modern Christianity teaches and wants you to believe.

If Christ was not in the grave for three full days and nights, as He said He would be, then He could not be our true Messiah, and He could not be God's only begotten Son. Instead, He would be a false Messiah, an imposter. *Do you see the importance of this? Do you see how crucial it is to know and understand the true biblical answers?*

To understand the full meaning of three days and three nights, we must ask **seven** basic but important questions and allow the Holy Bible to answer each one.

1. *How does God count days?* In **Genesis 1:4–5**, God tells us how He counts days. "And God saw the light, that it was good; and God divided the light from the darkness. God called the light Day, and the darkness He called Night. So, the evening and the morning were the first day."

One complete day is divided into two separate parts—the evening portion and the morning portion. So, the dark portion of the day God calls night, or evening, and the light portion God calls day, or morning. It is important to note that God begins days in the evening, at sunset, because He states, "So the evening and morning were the first day." The evening is mentioned first because God's days begin in the evening. The evening is followed by the morning and then followed by the next evening, which begins the next day. According to God, one day consists of an evening and a morning, and both parts added together equal one full day. Since creation week, a day has always consisted of these two parts—an evening and a morning—and that has never changed. Also, from sunset (the end of one day) to sunset (the beginning of the next day) has always been the same length of time—a full twenty-four hours. Of course, in winter the evenings are longer, and the mornings shorter, but a day is still twenty-four hours long. One day is how long it takes the earth to rotate one full turn.

If you read **Genesis 1**, you will find the phrase "and the evening and morning was the next day" scattered throughout the remainder of creation week. It is only because humans want to do things their own way that they changed the beginning of the new day to midnight. But remember that from the Bible, God's new day always begins in the evening at sunset.

2. *Is God exact in His timing of events?* In other words, does God do things on time and in a timely manner? "But when the fullness of the time had come, God sent forth His Son, born of a woman, born under the law" (**Galatians 4:4**). Notice that God does everything right on time, right on schedule—nothing is accidental to Him. Jesus, our Messiah, was born "when the fullness of time had come" (on time). He died right on time and was resurrected on time, not one hour early or one hour late.

Take a look at another example: "Jesus spoke these words, lifted up His eyes to heaven, and said: 'Father, the hour has come. Glorify Your

Son, that Your Son also may glorify You'" (**John 17:1**). Notice that "the hour has come." Even that specific hour of glorification was part of God's plan.

Look at another example of timing. "You go up to this feast. I am not yet going up to this feast, for My time has not yet fully come" (**John 7:8**). Since there was an exact time for Christ's birth, an exact time of His anointing and baptism, an exact time of His death, and an exact time for His resurrection, it should be of no great surprise that an exact time was to elapse between His burial and resurrection. That exact time was three full days and three full nights—exactly seventy-two hours.

3. *Where did the phrase "three days and three nights" come from?* The phrase came from Christ. Since the scribes and the Pharisees did not believe that Christ was the true Messiah, they asked Him to give them a sign to prove that He was truly the Messiah. "Then some of the scribes and Pharisees answered, saying, 'Teacher, we want to see a sign from You.' But He answered and said to them, 'An evil and adulterous generation seeks after a sign, and no sign will be given to it except the sign of the prophet Jonah. For as Jonah was three days and three nights in the belly of the great fish, so will the Son of Man be three days and three nights in the heart of the earth'" (**Matthew 12:38–40**). "The heart of the earth" simply means the grave. To prove that Christ was the prophesied Messiah, He gave the unbelieving religious leaders living at that time the sign of being in the grave three days and three nights. Christ quoted His words from the book of Jonah. "Now the LORD had prepared a great fish to swallow Jonah. And Jonah was in the belly of the fish three days and three nights" (**Jonah 1:17**).

As Jonah was in the belly of a great fish for three full days and three full nights, so was Christ to be "in the heart of the earth" (grave) for three full days and three full nights. That's the only sign Christ gave to the scribes and Pharisees to prove that He was the Messiah. This means that Christ was to be in the grave exactly seventy-two hours—no more and no less. Jesus spoke of the "temple" being destroyed and then raised in three days. "Jesus answered and said to them, 'Destroy this temple, and in three days I will raise it up.' Then the Jews said, 'It has taken forty-six years to build this temple, and will You raise it up in three days?' But He was speaking of the temple of His body" (**John 2:19–21**). In other words, Christ's body was to be resurrected from the dead just after three full days and three full nights of being in the grave.

4. *What is the biblical explanation for there being three days and three nights from 3:00 p.m. on Friday to early Sunday?* Whether By human reasoning or by God's reckoning of days, it is impossible to get three full days and three full nights from Friday afternoon to very early Sunday. Yet this is exactly what we have been taught by the Christian clergy, assuming it to be correct. But there is definitely something illogical with the widespread Christian belief about a Friday crucifixion and an early Sunday resurrection. And that is, it does not add up to seventy-two hours; in fact, it is a mere thirty-six hours. Yet Christ emphatically stated that He would be "in the heart of the earth" three days and three nights, just as the prophet Jonah was in the belly of a great fish. As has already been stated, God is an exacting God. He does things systematically and on time. He does not count one half day as a full day, as some people think. God counts only full days. Therefore, Christ could "not" have died on Friday if the resurrection was on Sunday.

5. *When did Christ actually die?* For the biblical answer, let's go to **Daniel 9:27**, where it tells us that Christ died in the middle of the week: "Then He [Christ] shall confirm a covenant with many for one week; But in the middle of the week, He shall bring an end to sacrifice and offering."

Christ's final Passover meal and death occurred in the middle of the week. Directly in the middle of the week is Wednesday. This is an astonishing biblical fact to most Christians. Sunday is the first day of the week, and the Sabbath (Saturday) is the seventh day of the week. Remember that by God's calculation, Tuesday evening, after sunset begins the next day, Wednesday. Again, God is an exacting God, a timely God, a God who does things on time. On Tuesday evening after sunset, Christ observed the Passover by using the new symbols of unleavened bread and wine. Unleavened bread symbolizes Christ's sinless body, and the wine symbolizes Christ's blood. "For I received from the Lord that which I also delivered to you: that the Lord Jesus on the same night in which He was betrayed took bread; and when He had given thanks, He broke it and said, 'Take, eat; this is My body which is broken for you; do this in remembrance of Me'" (**1 Corinthians 11:23–24**).

6. *At what time on Wednesday did Christ die?*

> And about the ninth hour Jesus cried out with a loud voice, saying, "Eli, Eli, lama sabachthani?" that is, "My God, My God, why have You forsaken Me?" Some of those who stood there, when they heard that, said, "This Man is calling for Elijah!" Immediately one of them ran and took a sponge, filled it with sour wine and put it on a reed, and offered it to Him to drink. The rest said, "Let Him alone; let us see if Elijah will come to save Him." And Jesus cried out again with a loud voice, and yielded up His spirit." (**Matthew 27:46–50**)

According to Hebrew scholars, the ninth hour, in Christ's day, was 3:00 p.m. Christ died at three o'clock on Wednesday afternoon. This is not a great surprise; the vast majority of Christians believe that Christ died around three o'clock. We know from Scripture that the Jews wanted Christ down from the cross before the high Sabbath day.

"Therefore, because it was the Preparation Day, that the bodies should not remain on the cross on the Sabbath (for that Sabbath was a High day), the Jews asked Pilate that their legs might be broken, and that they might be taken away" (**John 19:31**). Christ died on Wednesday at 3:00 p.m.

7. *What is a high Sabbath day?* It's important to note that the Sabbath mentioned above was a "High day." It should not be confused with the weekly Sabbath. This High day Sabbath was one of God's annual Sabbath days. Annual Sabbaths are God's feasts, which are to be observed once per year by all people, not just the Jews. God's annual days are thus called high Sabbath days. No customary work was/is to be done, either on annual High Sabbaths or the weekly Sabbath. In the Holy Bible, the weekly Sabbaths, while very important days that need to be observed, are not high holy days; they are referred to only as rest days.

The above Scripture states that Christ died on the preparation day which was also the Passover. In the week that Christ died, the Passover occurred on Wednesday (14 Abib) and was the preparation day for the annual high Sabbath day of the First Day of Unleavened Bread, Thursday (15 Abib). Christ's body was to be taken down "before" the beginning of the First Day of Unleavened Bread.

The preparation day for the annual High Sabbath day can occur on any day of the week and therefore changes from year to year. On the other hand, the preparation day for the weekly Sabbath always occurs on Friday; it never changes. The vast majority of Christians believe that Christ died on Friday because the Bible states "high Sabbath day," and they think that it refers to the weekly Sabbath or Saturday. They do not believe or understand that there is also a preparation day for each of God's annual high Sabbath days.

Most of today's Christianity reject God's annual feasts because they think they are "Jewish." But the Bible clearly states that God's annual Sabbaths are His feasts, given to all of humanity, not just the Jews.

Take a look at **Leviticus 23:4–8**, where God tells us about His seven annual high Sabbath days:

> These are the feasts of the LORD, holy convocations which you shall proclaim at their appointed times. On the fourteenth day of the first month at twilight is the LORD's Passover. And on the fifteenth day of the same month is the Feast of Unleavened Bread to the LORD; seven days you must eat unleavened bread. On the first day you shall have a holy convocation; you shall do no customary work on it. But you shall offer an offering made by fire to the LORD for seven days. The seventh day shall be a holy convocation; you shall do no customary work on it.

All of God's feasts are still binding for everyone today.

If Christ died at 3:00 p.m. on a Wednesday, then three days and three nights would end at 3:00 p.m. on the Sabbath—no more and no less than seventy-two hours. Christ rose from the dead shortly after 3:00 p.m. on the weekly Sabbath, Saturday. In addition, the Sabbath is Christ's day, not Sunday. He rose on His day. In many places in the Bible, Christ is called the Lord of the Sabbath. "Therefore, the Son of Man is also 'Lord of the Sabbath'" (**Mark 2:28**).

Let's look at each day of crucifixion week, with Bible events that took place from the time when Christ died until He was resurrected:

Passover. Preparation day, fourteenth day of the first month, Wednesday. Christ died about three o'clock in the afternoon. His body would have been taken down from the cross and placed in the tomb before sunset so that His death would not interfere with the high Sabbath of the First Day of Unleavened Bread, which began after sunset on Wednesday.

First Day. Feast of Unleavened Bread, fifteenth day of the first month, Thursday. As an annual high Sabbath day, no work was done on this day. The women who wanted to anoint Christ's body could "not" go out and buy spices and ointments because of their observance of this annual high Sabbath day.

Second Day. A regular work day, sixteenth day of the first month, Friday. The women journeyed out and bought spices and ointments to anoint Christ's body.

Third Day. The weekly Sabbath day, seventeenth day of the first month, Saturday. This was a day of rest, and no work was to be done on the weekly Sabbath. The women could not anoint Christ's body; they had to rest. Christ rose from the dead on His day, the weekly Sabbath, shortly after 3:00 p.m. After being in the "heart of the earth" for three full days and three full nights, Christ was resurrected by God the Father on time. After His resurrection, Christ appeared and was seen by many people. Christ fulfilled the three days/three-night requirement, authenticating that He was our true Messiah, just as He had told the scribes and Pharisees.

Fourth Day. A regular work day, eighteenth day of the first month, Sunday. Since the women had already purchased the spices, they went out early on this day, before daybreak, to anoint Christ's body. When the women entered the tomb to anoint Christ's body, they did "not" find Him there. He had already risen from the dead on the weekly Sabbath, about twelve hours before they arrived.

Knowing this vital information can help restore your faith in God the Father and His Son, Jesus the Christ. Both have always been faithful and true to us. The truth in this chapter was revealed through God's Holy Word. I hope this vital knowledge and truth will help your understanding of Christ's death, His resurrection, and the fulfillment of three full days and nights. Another piece of the giant jigsaw puzzle was put in place.

5.5   WHO SHOULD WE TRUST TO SAVE US?

In today's society, the character quality of trust is hard to find and is very elusive. Sometimes people look for trust in all the wrong places. When I was young, in the late 1950s, contracts were made by people shaking hands and promising to do something for a certain wage. The contract was verbal— "If you do this, I'll do that for you." There probably were not many formal written contracts back then; a firm handshake or verbal agreement was the contract, and it meant a lot to most people. It showed a trusting relationship between two people or groups of people—a promise to buy or do something. It showed respect.

If the promise to perform a job was kept and wages were paid in full, then trust took root. Advertisement back then was mostly done by word of mouth. Notice what God says about people speaking the right words at the right time: "A word fitly spoken is like apples of gold in settings of silver" (**Proverbs 25:11**). But like anything worthwhile, trust takes a long time to build and strengthen. When promises are broken, then the trust is also broken. All it takes is one wrong word, one wrong action, one wrong deed, or one unpaid wage, and the trust is broken. The trust that took so long to build, nurture, and mature can suddenly vanish. And once the trust is broken, it may take a long time to rebuild. In some cases, trust is lost forever.

In whom or in what should we place our total trust? What does the holy Word of God say about trust? Webster's Dictionary defines trust as a "firm belief in some quality of a person or a thing." Trust is having confidence in and reliance on the good qualities of a person, especially fairness, truthfulness, and honesty.

I believe there are **three** major categories where people place their trust today:

1. Most people place their trust in people. Some people trust their friends. Others trust people in high places, such as princes, kings, doctors, lawyers, and people who hold public offices (mayors,

governors, elected representatives, presidents, politicians). The Holy Bible is very specific about where we should place our trust. "Do not put your trust in princes, nor in a son of man, in whom there is no help. His [the son of a man's] spirit departs, he returns to this earth; In that very day his plans perish" (**Psalm 146:3–4**). Here, the Bible plainly states that we should "not" put our total trust in people.

"Do not trust in a friend; Do not put your confidence in a companion; Guard the doors of your mouth; From her who lies in your bosom" (**Micah 7:5**).

As a matter of fact, God said that He would curse the man or woman who places his or her complete trust in another person. Strong words are these, but they come from the One who cannot lie. "Thus says the LORD: 'Cursed is the man who trusts in man and makes flesh his strength, whose heart departs from the LORD'" (**Jeremiah 17:5**). *Why do you think God curses such a person?* Because if you totally trust a person and not God, that person becomes your god, breaking the first commandment of having no other gods in place of the true God. (Reference **Exodus 20:3**.) The minute you place your trust in man is the minute that your heart departs from God. Think about that—these words are from God Himself. We should not place our total trust in any human at any time.

Can we trust what people say? Many people trust what others tell them, and they do not bother to see if what they were told is true. These same people, including religious leaders, do not test all things, as the Bible admonishes us to do. "Test all things; hold fast what is good" (**1 Thessalonians 5:21**). Some Bibles translate the Greek words to read, "Prove all things; hold fast that which is good."

Let us take a closer look at this subcategory of trusting what people say. "Thus says the LORD of hosts, the God of Israel: 'Amend your ways and your doings, and I will cause you to dwell in this place. Do not trust in these lying words, saying, "The temple of the LORD, the temple of the LORD, the temple of the LORD are these"'" (**Jeremiah**

7:3–4). God plainly says not to trust in lying words. *How do you know if words are lying words?* Again, you must test and prove all things that pertain to God for yourself. Be sure to ask God to guide you in your quest for the truth. The only human who always spoke the truth was Christ.

Sometimes, people tell outright lies. Sometimes they tell you things that they have not proved and are therefore deceived. Isaiah was inspired to write the following, and it is for our admonition today: "Woe to those who call evil good, and good evil; Who put darkness for light, and light for darkness; Who put bitter for sweet, and sweet for bitter!" (**Isaiah 5:20**). *If someone says that something is good when you know its evil, isn't that a lie?* Yes, it is!

I have heard some youths say, "Hey, it's okay to steal as long as you don't get caught." Others say, "It's okay to live with someone before getting married because we want to see if we are compatible with each other." *If that were true, then why are divorce rates at an all-time high today?* Those are lying words. *Did Abraham have sex with Sarah before they were married?* I think not, because Abraham was very obedient to God and His laws. "Because Abraham obeyed My voice and kept My charge, My commandments, My statutes, and My laws" (**Genesis 26:6**). You cannot obey God without keeping His commandments.

Another subcategory is that of trusting oneself. You may think that if you can't trust other people or what they say, then surely you can trust yourself. Let's allow the Bible to address that. "Yes, we had the sentence of death in ourselves, that we should not trust in ourselves but in God who raises the dead, who delivered us from so great a death, and does deliver us; in whom we trust that He will still deliver us" (**2 Corinthians 1:9–10**).

"There is a way that seems right to a man, but its end is the way of death" (**Proverbs 14:12**). When you think you're absolutely right about something, without consulting God, read **Proverbs 14:12** and **2 Corinthians 1:9–1** again. What we think may be the right thing to do may not be right in God's eyes. Ask God in prayer to help you find the right solution to your problem, according to His will. That is the only true way to go.

The prophet Hosea also has something to say about trust. "You have plowed wickedness; You have reaped iniquity. You have eaten the fruit of lies, because you trusted in your own way, in the multitude of your mighty men" (**Hosea 10:13**). These Scriptures need no interpretation; the message is clear that we are not to put our total trust in ourselves either.

Solomon, the wisest man who ever lived, other than the Messiah, was deceived by his own wisdom. Imagine that! He erroneously thought he could trust himself.

> But King Solomon loved many foreign women, as well as the daughter of Pharaoh: women of the Moabites, Ammonites, Edomites, Sidonians, and Hittites from the nations of whom the LORD had said to the children of Israel, "You shall not intermarry with them, nor they with you. Surely they will turn away your hearts after their gods." Solomon clung to these in love. And he had seven hundred wives, princesses, and three hundred concubines; and his wives turned away his heart. For it was so, when Solomon was old, that his wives turned his heart after other gods; and his heart was not loyal to the LORD his God, as was the heart of his father David. For Solomon went after Ashtoreth the goddess of the Sidonians, and after Milcom the abomination of the Ammonites. Solomon did evil in the sight of the LORD, and did not fully follow the LORD, as did his father David. Then Solomon built a high place for Chemosh the abomination of Moab, on the hill that is east of Jerusalem, and for Molech the abomination of the people of Ammon. (**1 Kings 11:1–7**)

Being wise, Solomon thought he could place his total trust in himself and in his wives—and look what happened to him! Solomon did evil in the sight of God. What a shameful thing to do to your Creator.

2. People trust in things. Let's take a close look at a few examples. Many people put their trust in weapons of war, such as airplanes, fighter jets, tanks, ships, or cannons. They place their trust in chariots and horses, bows and arrows, guns, bombs, knives, and swords. David was inspired to write the following about placing total trust in weaponry: "For I will not trust in my bow, nor shall my sword save me" (**Psalm 44:6**). David told God that he would not place his total trust in weapons of war.

Many people also put their trust in things such as the stock market, cars, the economy, money, buildings, and franchises. "Those who trust in their wealth, and boast in the multitude of their riches, none of them can by any means redeem his brother, nor give to God a ransom for him—for the redemption of their souls is costly, and it shall cease forever—That he should continue to live eternally, and not see the Pit" (**Psalm 49:6–9**). In other words, no amount of wealth will save you or anyone else; only God has the power to save you.

"And the disciples were astonished at His words. But Jesus answered again and said to them, 'Children, how hard it is for those who trust in riches to enter the kingdom of God! It is easier for a camel to go through the eye of a needle than for a rich man to enter the kingdom of God'" (**Mark 10:24–25**). How plain and simple this teaching is.

3. People trust in God. Very few people place their total trust in God. But for true Christians, it is the only place where they should place their total trust.

"Trust in the LORD, and do good; Dwell in the land, and feed on His faithfulness. Delight yourself also in the LORD, and He shall give you the desires of your heart" (**Psalm 37:3–4**). If we place our total trust in God, He will see to it that the desires of our hearts are met.

"Trust in the LORD with all your heart, and lean not on your own understanding" (**Proverbs 3:5**). "Oh, how great is Your goodness, which You have laid up for those who fear You, which You have prepared for those who trust in You in the presence of the sons of men" (**Psalm 31:19**).

Young children are taught to trust Mom and Dad. Perhaps both of your parents held your hand as you learned to cross the street. As Mom and Dad see their child trusting them, their love for their child grows even more. God loves us when we, as grown-ups, place our total trust in Him. And trust is much like faith. "But without faith it is impossible to please Him, for he who comes to God must believe that He is, and that He is a rewarder of those who diligently seek Him" (**Hebrews 11:6**).

As His little children, we need to hold God's hand when we "cross the street" and totally trust Him. In His wisdom, God knows the people who put their total trust in Him. You cannot fool God. "The LORD is good, a stronghold in the day of trouble; and He knows those [men, women and children] who trust in Him" (**Nahum 1:7**).

Let us be sure that we always give thanks to God for all things. Let us also be sure to place our total trust only in the God family.

5.6 IS JUST "BELIEVING IN CHRIST" ENOUGH FOR SALVATION?

An often quoted and misunderstood Scripture by mainstream Christianity has to do with believing in Christ. It is found in **Acts 16:31** "So they said, 'Believe on the Lord Jesus Christ, and you will be saved, you and your household.'" Most people stop right here and assume that all they have to do is to believe that Jesus is Lord, and they think they are saved. Recall from section 5.1 that you cannot be saved and at the same time be human and walk this earth. Remember, salvation takes place at a resurrection, when we become immortal spirit beings and are finally in God's kingdom. Look at **Acts 16:31** again. *Does it say that when you believe in Christ you are saved?* No, it says "you will be saved"—future tense.

Now notice what the apostle James says about believing. If only believing is required for salvation, then, according to your Bible, it's not enough. "You believe that there is one God. You do well. Even the demons believe—and tremble!" (**James 2:19**). James clearly states that just believing in God is not enough to be saved, because even the demons believe and, as you know, demons are God's adversaries, as they rebelled against Him. But according to Scripture, there is much more to salvation than just believing in the name of Jesus, the Christ.

Please do not misunderstand—we must believe in Christ as the Son of God who died for us and that He is our Savior. Believing is a good beginning in a true Christian's life, but it's not the end. Even people in Christ's day believed in Him. "And many of the people believed in Him, and said, 'When the Christ comes, will He do more signs than these which this Man has done?'" (**John 7:31**).

The people in Christ's day, as well as most Christians today, believe in Him, but they simply don't believe what He said. "But why do you call Me 'Lord, Lord,' and not do the things which I say?" (**Luke 6:46**). "Many will say to Me in that day, 'Lord, Lord, have we not prophesied in Your name, cast out demons in Your name, and done many wonders in Your name?' And then I will declare to them, 'I never knew you; depart from Me, you who practice lawlessness!'" (**Matthew 27:22–23**). Christ said that He never knew them because they only believed in Him but still practiced "lawlessness."

Christ told the people the truth about the commandments, the feast days, the kingdom of God and the plan of salvation, but they did not believe what He said. "But now you seek to kill Me, a Man who has told you the truth which I heard from God. Abraham did not do this" (**John 8:40**).

A true Christian must not only believe in Christ and what He says but must also have faith.

5.7   IS JUST "HAVING FAITH IN GOD" ENOUGH FOR SALVATION?

Another often quoted and misunderstood Scripture has to do with the phrase "having faith." Mainstream Christians seem to think that having faith is all that is required to be saved. But again, they omit other essential Scriptures that are needed to obtain the true understanding and the true meaning of having faith in God.

Let's allow the Bible to tell us exactly what faith is. "Now faith is the substance of things hoped for ..." (**Hebrews 11:1**). Having faith includes **two** important thoughts:

1.   Faith is the "substance of things hoped for." Our hope should be to become immortal spirit beings and to someday be in the kingdom of God. That is what we hope for and have faith in. Now read the second half of **Hebrews 11:1**, which tells us "the evidence of things not seen."

2.   Faith is the "evidence of things not seen." *Do we see God?* No! But we have ample evidence of His existence by the physical things He created. Physical things are what we see—birds, flowers, trees, animals, and stars. We also see that we live on this beautiful planet that was made specifically for us. We know that the earth miraculously and effortlessly rotates around the sun. *How does it do that?* It is done by the unseen yet mighty hand of God. That is having faith. Putting your total trust and confidence in God that He will save us in the future also means you have faith in Him.

How do you obtain faith? "So, then faith comes by hearing, and hearing by the word of God" (**Romans 10:17**). God says you obtain faith by hearing His Word, the Holy Bible. When you go to a church of God to hear the Bible expounded upon, you obtain faith. Most people today seem to think that they have enough faith to be saved. Notice what Christ says: "I tell you that He [God the Father] will avenge them speedily. Nevertheless, when the Son of Man comes, will He really find faith on the earth?" (**Luke 8:18**). From this Scripture, it does not seem likely that very many people will have the necessary faith to be saved when Christ returns.

Nevertheless, if you want to please God, you must have faith in Him and His beloved Son, Christ. "But without faith it is impossible to please Him, for he who comes to God must believe that He is, and that He is a rewarder of those who diligently seek Him" (**Hebrews 11:6**).

Having faith is very important to God. It pleases Him. *But is having faith enough for salvation?*

> What does it profit, my brethren, if someone says he has faith but does not have works? Can faith save him? If a brother or sister is naked and destitute of daily food, and one of you says to them, "Depart in peace, be warmed and filled," but you do not give them the things which are needed for the body, what does it profit? Thus, also faith by itself, if it does not have works, is dead. But someone will say, "You have faith, and I have works. Show me your faith without your works, and I will show you my faith by my works." (**James 2:14–18**)

James explicitly states that without doing good works, a person's faith is dead.

So far, we have proved that true Christians must believe in God and believe what He says by obeying all of His commandments. Christians must also have faith in order to please God. *But again, is that all that is needed to be saved?*

5.8   IS JUST "DOING GOOD WORKS" ENOUGH FOR SALVATION?

Another often quoted and misunderstood Scripture by mainstream Christianity has to do with "doing good works." Many of today's

Christian minister proudly say that doing good works was done away with. They often quote **Ephesians 2:8–9** to try to prove their belief: "For by grace you have been saved through faith, and that not of yourselves; it is the gift of God, not of works, lest anyone should boast."

People who quote this Scripture freely teach and preach the doctrine of "no works." They say, in essence, "Hey, you don't have to do anything; you are saved by grace through faith, not by works." These same people fail to read the very next verse: "For we are His workmanship, created in Christ Jesus for good works, which God prepared beforehand that we should walk in them" (**Ephesians 2:10**). The Bible clearly says that humans were created to do good works, not do away with them! Let us notice **James 2:14–17** again: "What does it profit, my brethren, if someone says he has faith but does not have works? Can faith save him? If a brother or sister is naked and destitute of daily food, and one of you says to them, 'Depart in peace, be warmed and filled,' but you do not give them the things which are needed for the body, what does it profit? Thus, also faith by itself, if it does not have works, is dead." Again, just having faith is dead, without doing good works. That's what your Bible says.

It is true that just doing good works does not save you. God may save you through grace, but that does "not" excuse you from doing good works. James makes the truth of God very plain about faith and works— "faith by itself, if it does not have works, is dead" (**James 2:17**).

It is also true that grace is unmerited pardon; it is a gift from God, and a person cannot earn it. But as true Christians, we are "not" exempt from believing, having faith, and doing good works. We must be willing to do all of the above because that's what the Holy Bible clearly teaches us to do. If we do our part in believing, having faith, and doing good works, then God will grant us grace. He is a just and merciful God.

Continue this powerful thought. "But someone will say, 'You have faith, and I have works.' Show me your faith without your works, and I will show you my faith by my works. You believe that there is one God. You do well. Even the demons believe—and tremble! But do you want to know, O foolish man, that faith without works is dead? Was not Abraham our father justified by works when he offered Isaac his son on the altar? Do you see that faith was working together with his works, and by works faith was made perfect?" (**James 2:18–22**). "But do not forget to do good and to share, for with such sacrifices God is well pleased" (**Hebrews 13:16**).

Clearly, the Holy Bible teaches that we must believe Christ. We also need faith in addition to doing good works. As true Christians, we must never stop helping others by doing good works for them. Remember the two great commandments: love God (which includes the first four commandments) and love your neighbor (the last six). Another of the giant jigsaw puzzle has been put in place.

Chapter 6
GOD'S TRUTH ABOUT GOD'S LAW

6.1 HAS GOD'S LAW, THE TEN COMMANDMENTS, BEEN DONE AWAY?

In addition to believing in God and what He says, true Christians must also have faith, accompanied by good works. Doing good works (helping others) has not been done away with. This leads us to an often-quoted Scripture that is misunderstood and misapplied by modern Christians, who leave out important, supplemental Scriptures that are required to obtain God's true meaning. Most Christians believe that God's Law, which includes the Ten Commandments, His feast days, and observing the Sabbath day, were done away with. They erroneously believe that if you keep the Law, then you are doing works and are under bondage. They also falsely teach that the Ten Commandments were nailed to the cross when Christ died.

The Scripture they usually quote is found in **Romans 3:20**. "Therefore, by the deeds of the law no flesh will be justified in His sight ..." From this Scripture, Christians gather **two** beliefs:

1. If you are doing the deeds of God's Law, that, in itself, will not make you right in God's sight. This belief is actually true! Observing

God's Law by itself does not make anyone right in God's sight, but that does not mean that we should not observe the Law.

2. *Today's Christians falsely reason that if keeping God's Law doesn't make you right in His sight, why keep it?* We need to always keep God's Law, even though it does not justify us because God says to. When we sin, we no longer maintain our connection with God. When Christ paid the death penalty for our sins, He reconciled us to the Father. "Now all things are of God, who had reconciled us to Himself through Jesus Christ, and has given us the ministry of reconciliation" (**2 Corinthians 5:18**). The fact that Christ reconciled us to the Father does not mean that we should "not" keep God's Law.

Look at the remainder of **Romans 3:20**, where Paul says, "For by the law is the knowledge of sin." If you do away with the Law, you are also doing away with knowing what sin is. God's Law tells us what is right and what is wrong. It tells us what sin is, and that is precisely why we need to keep the Law today. Without the Law, we would have lawlessness and chaos. We would have all people deciding for themselves what is right or wrong. That's the sin that Adam and Eve committed by eating the forbidden fruit. With the influence of Satan, they decided for themselves to eat of the forbidden fruit, disbelieving God.

The Israelites in Moses' day committed the same sin. "In those days there was no king in Israel; everyone did what was right in his own eyes" (**Judges 17:6**). The Ten Commandments tell us not to steal, not to commit adultery, not to lie, not to kill. We desperately need God's Law, and we wholeheartedly need to keep it. God's Law clearly tells us what is right or wrong through the eyes of almighty God. "You shall not at all do as we are doing here today—every man doing whatever is right in his own eyes" (**Deuteronomy 12:8**). We need to rely on God's law to help us discern good from evil because, in all honesty, humans do not know what is good or evil. It is clear that God's Law has not been done away with, even though it does not justify us.

Paul does write about another law that was actually done away with. The Bible calls it the "handwriting of requirements" or "sacrificial laws," used in the temple by ancient Israel. Each year at Passover, a year-old male lamb or goat, without blemish, was sacrificed in the temple of God. Its blood was used as a symbol to blot out the sins of Israel, which they committed throughout the year. These sacrificial laws were handwritten to give detailed instructions on temple worship, cleanliness, and the use of animal blood and fats. These sacrificial laws were the handwriting of requirements that Paul spoke about. "And you, being dead in your trespasses and the un-circumcision of your flesh, He has made alive together with Him, having forgiven you all trespasses, having wiped out the handwriting of requirements that was against us, which was contrary to us. And He has taken it out of the way, having nailed it to the cross. Having disarmed principalities and powers, He made a public spectacle of them, triumphing over them in it" (**Colossians 2:13–15**).

Since Christ took the place of animal sacrifices as the Lamb of God, the handwriting of requirements was no longer necessary. They were done away with—wiped out. They were "nailed to the cross" by Christ's death. It was the handwriting of requirements that was against us and contrary to us, not the Ten Commandments. Therefore, God's Laws, the Ten Commandments, were never done away with. They were binding on the Israelites of old, and they are binding on us, today and forever.

Notice the question Paul posed: "What purpose then does the law serve? It was added because of transgressions, till the Seed [Christ] should come to whom the promise was made; and it was appointed through angels by the hand of a mediator" (**Galatians 3:19**). In other words, Paul said sacrificial laws were added because we sinned. Remember, animal sacrifices were only a temporary solution for removing sins. Christ's sacrifice for humanity was the permanent solution to remove people's sins, once they repented of them. Christ took the place of all animal sacrifices and all sacrificial laws, He abolishing them.

Paul never said, "Don't keep the Law," referring to the Ten Commandments. Paul clearly said to keep the Law because it tells us what sin is. "What shall we say then? Is the law sin? Certainly not! On the contrary, I would not have known sin except through the law. For I would not have known covetousness unless the law had said, 'You shall not covet.' ... Therefore, the law is holy, and the commandment holy and just and good" (**Romans 7:7, 12**). Paul explicitly states many times that God's Law (His commandments) is holy, just, and good! *How can Christians and clergy, in good conscience, say that the commandments are done away with?* In all honesty, they cannot!

Further, notice what Paul says: "for not the hearers of the law are just in the sight of God, but the doers of the law will be justified" (**Romans 2:13**). This means that it's not just those who hear or learn the Law who are made right in God's sight but the doers of the Law. Notice the future tense in the above Scripture. *Who will be justified?* The doers of the Law! Paul is simply telling the church in Rome and us today that we need to **do** God's Law, and God will see to it that we will be justified in His sight in a future resurrection.

What kind of a world would it be if we did away with the Ten Commandments? We would have what we have today—total chaos and confusion everywhere, with everyone doing what is right in their own eyes. When Paul wrote that the Law is good, just, and holy, he was referring to the Ten Commandments. The Ten Commandments are spiritual laws that will remain in effect forever. The teachings of the Bible are plain and simple for those who have God's Holy Spirit and for those who have an ear to hear. Understanding the purpose of God's Law adds another vital piece to the giant jigsaw puzzle.

6.2   TWO OFTEN QUOTED/MISAPPLIED SCRIPTURES

Two additional Scriptures are used by Christians to try to prove that God's Law was done away with.

1. **Romans 10:4** "For Christ is the end of the law for righteousness to everyone who believes."

The word "end" used here is from the Greek word "telos." To properly understand the translated word, "end" in the above verse, we must determine Paul's intended meaning. To illustrate, a person might ask a college student, *"To what end are you attending college?"* In this context, "end" would refer to the end result or goal the student has in mind by attending college. Receiving a college degree would be the student's goal. Paul uses "telos" to convey that the objective or goal of the Law—its aim and purpose—is to point us to the mind and character of Christ. Jesus epitomized the Law. He embodied the Law. He always kept it perfectly, never once sinning.

Paul is telling us that as true Christians our end result should be to become like Christ. Paul reinforces this same thought of being like Christ to the Galatian church. "My little children, for whom I labor in birth again until Christ is formed in you" (**Galatians 4:19**). And again, in **Philippians 2:5**, Paul states, "Let this mind be in you which was also in Christ Jesus." Christ emphatically stated in **Matthew 5:17**, "Do not think that I came to destroy the Law or the Prophets. I did not come to destroy but to fulfill." Christ came to earth to fulfill what was written in the Law, not do away with it.

By revealing the Law's deep spiritual meaning and application in human behavior, Christ fulfilled or epitomized the Law. **Matthew 5:27–28** offers an example of how Christ epitomized the Law: "You have heard that it was said to those of old, 'You shall not commit adultery.' But I say to you that whoever looks at a woman to lust for her has already committed adultery with her in his heart." This law clearly states that we should not only abstain from committing physical adultery, but we should also abstain from committing spiritual adultery in the heart. This is an example of fulfilling the physical and spiritual implication of the Law. The Law has not been done away with.

The vast majority of Christians have the illogical assumption that having faith makes the Law void. Notice what Paul says about the Law and faith: "Do we then make void the law through faith? Certainly not! On the contrary, we establish the law" (**Romans 3:31**). Paul emphatically states that we establish the Law through faith, not end it. "Therefore, the law is holy, and the commandment holy and just and good" (**Romans 7:12**). *In understanding these Scriptures, how can anyone say the Law has been done away with?* In all good conscience, they cannot!

The apostle Peter strongly warns not to twist the meaning of Scripture. "And consider that the longsuffering of our Lord is salvation—as also our beloved brother Paul, according to the wisdom given to him, has written to you, as also in all his epistles, speaking in them of these things, in which are some things hard to understand, which untaught and unstable people twist to their own destruction, as they do also the rest of the Scriptures" (**2 Peter 3:15–16**). True Christians, hungering and thirsting for truth, should never twist Scriptures to fit their own beliefs. Rather, we should change our beliefs to fit with what the Bible teaches.

2. **Romans 7:6**. "But now we have been delivered from the law, having died to what we were held by, so that we should serve in the newness of the Spirit and not in the oldness of the letter."

Many Christians and clergy try to argue that God's Law, Sabbath, and feast days were abolished by keying in on the phrase, "We have been delivered from the law."

But Paul is very clear about his love for God's Law, which is found in several places in the same chapter. "For I delight in the law of God according to the inward man" (**Romans 7:22**). No interpretation or guesswork is needed to understand this Scripture. The message is clear and powerful. Paul loved and kept God's Law. Yet, he states in Romans 7 that "we have been delivered from the law." *So, which is it? Is this a Bible contradiction? Which law is Paul talking about here?*

Let's take a sincere look at the beginning of **Romans 7** to obtain a clear understanding of which law Paul was talking about.

> Or do you not know, brethren (for I speak to those who know the law), that the law has dominion over a

man as long as he lives? For the woman who has a husband is bound by the law to her husband as long as he
lives. But if the husband dies, she is released from the
law of her husband. So then if, while her husband lives,
she marries another man, she will be called an adulteress; but if her husband dies, she is free from that law,
so that she is no adulteress, though she has married
another man. (**Romans 7:1–3**)

What is the context of these verses? Clearly, Paul is talking about
the marriage law that binds a husband and a wife together, until
the death of one releases the other spouse from the marriage law.
Therefore, upon death, the survivor is delivered from the marriage
law but not from the Ten Commandments. The survivor is free to
marry again without committing adultery. It is important to note
that the penalty for committing adultery under the Old Testament
marriage law was death. Christ took that penalty upon Himself
because of our sins.

"Therefore, my brethren, you also have become dead to the law
through the body of Christ, that you may be married to another—
to Him who was raised from the dead, that we should bear fruit
to God" (**Romans 7:4**). Paul is telling the church of God in Rome
that since Christ died for them, they are no longer bound to the
marriage law and are "dead to that law." Therefore, they are free to
"marry another, to Him who was raised from the dead." In other
words, the brethren are free to marry a risen Christ, using the New
Testament agreement.

It is important to note that ancient Israel was actually married to
Christ in Old Testament times. "For your Maker is your husband, the
LORD of hosts is His name; And your Redeemer is the Holy One of
Israel; He is called the God of the whole earth" (**Isaiah 54:5**).

It is equally important to note that Israel (Christ's wife) committed adultery by worshipping false gods and breaking the Sabbath.
Instead of Israel's dying for committing adultery, Christ died for her,

releasing Israel from the marriage law. His death on the cross terminated His marriage to Israel and, at the same time, released her from the death penalty.

Israel now can continue to live, repent, and have another chance at marriage under the new covenant. Once Christ died and was resurrected, true Christians (spiritual Israel/the church) can now be engaged to Christ again, as a future husband under the new covenant. Notice the deep meaning in **2 Corinthians 11:2**, which says, "For I am jealous for you with godly jealousy. For I have betrothed you to one husband, that I may present you as a chaste virgin to Christ."

Under the new covenant, true baptized Christians are engaged to be married to a risen Christ and are to be partakers in a future marriage supper. This future marriage to Christ will take place shortly after the first resurrection, when He marries His bride, the church. "Let us be glad and rejoice and give Him glory, for the marriage of the Lamb has come, and His wife has made herself ready. And to her it was granted to be arrayed in fine linen, clean and bright, for the fine linen is the righteous acts of the saints. Then he said to me, 'Write: "Blessed are those who are called to the marriage supper of the Lamb!"' And he said to me, 'These are the true sayings of God'" (**Revelation 19:7–9**).

"For when we were in the flesh, the sinful passions which were aroused by the law were at work in our members to bear fruit to death" (**Romans 7:5**). Paul is saying that in the flesh we sin and the fruit we bear is death. "But now we have been delivered from the law, having died to what we were held by, so that we should serve in the newness of the Spirit and not in the oldness of the letter" (**Romans 7:6**). Since Christ was put to death, Christians are free from the marriage law and can now bear the fruit of the Spirit. (Please reference **Galatians 5:22–23** for the fruit of the Spirit.)

"What shall we say then? Is the law sin? Certainly not! On the contrary, I would not have known sin except through the law. For I would not have known covetousness unless the law had said, 'You shall not covet'" (**Romans 7:7**). It becomes very clear that we are to continue to observe and obey God's laws and commandments in the newness of the Spirit and not in the oldness of the letter. **Romans 7:7** does "not" say that we are released from keeping God's Law and the Ten Commandments.

Notice what Christ says:

> Do not think that I came to destroy the Law or the Prophets. I did not come to destroy but to fulfill. For assuredly, I say to you, till heaven and earth pass away, one jot or one tittle will by no means pass from the law till all is fulfilled. Whoever, therefore breaks one of the least of these commandments, and teaches men so, shall be called least in the kingdom of heaven; but whoever does and teaches them, he shall be called great in the kingdom of heaven. For I say to you, that unless your righteousness exceeds the righteousness of the scribes and Pharisees, you will by no means enter the kingdom of heaven. (**Matthew 5:17–20**)

If heaven and earth have not passed away, neither has God's Law.

For those people who still think the Law was abolished, nailed to the cross, done away with, or is a burden, consider the following scenario:

> If the law is abolished, there would be no sin.
> If there is no sin, there would be no need for forgiveness.
> If there is no forgiveness, there would be no need for a Savior.
> If there is no Savior, then Christ died in vain.

Such reasoning leads to the conclusion that man is completely self-sufficient and needs nothing from God. Notice what Christ says: "Whoever, therefore breaks one of the least of these commandments, and teaches men so, shall be called least in the kingdom of heaven; but whoever does and teaches them, he shall be called great in the kingdom of heaven" (**Matthew 5:19**).

Obedience to the laws and commandments of God result in many blessings for us. Notice some of the blessings:

> Now it shall come to pass, if you diligently obey the voice of the LORD your God, to observe carefully all His commandments which I command you today, that the LORD your God will set you high above all nations of the earth. And all these blessings shall come upon you and overtake you, because you obey the voice of the LORD your God: "Blessed shall you be in the city, and blessed shall you be in the country. "Blessed shall be the fruit of your body, the produce of your ground and the increase of your herds, the increase of your cattle and the offspring of your flocks." (**Deuteronomy 28:1–4**)

Be sure to read all of **Deuteronomy 28**.

How could God's Law, which is perfect and righteous and given by a righteous God, be a curse? "For certain men have crept in unnoticed, who long ago were marked out for this condemnation, ungodly men, who turn the grace of our God into lewdness and deny the only Lord God and our Lord Jesus Christ" (**Jude 4**).

Without a doubt, Paul taught all Gentile converts in every church he established to observe the same things. "But as God has distributed to each one, as the Lord has called each one, so let him walk. And so, I ordain in all the churches" (**1 Corinthians 7:17**). Christ tells us in **Matthew 4:4**, "But He answered and said, 'It is written, "Man shall not live by bread alone, but by every word that proceeds from the mouth of God."'"

6.3 ACCORDING TO GOD'S LAW, WHICH DAY IS GOD'S TRUE DAY OF REST?

Most Christians automatically accept Sunday as their day of rest and worship. Some people call Sunday their Sabbath day. *Can Sunday legitimately be called the Sabbath? Aren't Saturday and Sunday two separate and distinct days of the week? How can you call Sunday a Saturday?* The answer is that you cannot!

The Muslims observe Friday as their day of rest. Some Jewish people observe the seventh day or Saturday, as their day of rest and worship. *Which day is God's true day of rest?* After all, God only created one day of rest. *Does it even matter which day is observed, as long as it is observed in honor of God? What exactly does the Bible say about the day of rest?* These are questions that demand a true biblical answer.

It does not matter what a person thinks or what Christian denominations believe about rest days; it only matters what the almighty creator God tells us. Let us begin with **seven** biblical proofs about the true day of rest and worship.

> **Proof 1.** Saturday is the seventh day of the week. Since time began, in almost all cultures, every week begins with the first day of the week, Sunday. If you look at the majority of calendars used around the world, you will find each week begins with Sunday (reading from left to right) and ends seven days later on Saturday. This makes Sunday the first day of the week, while Saturday is the last or seventh day.

Although man has modified calendars through the centuries, the seven-day weekly cycle has remained intact throughout history. The days of the week have always remained in their proper order, with Sunday as the first day and Saturday as the seventh day. Because each day is its own separate day, Saturday cannot be called Sunday, or vice versa. The "oracles of God" were entrusted to the Jewish people (God's chosen people). The seventh day Sabbath has been faithfully preserved by them since before Christ's time, even to this very day. "What advantage then has the Jew, or what is the profit of circumcision? Much in every way! Chiefly because to them were committed the oracles of God. For what if some did not believe? Will their unbelief make the faithfulness of God without effect?" (**Romans 3:1–3**).

> **Proof 2.** Since darkness covered the expanse of space, God made light on the first day. God Himself worked on the very first day of creation week, Sunday. He did not rest on Sunday but made light on the first day of the week. "The earth was without form, and void; and darkness was on the face of the deep. And the Spirit of God was hovering over the face of the waters" (**Genesis 1:2**). By making light and separating it from darkness, God made our current days.

God worked and created many lights over the expanse of the entire universe. "Then God said, 'Let there be light;' and there was light. And God saw the light, that it was good; and God divided the light from the darkness. God called the light Day, and the darkness He called Night. So, the evening and the morning were the first day" (**Genesis 1:3–5**). According to God, the day begins and ends at sunset. One day begins while the previous day ends. The length of darkness and length of daylight have remained about the same—roughly twelve hours of night and twelve hours of light, totaling twenty-four hours.

> **Proof 3**. God made the Sabbath rest as the seventh day of the week. It is true that some Jewish people observe the Sabbath, but the Sabbath was created long before Jews came into existence. Recall that the children of Israel descended from Abraham, Isaac, and Jacob. Later, God changed Jacob's name to Israel. Israel had twelve sons. Judah was only one of Israel's sons. *Where are the remaining eleven brothers of Judah?* If you aren't Jewish, you could very well be a descendant from one of the remaining eleven brothers. Regardless, the Sabbath was not just made for the Jews; it was made for

"all" of humankind. The Sabbath is not a Jewish day; it is God's Day, and He rested on that particular day.

"And He [Christ] said to them, 'The Sabbath was made for man, and not man for the Sabbath'" (**Mark 2:27**). This verse explicitly says that the Sabbath was made for man's benefit. It also implies that man is more important to God than the Sabbath. Some people think the Sabbath was made only for the Jews, but that is "not" what the Bible says. It says that the Sabbath was made for man—for "all" of humankind. Therefore, if we are to obey God, we all must observe the seventh day Sabbath (Saturday) and keep it holy by resting and worshipping God. No other day will do, only the Sabbath.

Besides creating light, air, trees, stars, animals, and man, God created the Sabbath day too. "Thus, the heavens and the earth, and all the host of them, were finished. And on the seventh day God ended His work which He had done, and He rested on the seventh day from all His work which He had done. Then God blessed the seventh day and sanctified it because in it He rested from all His work which God had created and made" (**Genesis 2:1–3**). By resting on the seventh day Sabbath, God set it apart (sanctified it) from the remaining days of the week.

Not only did God create the seventh day Sabbath, but He called it by a special name, the Sabbath. Notice that God did not place a name on any other day of the week except that special seventh day. The Sabbath day on which God rested was not Friday or Sunday or any other day of creation week. God worked six days and rested on the seventh day of the week.

> **Proof 4.** God made the seventh day Sabbath holy. "For in six days the LORD made the heavens and the earth, the sea, and all that is in them, and rested the seventh day. Therefore, the LORD blessed the Sabbath day and hallowed it [made it Holy]" (**Exodus 20:11**).

When we work six days a week and carefully observe God's true holy day, the Sabbath, we honor Him. "If you turn away your foot from the Sabbath, from doing your pleasure on My holy day, and call the Sabbath a delight, the holy day of the LORD honorable, and shall honor Him, not doing your own ways, nor finding your own pleasure, nor speaking your own words, then you shall delight yourself in the LORD; And I [God] will cause you to ride on the high hills of the earth, and feed you with the heritage of Jacob your father. The mouth of the LORD has spoken" (**Isaiah 58:13–14**).

If you correctly observe God's Sabbath by not working or doing your own thing on His holy day, then God will bless you immensely, not only while living on earth but also in the future.

> **Proof 5**. God commands us over and over to always remember the Sabbath day. Look at Exodus, where the Lord God thundered out the Ten Commandments. "Remember the Sabbath day, to keep it holy. Six days you shall labor and do all your work, but the seventh day is the Sabbath of the LORD your God. In it you shall do no work: you, nor your son, nor your daughter, nor your male servant, nor your female servant, nor your cattle, nor your stranger who is within your gates. For in six days the LORD made the heavens and the earth, the sea, and all that is in them, and rested the seventh day. Therefore, the LORD blessed the Sabbath day and hallowed it" (**Exodus 20:8–11**).

Can you see the importance that almighty God places on observing His special Sabbath day? No other weekday is as important to God as His Sabbath day. Worshipping God on any other day except His Sabbath is worshipping Him in vain. You are disobeying God when you worship Him on a day that He did not make holy. "And in vain they worship Me, teaching as doctrines the commandments of men" (**Matthew 15:9**). The vast majority of Christian churches today worship God on Sunday. Sunday worship began with a proclamation by the Roman emperor Constantine at the Council of Nicaea in AD 364. Sunday observance is, therefore, a man-made commandment and did not originate from God. According to God, the Sabbath should be remembered as His rest and worship day, not Sunday!

> **Proof 6.** The word "Sabbath" means "to rest" in many languages. The Latin word for Sabbath is "Sabbatum," and it means "to rest" and is translated as "Saturday" in English. The Latin word for Sunday is "Dominica," which means "dominant light" and refers to God's creating our dominant source of light, our sun. Remember God made light on the first day of the week and separated it from darkness.

The Italian word "Sabbato" literally means "to cease from work" or "to rest," and it is translated into English as Saturday. The Italian word for Sunday is "Domenica," and it also means "dominant light." In Spanish, the Sabbath is called "Sabado," and it is translated as Saturday. Sunday in Spanish is "Domingo" and is similar to the Italian meaning. The English word "sabbatical" comes from the Latin word "Sabbatum" and also means "to rest" or "to take a vacation." A sabbatical means "restful vacation." *Can there be any doubt that the seventh day, Saturday, is in fact the Sabbath of the Holy Bible?* I don't think so!

> **Proof 7.** Sunday is not God's Day of rest. This last proof is found in **Revelation 12:9.** "So the great dragon was cast out, that serpent of old, called the Devil and Satan, who deceives [present tense] the whole world; he was cast to the earth, and his angels were cast out with him." This Scripture clearly tells us that Satan was cast down to the earth and has successfully deceived and is deceiving the entire world in many ways. He has deceived the whole world into believing that Sunday

is God's Day of rest and worship, when, in reality, it is
Satan's day of worship.

Look carefully at the following question posed by Christ: "But why
do you call Me 'Lord, Lord,' and not do the things which I say?" (**Luke
6:46**). Most Christians call on the Lord God in prayer but do not
observe the day that He kept while on earth. Christ kept the Sabbath.
He is Lord of the Sabbath.

Christians say that they worship on Sunday because they believe
Christ rose from the dead on Sunday (please refer to section 5.4 to
learn when Christ truly rose from the dead). As you have seen with
these seven proofs and according to your own Bible, the Sabbath is
God's true day of rest and worship.

This is yet another huge piece of the giant jigsaw puzzle that has
been correctly placed to help us see the overall picture God is showing
us. "You shall walk in all the ways which the LORD your God has commanded you, that you may live and that it may be well with you, and
that you may prolong your days in the land which you shall possess"
(**Deuteronomy 5:33**).

6.4   WHY SHOULD GOD'S SABBATH DAY BE
IMPORTANT TO YOU?

We now know for certain that the seventh day Sabbath is Saturday, and
it is the day on which God rested and made holy. We have proved that
the Sabbath was not done away with by Christ's sacrifice, nor was/is it
a burden to observe it. In fact, it is a delight to observe the Sabbath! "If
you turn away your foot from the Sabbath, from doing your pleasure
on My holy day, and call the Sabbath a delight, the holy day of the LORD
honorable, and shall honor Him, not doing your own ways, nor finding
your own pleasure, nor speaking your own words" (**Isaiah 58:13**).

Before going any further, we must remember that God is allowing
Satan to deceive some people concerning the Sabbath day. There are
three important points to remember:

1. Satan is the "god of this world" **(2 Corinthians 4:4);**

2. Satan is being used to fulfill God's purpose for humanity; and

3. God is allowing Satan to deceive some people because they are not spiritually ready to be called by God **(Revelation 12:9).**

This is part of God's plan of salvation. He is not calling everyone in the world at this time. "No one can come to Me unless the Father who sent Me draws him; and I will raise him up at the last day" **(John 6:44).** Through the millennia, God has called a relatively small number of people who have kept His commandments and feasts, of which the Sabbath is one. *Does that mean that God is unfair or has favorites?* Not at all! All people will be given an opportunity to be saved. For some, it is right now; for others, it will occur later.

I would like to provide **six** biblical reasons as to why the Sabbath should be important to you.

1. God, Himself, created and observed the seventh day Sabbath (Saturday) as a day of rest from His labor. "Thus, the heavens and the earth, and all the host of them, were finished. And on the seventh day God ended His work which He had done, and He rested on the seventh day from all His work which He had done. Then God blessed the seventh day and sanctified it because in it He rested from all His work which God had created and made" **(Genesis 2:1–3).**

2. All of God's faithful people observed the Sabbath. Abel, Enoch, Noah, Abraham, King David, Paul, and others all observed the seventh day Sabbath. Let's look at a few examples:

"That on you may come all the righteous bloodshed on the earth, from the blood of righteous Abel to the blood of Zechariah, son of Berechiah, whom you murdered between the temple and the altar"

(**Matthew 23:35**). "And did not spare the ancient world, but saved Noah, one of eight people, a preacher of righteousness, bringing in the flood on the world of the ungodly" (**2 Peter 2:5**). A person cannot be called righteous by God and not observe His holy Sabbath day.

"After he begot Methuselah, Enoch walked with God three hundred years, and had sons and daughters" (**Genesis 5:22**). Again, a person cannot "walk with God" without observing His Sabbath day. "Because Abraham obeyed My voice and kept My charge, My commandments, My statutes, and My laws" (**Genesis 26:5**).

King David was inspired to write the following about God's commandments, of which the Sabbath is fourth: "My [King David's] tongue shall speak of Your word, for all Your commandments are righteousness" (**Psalm 119:172**). Observe Paul's custom in **Acts 17:2**, "Then Paul, as his custom was, went in to them, and for three Sabbaths reasoned with them from the Scriptures." Paul observed and preached on the Sabbath. All the people mentioned above obeyed God by observing His Sabbath. To be God's true servant, you must observe His Sabbath.

3. Christ, our Savior, observed it. "So, He [Christ] came to Nazareth, where He had been brought up. And as His custom was, He went into the synagogue on the Sabbath day, and stood up to read" (**Luke 4:16**). Remember also that Christ is "Lord of the Sabbath." We proved in the preceding section that Christ did "not" do away with the Law or the Sabbath. He kept both. "And He [Christ] said to them, 'The Sabbath was made for man, and not man for the Sabbath. Therefore, the Son of Man is also Lord of the Sabbath'" (**Mark 2:27–28**). The Bible plainly says that the Sabbath was made for man, not just for the Israelites and not just for the Jews. God, being neither Israelite nor Jew, observed it. It amazes me that Christians worship a Jewish Messiah on Sunday, a day which He Himself never observed. They worship a Jewish Messiah, but don't do as He did.

4. God made the Sabbath as a sign between Him and His people. Take a close look at the following:

> "Speak also to the children of Israel, saying: 'Surely My Sabbaths you shall keep, for it is a sign between Me and you throughout your generations, that you may know that I am the LORD who sanctifies you. You shall keep the Sabbath, therefore, for it is holy to you. Everyone who profanes it shall surely be put to death; for whoever does any work on it, that person shall be cut off from among his people. Work shall be done for six days, but the seventh is the Sabbath of rest, holy to the LORD. Whoever does any work on the Sabbath day, he shall surely be put to death. Therefore, the children of Israel shall keep the Sabbath, to observe the Sabbath throughout their generations as a perpetual covenant. It is a sign between Me and the children of Israel forever; for in six days the LORD made the heavens and the earth, and on the seventh day He rested and was refreshed.'" (**Exodus 31:13–17**)

Who are God's people? In the New Testament, we find that God loves everyone, whether Greek or Jew. "There is neither Jew nor Greek, there is neither slave nor free, there is neither male nor female; for you are all one in Christ Jesus. And if you are Christ's, then you are Abraham's seed, and heirs according to the promise" (**Galatians 3:28–29**).

Observing God's Sabbath distinguishes those people who believe what God says from those who rely on their own reasoning to determine how they should live and on which day they should worship God. Those who keep holy His Sabbath day proclaim, by their actions, obedience to God and their acceptance that God is the supreme authority over how they should live, think, and worship.

5. The Sabbath is a delight. "If you turn away your foot from the Sabbath, from doing your pleasure on My holy day, and call the Sabbath a delight, the holy day of the LORD honorable, and shall honor Him, not doing your own ways, nor finding your own pleasure, nor speaking your own words" (**Isaiah 58:13**). Look at what Paul says: "For I delight in the law of God according to the inward man" (**Romans 7:22**). Paul never tried to do away with God's Sabbath day; to the contrary, he called it "a delight." Paul affirmed that God's law is holy. "Therefore, the law is holy, and the commandment holy and just and good" (**Romans 7:12**). Contrary to what most Christians think, Paul never looked at his writings (which became the New Testament) as replacing the Old Testament. All he had to read, study, and meditate on was the Old Testament. Look at what else Paul says: "But keeping the commandments of God is what matters" (**1 Corinthians 7:19**). The Sabbath is the fourth commandment, and God emphatically wants us all to observe that special day.

6. The Sabbath has a future fulfillment. The weekly physical rest of the Sabbath serves as a reminder of a future spiritual rest. That spiritual rest will come when the kingdom of God is finally established on earth, at the second coming of Christ. The weekly Sabbath reminds us of God's coming and restful kingdom. Christ is the Lord of the Sabbath. Not only does the Sabbath day retain its Old Testament meaning of a physical rest, but it also points to another rest, leading us to the kingdom of God. "Therefore, since a promise remains of entering His rest, let us fear lest any of you seem to have come short of it. For indeed the gospel was preached to us as well as to them; but the word which they heard did not profit them, not being mixed with faith in those who heard it. For we who have believed do enter that rest, as He has said: 'So I swore in My wrath, "They shall not enter My rest"'" (**Hebrews 4:1–3**). (The quote within the verse is from **Psalm 95:11**.)

Let's continue the thought of the Sabbath as a future fulfillment. "For if Joshua [Jesus] had given them rest, then He [Jesus] would not afterward have spoken of another day. There remains therefore, another rest for the people of God. For he who has entered His rest has himself also ceased from his works as God did from His. Let us therefore, be diligent to enter that rest, lest anyone fall according to the same example of disobedience" (**Hebrews 4:8–11**).

"Blessed and holy is he who has part in the first resurrection. Over such the second death has no power, but they shall be priests of God and of Christ, and shall reign with Him a thousand years" (**Revelation 20:6**). Yes, those who faithfully observe God's Law, including His Sabbath day, are destined to reign with God and His beloved Son for one thousand years on earth. The one thousand years of Christ's reign on earth is an extension and a future fulfillment of the weekly Sabbath day. That's why the Sabbath is so important. God's kingdom, picturing His Sabbath, will be the only kingdom to bring lasting peace and rest to this earth, once and for all.

What a wonderful future meaning the Sabbath has, and what an awesome plan God has for those who love Him and obey His commands. Proper observance of the weekly Sabbath means turning away from doing your own thing and your own pleasure and speaking idle words. Proper observance of the Sabbath is to rest from your work and to worship God in spirit and in truth. That's how important the Sabbath is to God and why it should be very important to you. Physically, the Sabbath is a time of rest, to be used for building a relationship with God while we live on this earth. Spiritually, the Sabbath means to enter God's "rest," which is God's everlasting kingdom. God intended the Sabbath to be a delight, not a burden, now and forever.

Chapter 7
GOD'S TRUTH ABOUT THE KINGDOM OF GOD

7.1 FIVE COMMON MISCONCEPTIONS ABOUT THE KINGDOM OF GOD

There are many misconceptions about what the kingdom of God is and where it is, even for those very few true Christians who believe in it. Let's first look at what the kingdom of God is "not," from the Holy Bible. "For the kingdom of God is not eating and drinking, but righteousness and peace and joy in the Holy Spirit" (**Romans 14:17**). "For the kingdom of God is not in word but in power" (**1 Corinthians 4:20**).

I would like to focus on **five** common misconceptions about the kingdom of God. In doing so, we will find out more information about what the kingdom of God really is.

1. Some people think that the kingdom of God is everyone, all human governments working together in harmony, so as to bring universal peace, brotherly love, and tolerance for one another. Perhaps they mean something like the United Nations, where various forms of human government get together to set goals and achieve peace through talks, treaties, and agreements. *Working together in harmony sounds like a good idea, but can it be successful with men ruling over men with the influence of Satan, the adversary?* "All this

I have seen, and applied my heart to every work that is done under the sun: There is a time in which one man rules over another to his own hurt" (**Ecclesiastes 8:9**).

Also, notice how God answers the question of human governments working in harmony to achieve peace with one another: "The way of peace they have not known, and there is no justice in their ways; they have made themselves crooked paths; whoever takes that way shall not know peace" (**Isaiah 59:8**). Almighty God says that humanity, its ways, and its governments do not know the way to achieve lasting peace and harmony.

Humanity has tried for about six thousand years, and the end result has almost always been war. Humans have never been successful in establishing true peace. Everlasting peace can only come from almighty God. He is the only One who knows the right way to achieve true, lasting peace. *Where do wars come from?* Notice what James says: "Where do wars and fights come from among you? Do they not come from your desires for pleasure that war in your members? You lust and do not have. You murder and covet and cannot obtain. You fight and war. Yet you do not have because you do not ask. You ask and do not receive, because you ask amiss, that you may spend it on your pleasures" (**James 4:1–3**). War comes from people desiring what other people have, whether it's land, sea gates, power, material goods or wealth.

The kingdom of God will not be set up by any human being or any human organization. It will be a divinely set-up world-ruling government that will last forever and ever. True justice and peace will prevail at that time as we will soon see. The kingdom of God is not all humans working together in harmony!

2. Others believe that the kingdom of God is not a real, literal government or kingdom. Maybe they think that the kingdom of God is just a nice sentiment established in the hearts of men and women. Yet the One who modern Christians claim to worship,

Jesus the Christ, did not say it was a nice sentiment set up in the hearts of people. He powerfully preached the good news of a very real and soon-coming kingdom of God to this earth. "Now after John was put in prison, Jesus came to Galilee, preaching the gospel of the kingdom of God, and saying, 'The time is fulfilled, and the kingdom of God is at hand. Repent, and believe in the gospel'" (**Mark 1:14–15**). *Was the Son of the living God just saying these words and not really meaning what He said, or was Christ speaking of a literal coming kingdom of God?* Christ said and meant each and every word that He ever spoke, and He said that the kingdom of God is at hand. In other words, the kingdom of God is a real, literal government, and it's soon coming to this earth—that's what Christ said. We know that the kingdom of God is very real.

Even the apostle Paul, who was personally taught by Christ, preached about a very real coming kingdom of God to all the churches of God in Asia Minor. The prophets and other holy men of God, such as Isaiah, Daniel, Ezekiel, Haggai, and others, prophesied about horrible world conditions that would exist in the last days. Unless God Himself would intervene in human affairs and bring true world peace, humans would self-destruct. With the making of the atom and hydrogen bombs, as well as the development of biological warfare, people eventually would self-destruct. The book of Matthew states the following: "And unless those days were shortened, no flesh would be saved; but for the elect's sake those days will be shortened" (**Matthew 24:22**). All it would take would be a power-hungry dictator like Hitler, Mussolini, or Stalin to bring about mass destruction and misery. (Read all of **Matthew 24** for context.)

3. Some people believe that the kingdom of God is already on this earth. Many of today's Christians believe that Christianity itself is the kingdom of God. *Is it really, with all the religious confusion out there?* Catholicism teaches that the Roman Catholic Church and the Vatican is the kingdom of God, and it is right here, right

now, on this earth, with an infallible pope representing God. They say that the pope is the "vicar" of Christ. The word "vicar" means "in place of or representative of." The word "infallible" means a person who never makes a mistake. But the Bible plainly says that all humans have sinned and come short of the glory. "For all have sinned and fall short of the glory of God" (**Romans 3:23**). *How is it that the pope never makes a mistake?* Yet, that is precisely what most Catholics believe. They have no idea what they are saying.

Jehovah's Witnesses also believe that when they walk into their Kingdom Hall every Sunday, that is God's kingdom. Here again, these are people's opinions, which are not provable in the Holy Bible.

We also know that it cannot be right here, right now, simply because of all the hatred, jealousy, murders, injustices, corruption, greed, pollution, wars, and diseases running rampant today, not to mention the financial, global, racial and economic crisis looming before us. But rest assured that God has put it in His Holy Word that when His kingdom is established on earth, there will be no more wars or weapons of mass destruction. Christ will finally bring about true, lasting peace and happiness. "He shall judge between many peoples, and rebuke strong nations afar off; They shall beat their swords into plowshares, and their spears into pruning hooks; Nation shall not lift up sword against nation, neither shall they learn war anymore" (**Micah 4:3**).

4. Some people today believe that they can actually "see" the kingdom of God. "Jesus answered and said to him [Nicodemus] 'Most assuredly, I say to you, unless one is born again [margin has it as "born from above"], he cannot see the kingdom of God'" (**John 3:3**). Christ plainly said to Nicodemus and is telling us today that as human beings, we cannot see the kingdom of God unless we are "born from above," which means to become a spirit being through a resurrection. Once you become a spirit-being, you will finally be able to see God's kingdom. (See section 5.1 to learn more about being born again.)

Notice also what the apostle Paul states about flesh and blood inheriting the kingdom of God. "Now this I say, brethren, that flesh and blood cannot inherit the kingdom of God; nor does corruption inherit incorruption" (**1 Corinthians 15:50**). *How can the kingdom of God be inherited if we are all flesh and blood?* It cannot! Humans are made corruptible right now because we die. To be made incorruptible means to never die. We can only see and inherit the kingdom of God when we are resurrected and become spirit beings who cannot die.

5. Other people get confused when they read that God's kingdom "has come near you." This Scripture is found in Luke. "Whatever city you [the seventy men] enter, and they receive you, eat such things as are set before you. And heal the sick there and say to them 'the kingdom has come near you'" (**Luke 10:8–9**). The seventy men that Christ sent out to preach the gospel and heal the sick were representatives of the coming kingdom of God, and therefore Christ said, "The kingdom has come near you."

Another Scripture where people seem to get confused is found also in Luke where it states God's Kingdom "is within you." "Now when He was asked by the Pharisees when the kingdom of God would come, He answered them and said, 'The kingdom of God does not come with observation; nor will they say, "See here!" or "See there!" For indeed, the kingdom of God is within [among] you'" (**Luke 17:20–21**). Christ clearly said that the Kingdom of God is "not" coming so you can see it. Rather, the Kingdom of God was in their "midst," meaning that Christ, the future ruler of God's kingdom, was near or "among" them.

In summary, the Kingdom of God is not a nice sentiment set up in the hearts of men, and it is certainly not right here, right now. The kingdom of God is an unseen, spiritual but very real, soon-coming, divine government that will only be seen when we become spirit beings in a future resurrection. God's kingdom will destroy all forms human government, enforce keeping God's laws, and bring lasting joy, peace and happiness to humankind. Imagine that! "And in the days of these kings the God of heaven will set up a kingdom which shall never be destroyed; and the kingdom shall not be left to other people; it shall break in pieces and consume all these kingdoms [human governments], and it shall stand forever" (**Daniel 2:44**). "Then to Him (Christ) was given dominion and glory and a kingdom. That all peoples, nations, and languages should serve Him. His dominion is an everlasting dominion, which shall not pass away, and His kingdom the one which shall not be destroyed" (**Daniel 7:14**).

God has to force us to be really and truly happy; we cannot do it ourselves. It will take God's kingdom on this earth to finally bring true, lasting peace, justice and prosperity for all. Almighty God, through His Word, will make this happen. *How will it come about?* "For the mouth of the Lord has spoken" (**Micah 4:4**). God's going to make it happen through the power of His spoken word! Living as a spirit being in God's wonderful kingdom is part of your awesome destiny.

7.2   WHAT EXACTLY IS THE KINGDOM OF GOD?

It's the good news of the coming kingdom (or government) of God to this earth. That's what Christ preached in all of Judea. That's what we should be preaching today! Recall that the word "gospel" comes from the Greek, and it literally means "good news." (Refer to section 2.3 for more about Christ's mission on earth.)

Today, it seems that almost all of mainstream Christian churches have lost the true gospel that Christ came to preach at His first coming. Instead, they preach a message about Christ, who He was, and the miracles He performed. They preach about the person of Christ, instead of the important "good news" He brought to us.

Let's consider **three** false gospels that are preached in some of today's modern Christian churches:

1. Some Christian denominations proclaim "the gospel of grace," which states that all you have to do is "believe and accept Christ as your personal Savior" and you will be saved. (Refer to section

5.6 for the truth about believing.) But notice what is stated in **Jude 4**: "For certain men have crept in unnoticed, who long ago were marked out for this condemnation, ungodly men, who turn the grace of our God into lewdness and deny the only Lord God and our Lord Jesus Christ." "Grace" simply means unmerited pardon from God. It does not mean to keep doing what you are doing and think God will forgive you. God only grants grace to those who truly acknowledge their sins, repent, and are correctly baptized, according to the Bible. True Christians must love God and whole-heartedly keep all of His commandments.

2. Other Christian denominations preach "the gospel of salvation." This approach happens when people go knocking door-to-door or go around asking questions like, *"Are you saved?"* or *"Did you give your heart to the Lord?"* (Refer to sections 5.1 and 5.2 for the biblical meaning of salvation.)

3. Still others preach "the gospel of prosperity," where lay people are asked to give money or make a pledge to sponsor a church or denomination so that they might receive blessings or healings from God, all the while, turning the church and God's Word into a money-making business. Clearly, these "gospels" are not the true gospel that Christ or the apostles preached.

The true gospel Christ preached has been changed to the false gospels mentioned above. Notice what Paul says to the church in Galatia about turning to different gospels. "I marvel that you are turning away so soon from Him who called you in the grace of Christ, to a different gospel, which is not another; but there are some who trouble you and want to pervert the gospel of Christ" (**Galatians 1:6–7**).

Christ preached about the kingdom of God coming to this earth; that was His message to the world. Christ preached it freely to anyone who was willing to listen. All of God's people, prophets, and apostles preached the same message, free of charge. Their message of hope is the same message that should be preached "in all the world as a witness" by the true church today. "And this gospel of the kingdom will be preached in all the world as a witness to all the nations, and then the end will come" (**Matthew 24:14**).

Christ was the messenger sent by God the Father to preach the good news of God's coming kingdom to earth. "The beginning of the gospel of Jesus Christ, the Son of God" (**Mark 1:1**). "Now after John was put in prison, Jesus came to Galilee, preaching the gospel of the kingdom of God, and saying, 'The time is fulfilled, and the kingdom of God is at hand. Repent, and believe in the gospel'" (**Mark 1:14–15**).

Not only did Christ travel throughout Judea preaching the good news of the coming kingdom of God, but He commissioned seventy men and commanded them to preach that same gospel wherever they went. "Whatever city you [the seventy] enter, and they receive you, eat such things as are set before you. And heal the sick there, and say to them, 'The kingdom of God has come near to you'" (**Luke 10:8–9**). Christ also sent the apostles to preach the kingdom of God. "Then He called His twelve disciples together and gave them power and authority over all demons, and to cure diseases. He sent them to preach the kingdom of God and to heal the sick" (**Luke 9:1–2**).

Remember that the apostle Paul preached the gospel of the kingdom of God to the Gentiles during his time on earth. "For I speak to you Gentiles; inasmuch as I am an apostle to the Gentiles, I magnify my ministry" (**Romans 11:13**). "They wrote this letter by them: The apostles, the elders, and the brethren, to the brethren who are of the Gentiles in Antioch, Syria, and Cilicia: Greetings" (**Acts 15:23**). That should be the mission of God's true church today—to preach the gospel to the world and to heal the sick.

The kingdom of God is a literal spiritual kingdom to be established on earth by Christ, wherein you will receive everlasting life, righteousness, peace, joy, and power. God's kingdom is a very real kingdom! It will be as real as many powerful human kingdoms that were established on earth.

In the book of Daniel, we find examples of **four** powerful human empires that existed.

1. Babylon was ruled by king Nebuchadnezzar (reference **Daniel 2:28–30**).

2. The Media-Persian Empire, ruled by King Cyrus (reference **Daniel 6:15**).

3. The Greco-Macedonian Empire was ruled by Alexander the Great (reference **Daniel 6:20–21**).

4. The Roman Empire ruled by Julius Caesar (reference **Daniel 2:40**).

God's kingdom, when established at Christ's return to earth, will destroy all man-made governments and will last forever. That's how real the kingdom of God will be. "Then comes the end, when He [Christ] delivers the kingdom to God the Father, when He puts an end to all rule and all authority and power. For He must reign till He has put all enemies under His feet" (**1 Corinthians 15:24–25**).

"Then the seventh angel sounded: And there were loud voices in heaven, saying, 'The kingdoms of this world have become the kingdoms of our Lord and of His Christ, and He shall reign forever and ever!'" (**Revelation 11:15**).

After Christ sits on His throne in Jerusalem, notice what is stated: "Many nations shall come and say, 'Come, and let us go up to the mountain [government] of the LORD, to the house of the God of Jacob; He will teach us His ways, and we shall walk in His paths. For out of Zion [Jerusalem] the law shall go forth, and the word of the LORD from Jerusalem'" (**Micah 4:2**).

Jerusalem will be the headquarters for the kingdom of God, and His law will flow out from there. "And in that day His feet will stand on the Mount of Olives, which faces Jerusalem on the east. And the Mount of

Olives shall be split in two, from east to west, making a very large valley; half of the mountain shall move toward the north, and half of it toward the south" (**Zechariah 14:4**). Imagine a mountain being split in two at Christ's return to Jerusalem! What power and majesty Christ has!

What you have just read is the true gospel of the kingdom of God. This is yet another wonderful piece of the giant jigsaw puzzle that has been correctly placed.

7.3 IS BAPTISM NECESSARY TO BE IN THE KINGDOM OF GOD?

We have already referenced Scriptures that show that baptism is necessary to be in God's kingdom. But to confirm, let's turn to **Mark 16:15–16**. "And He [Christ] said to them [the apostles], 'Go into all the world and preach the gospel to every creature. He who believes and is baptized will be saved; but he who does not believe will be condemned.'" *Did you catch it?* He who is baptized "will be saved." Notice that the person "will be saved" sometime in the future. He is "not" saved at baptism or when in the flesh but at some time in a future resurrection. (Refer to sections 5.1 and 5.2 on salvation.)

If you do not have the spirit of Christ (Holy Spirit), you cannot rule with Him in His kingdom during His one thousand year reign on earth. "Blessed and holy is he who has part in the first resurrection. Over such the second death has no power, but they shall be priests of God and of Christ, and shall reign with Him a thousand years" (**Revelation 20:6**).

The conditions set forth in the Holy Bible on salvation by God include: Repentance, Conversion, Baptism, receiving the gift of the Holy Spirit, observing God's commandments and feast days, and loving one another. "A new commandment I give to you, that you love one another; as I have loved you, that you also love one another" (**John 13:34**).

This is yet another piece of the giant jigsaw puzzle in the Bible that few people know and understand.

7.4 SEVEN BIBLICAL TRUTHS THAT LEAD TO YOUR AWESOME DESTINY

God clearly spells out the awesome human destiny in His Holy Word, the Bible. It is not a theory or assumption or anything like that. *Do you know what your awesome destiny is? Do you know what God has planned for you after this present physical life?* Prepare yourself for exciting, new revealed knowledge. This knowledge tells us the reason we find ourselves in our present state of unrest and chaos. Science, education, businesses, and most religions do not know God's plan for humanity. The so-called intellectuals of the world do not know what it is. The most powerful, famous, and rich people of this world do not know what it is. No one seems to know what their awesome destiny is.

The primary reason why these institutions and intellectuals do not know their awesome destiny is because almost all of them have rejected revealed knowledge in the Bible in favor of man-made theories.

This revealed knowledge also carries the most monumental good news that has ever been revealed by our maker to humankind.

Let's take a look at the **seven** biblical truths that will lead you to your awesome destiny.

1. Your awesome destiny includes a resurrection from the dead after living your physical life. God has outlined two separate resurrections for two distinct and separate groups of people. To review, the first resurrection includes all the people God has chosen through the ages and who have died or were martyred, such as Abel, Noah, Moses, Isaac, and many more. "And I saw thrones, and they sat on them, and judgment was committed to them. Then I saw the souls of those who had been beheaded for their witness to Jesus and for the word of God, who had not worshiped the beast or his image, and had not received his mark on their foreheads or on their hands. And they lived and reigned with Christ for a thousand years" (**Revelation 20:4**).

A. The **first** resurrection also includes people who were chosen by
    God and are still alive when Christ returns. "For this we say to
    you by the word of the Lord, that we who are alive and remain
    until the coming of the Lord will by no means precede those
    who are asleep" (**1 Thessalonians 4:15**). "Behold, I tell you a
    mystery: We shall not all sleep, but we shall all be changed—in
    a moment, in the twinkling of an eye, at the last trumpet. For
    the trumpet will sound, and the dead will be raised incorrupt-
    ible, and we shall be changed. For this corruptible must put
    on incorruption, and this mortal must put on immortality. So,
    when this corruptible has put on incorruption, and this mor-
    tal has put on immortality, then shall be brought to pass the
    saying that is written: "Death is swallowed up in victory" (**1
    Corinthians 15:51–55**).

Together, these saints (the elect of God) will meet Christ in the air,
just like a special entourage would meet an important dignitary. After
a short while, Christ and all His elect will descend to Jerusalem and
begin divine rulership on earth for one thousand years.

B. Immediately after the one thousand year reign of Christ, a **sec-
    ond** group of people will be resurrected. The Bible calls this
    group of people "the great white throne judgment or the rest
    of the dead." It is also referred to by some as the second resur-
    rection and includes all people who have ever lived but were
    not chosen by God during their lifetimes. *Does that mean that
    God has favorites or is partial to some people?* NO! (More on
    partiality in the second truth.) "But the rest of the dead did
    not live again until the one thousand years were finished....
    (**Revelation 20:5**). Your awesome destiny includes a resurrec-
    tion and the potential to live forever as a spirit being. (Refer to
    section 5.1 for information on the resurrections.)

2. Your awesome destiny includes an everlasting life with a just, loving, and merciful God who has no partiality. God does not have favorites. "For there is no partiality with God" (**Romans 2:11**). "But from those who seemed to be something—whatever they were, it makes no difference to me; God shows personal favoritism to no man—for those who seemed to be something added nothing to me, says God" (**Galatians 2:6**). The reason why God calls someone instead of another is because He looks at that person's heart. "But the LORD said to Samuel, 'Do not look at his appearance or at his physical stature, because I have refused him. For the LORD does not see as man sees; for man looks at the outward appearance, but the LORD looks at the heart'" (**1 Samuel 6:7**). The people whom God chose during their lifetime must also fight Satan and are being judged by God now. "For the time has come for judgment to begin at the house of God; and if it begins with us first, what will be the end of those who do not obey the gospel of God?" (**1 Peter 4:17**). The phrase "house of God" refers to God's chosen people.

3. Your awesome destiny includes living a life without Satan and his demons. We fight Satan every day, trying to overcome the forces of evil. But God says that during His one thousand year reign on earth, Satan—the liar and arch-deceiver of humankind—and his demons will be "shut up" for one thousand years. "Then I saw an angel coming down from heaven, having the key to the bottomless pit and a great chain in his hand. He laid hold of the dragon, that serpent of old, who is the Devil and Satan, and bound him for a thousand years; and he cast him into the bottomless pit, and shut him up, and set a seal on him, so that he should deceive the nations no more till the thousand years were finished. But after these things he must be released for a little while" (**Revelation 20:1–3**).

We proved in section 3.3 that the primary cause of "all" human troubles and suffering is Satan, "the god of this age." Sometimes God allows Satan to blind people's minds. "Whose minds the god of this age has blinded, who do not believe, lest the light of the gospel of the glory of Christ, who is the image of God, should shine on them" (**2 Corinthians 4:4**). Satan also works in the "sons of disobedience." "In which you once walked according to the course of this world, according to the prince of the power of the air, the spirit who now works in the sons of disobedience" (**Ephesians 2:2**).

4. Your awesome destiny includes an everlasting life without pain, suffering, sorrow, or death. "And God will wipe away every tear from their eyes; there shall be no more death, nor sorrow, nor crying. There shall be no more pain, for the former things have passed away" (**Revelation 21:4**). Think about this awesome Scripture!

How many people have pain, cry, suffer, and maybe will even die today? Everyone does at some point in time, but God will wipe away all these anomalies from your life. God will make your awesome destiny a reality!

5. Your awesome destiny includes a life without war or war-making machinery. Take a look at the following wonderful and inspiring Scripture: "He [God] shall judge between the nations, and rebuke many people; They shall beat their swords into plowshares, and their spears into pruning hooks; Nation shall not lift up sword against nation, neither shall they learn war anymore" (**Isaiah 2:4**).

War has plagued humanity since the beginning of time. But during the one thousand year- reign of Christ on earth and thereafter, people will **not** learn war any more. *Why?* Because God will finally be ruling this earth as "King of Kings and Lord of Lords." "And He has on His robe and on His thigh a name written: KING OF KINGS AND LORD OF LORDS" (**Revelation 19:16**).

6. Your awesome destiny includes a life wherein God will "make all things new." Yes, all things! "Then He who sat on the throne

said, 'Behold, I make all things—new'" (**Revelation 21:5**). "Now I saw a new heaven and a new earth, for the first heaven and the first earth had passed away. Also, there was no more sea. Then I, John, saw the holy city, New Jerusalem, coming down out of heaven from God, prepared as a bride adorned for her husband" (**Revelation 21:1–2**).

7. Your awesome destiny includes God dwelling among us. "And I heard a loud voice from heaven saying, 'Behold, the tabernacle [dwelling place] of God is with men, and He will dwell with them, and they shall be His people. God Himself will be with them and be their God. And God will wipe away every tear from their eyes; there shall be no more death, nor sorrow, nor crying. There shall be no more pain, for the former things have passed away'" (**Revelation 21:3–4**).

What a wonderful picture, and what an incredible, awesome plan God has for us. It is all part of your awesome destiny. But even with this wonderful knowledge, we still do not know—nor can we fathom—"everything" that God has planned for those who love Him. "But as it is written: Eye has not seen, nor ear heard, nor have entered into the heart of man, the things which God has prepared for those who love Him" (**1 Corinthians 2:9**).

No human could have thought of such a marvelous plan of salvation, only our loving God. Our awesome destiny is to become immortal spirit beings, ruling with Christ throughout the entire universe, forever and ever, with true peace and everlasting happiness surrounding us wherever we go. I cannot wait for that wonderful day to finally happen. This is your awesome destiny!

7.5 CHARACTER TRAITS OF OUR FUTURE SPIRITUAL KING

Have you ever thought of what it will be like to work for the God family in their kingdom? Notice Christ's recorded words: "Now I am no longer in the world, but these [people] are in the world, and I come to You. Holy Father, keep through Your name those whom You have given Me, that they may be one as We are" (**John 17:11**). (Refer to section 2.1 for information on understanding the oneness of God.) The God family wants us to become like them—spirit beings. What awesome creators we have!

God the Father is the supreme ruler, and directly under Him in authority is Jesus, the Christ, our Messiah, our future spiritual king. *What character traits do the Father and Christ possess, and how would those traits compare with the physical bosses we might have today?*

Most of us have experienced working for supervisors in our jobs. Throughout my twenty-five–year career in the United States Air Force as a civil servant and prior to that as a music teacher in the Ohio public school system, I experienced many supervisors with varying skills, abilities, and character traits.

I want to focus on **three sets** of character traits—because the Holy Bible groups them in sets—that I have noticed in my physical bosses and compare those traits with the character traits of the God family. I am certain you will recognize some of the same traits in bosses for whom you work for. In general, it seems that the vast majority of workers today are not happy with their jobs or their bosses, sometimes. I hope this section will provide much needed hope for a spiritual King in the near future.

1. The **first set** of human character traits include the burning desire to get ahead and be promoted, whether for power, status, prestige, or money. It also seems that most bosses do not care who perishes in the process of their being promoted. It may not matter to them if they tell a little white lie here and there or even a blatant lie along the way. It is all done in the name of "climbing that corporate ladder."

What can we expect from our future spiritual King? Will He look for a promotion? Will He try to obtain prestige, status, or money? "That they may know that You, whose name alone is the LORD, are the Most High over all the earth" (**Psalm 83:18**). Our future perfect King, Jesus the Christ, will not look for His next promotion. Christ is part of the God family, but He will be the "Most High over all the earth." It is true that God the Father is supreme in authority, but all authority, in heaven and on earth, was given to Christ. "And Jesus came and spoke to them, saying, 'All authority has been given to Me in heaven and on earth'" (**Matthew 28:18**). God the Father has complete trust in Christ, His beloved Son. God owns all things, including precious metals. "'The silver is Mine, and the gold is Mine,' says the LORD of hosts" (**Haggai 2:8**). God owns "all" things, and there is no one richer than God.

Does God care about who perishes or gets hurt? Indeed, He does! God cares for and loves us and does not want anyone to perish. *How much does He care for us?* "For God so loved the world that He gave His only begotten Son, that whoever believes in Him should not perish but have everlasting life" (**John 3:16**). *Would you allow your only son to die so that others may live?* That is what the Father did for you and His Son willingly suffered death so that we may someday live again. The truth is that God does not want any human to perish but to have everlasting life at a resurrection. The vast majority of the time, we humans hurt ourselves by doing what God tells us **not** to do and, conversely, by not doing what God tells us **to** do.

We think we know more than God knows. We do things our way and get hurt in the process, and afterward, we blame God for our troubles and difficulties. God wants to give us everlasting life! But first, we need to learn to always love Him and obey His commands. *After all, His commands are for our own good, so why not obey God?* As physical parents love their children and sometimes disciplines them, so God does with us. "You should know in your heart that as a man chastens his son, so the LORD your God chastens you" (**Deuteronomy 8:5**).

Does God sometimes tell us little white lies, as some of our physical bosses do? "Thus God, determining to show more abundantly to the heirs of promise the immutability of His counsel, confirmed it by an oath, that by two immutable things, in which it is impossible for God to lie, we might have strong consolation, who have fled for refuge to lay hold of the hope set before us" (**Hebrews 6:18–19**). In short, it is impossible for God to lie. Think of it—no more white lies, no more blatant lies, no more half-truths, and no more devious omissions or cover-ups, only the truth from a loving God.

So far, our future King is the total opposite of most human bosses. Thank God for God.

2. The **second set** of character traits includes being quick to punish. Many human bosses get upset and angry quickly and show little compassion for people who might be enduring many of life's difficulties. Most human bosses show little or no mercy to their workers. And they are ever so slow to reward.

What can we expect from our future spiritual King? "So, rend your heart, and not your garments; Return to the LORD your God, for He is gracious and merciful, slow to anger, and of great kindness; And He relents from doing harm" (**Joel 2:13**). Our future spiritual King is ready to pardon, is slow to anger, and shows great kindness. Come to God with a humble heart, not with torn clothes, because He is gracious and merciful.

The Bible gives many examples of God's relenting of an act He said He would do to disobedient nations if people would repent of their sins. I never knew of a physical boss who ever said I'm sorry or held back an undeserved review. *Do you know of any?* "The instant I speak concerning a nation and concerning a kingdom, to pluck up, to pull down, and to destroy it, if that nation against whom I have spoken turns from its evil, I will relent of the disaster that I thought to bring upon it" (**Jeremiah 18:7–8**). If people and nations would just turn from their evil ways and humble their hearts toward God and repent, He would stop His punishment toward them. What a wonderful and merciful God and King we will have.

Do most physical bosses reward employees in a timely manner for a job well done? In appreciation for a job well done on a special project

I was given; it took the Air Force about a year to send me a congratulatory letter and bonus. When Christ returns to rule this earth at the sound of the seventh trumpet, He will have His reward with Him, ready to give. "And behold, I am coming quickly, and My reward is with Me, to give to everyone according to his work" (**Revelation 22:12**). Not only does God have His reward with Him, but He is coming quickly. "They refused to obey, and they were not mindful of Your wonders that You did among them. But they hardened their necks, and in their rebellion, they appointed a leader to return to their bondage. But You are God, ready to pardon, gracious and merciful, slow to anger, abundant in kindness, and did not forsake them" (**Nehemiah 9:17**). Our future spiritual King possesses character traits that are opposite of many human bosses.

3. The **third set** of character traits includes forgetting the people who worked so hard to help them get promoted. They forget the very people who helped them achieve their status, their successes, and their goals. And sometimes, they forget their promises. *Have you ever experienced broken promises?* I believe we all have. Moreover, once physical bosses reach top level positions, they tend to change—they often become moody and haughty. It is like "they never knew you."

What can we expect from our future spiritual King? Will God forget His promises to us? **Deuteronomy 4:31** tells us, "(for the LORD your God is a merciful God), He will not forsake you nor destroy you, nor forget the covenant of your fathers which He swore to them." God will not forget His covenant, which contains eternal promises that He swore to our forefathers, Abraham, Isaac, and Jacob. God will not forget His promises to them or to us, but we must obey God in all things, as they did.

Is God moody? Does He change his mind on a daily basis? Absolutely not! "For I am the LORD, I do not change; Therefore, you are not consumed, O sons of Jacob" (**Malachi 3:6**). Let us see if God changed in any way in the New Testament. "Jesus Christ is the same yesterday, today, and forever" (**Hebrews 13:8**). *Is God haughty?* No, God is gentle and lowly in heart. We can expect our world-ruling spiritual King to never change and never be moody but always remain the same: holy, just, gentle, loving, good, and upright. "Take My yoke upon you and learn from Me, for I am gentle and lowly in heart, and you will find rest for your souls" (**Matthew 11:29**).

"Good and upright is the LORD; Therefore, He teaches sinners in the way. The humble He guides in justice, and the humble He teaches His way" (**Psalm 25:8–9**). God loves humble people because they are teachable. Moses was a humble person. "Now the man Moses was very humble, more than all men who were on the face of the earth" (**Numbers 12:3**). "But He gives more grace. Therefore, He says: 'God resists the proud, but gives grace to the humble'" (**James 4:6**). "He has shown you, O man, what is good; And what does the LORD require of you but to do justly, to love mercy, and to walk humbly with your God?" (**Micah 6:8**).

Isaiah, the prophet, was inspired to write some awesome titles that fit our perfect, spiritual King. "For unto us a Child is born, unto us a Son is given; And the government will be upon His shoulder. And His name will be called Wonderful, Counselor, Mighty God, Everlasting Father, Prince of Peace" (**Isaiah 9:6**). The same words were put to music in Handel's *Messiah*. I wonder how many people really understand the deep meaning of this Scripture.

While on earth, as both God and man, Christ showed us more of His character traits. "Greater love has no one than this, than to lay down one's life for his friends. You are My friends if you do whatever I command you. No longer do I call you servants (an employee, a slave), for a servant does not know what his master is doing; but I have called you friends, for all things that I heard from My Father I have made known to you" (**John 15:13–15**).

Has your physical boss ever called you, his friend? Would your boss die for you so you could remain alive? Has he ever told you the plans he has for you and the company? Christ has made known to us all that the Father has declared to Him, thus making us His friends. In all my years of work, I never had a boss or supervisor call me his friend, but our Savior and Lord has done just that!

Let us be reminded daily of the special character traits of our future perfect, spiritual King. How wonderful it will be to work with a loving, just, kind, merciful, never-changing, willing-to-forgive creator God, who cannot lie, cheat, or steal and is not looking for a promotion.

As true Christians, we need to develop these same character traits of the God family, in ourselves, if we are to see our spiritual King as He is, in all His glory. This is another important piece to the giant jigsaw puzzle found in the Bible.

7.6 GOD'S EXTREME MAKEOVER

About ten years ago, there was a popular TV reality show called *Extreme Makeover: Home Edition.* The purpose of this program was to find a family who was in need of extreme help due to a crisis in life, health, job, or income. The goal was to demolish the home of the selected family and build a brand-new home for them in just seven days. The contractor teams worked twenty-four hours a day for those seven days to make this dream come true.

The design construction companies and many volunteers were needed to accomplish the task, while the needy family was sent away on an exotic vacation. In addition to a new dwelling, the hosts provided home furnishings and gifts that would help the family overcome their hardships and difficult circumstances.

Unlike oftentimes worthless television shows that just entertain, this show inspired, encouraged, taught, uplifted, and motivated people to help one another. Remember the second great commandment: "Love your neighbor as yourself." Perhaps most of all, this show provided hope for people who were struggling. As you may already know, God is our ultimate hope. "For I know the thoughts that I think toward you, says the LORD, thoughts of peace and not of evil, to give you a future and a hope" (**Jeremiah 29:11**). He is the

One who wants to give us the gift of everlasting life, but we must always obey Him.

Isn't it nice to hear and watch some good news sometimes? Wouldn't it be great to give hope to a person or a family who is really down and out? Well, someday, Christ Himself will direct and produce many very extreme makeovers involving humankind, animal-kind, and earth itself. His reality program is coming to your world. When our Messiah descends from the third heaven as King of Kings and Lord of Lords, He will perform "extreme makeovers"—not for just a few select families but for everyone worldwide.

Let's discover **five** of the extreme makeovers that will take place in this world at Christ's second coming.

1. God will reeducate humanity to His way of life. During His reign on earth, God will open the eyes, ears, and minds of the physically, mentally, and spiritually handicapped people all over the world so that His biblical truths can finally be understood. At His second coming, Christ will open all deceived minds, ultimately bringing them to voluntary repentance and baptism. Only God can perform this extreme makeover.

At that time, people will be very excited about and look forward to learning God's way of life. Notice what people will say: "Come, and let us go up to the mountain of the LORD, to the house of the God of Jacob; He will teach us His ways, and we shall walk in His paths. For out of Zion shall go forth the law, and the word of the LORD from Jerusalem" (**Isaiah 2:3**). God's law and His Holy Spirit will begin to flow out from Jerusalem to all people in the world. Everyone will know and participate in keeping God's commandments and feast days.

2. God will freely give of His Holy Spirit to all people. "And in that day, it shall be that living waters shall flow from Jerusalem, half of them toward the eastern sea and half of them toward the western sea; In both summer and winter it shall occur" (**Zechariah 14:8**).

Living waters refers to God's Holy Spirit and the gift of everlasting life. It is going to flow out from Jerusalem to the outermost parts of the earth. "The woman said to Him, 'Sir, You have nothing to draw with, and the well is deep. Where then do You get that living water? Are You greater than our father Jacob, who gave us the well, and drank from it himself, as well as his sons and his livestock?' Jesus answered and said to her, 'Whoever drinks of this water will thirst again, but whoever drinks of the water that I shall give him will never thirst. But the water that I shall give him will become in him a fountain of water springing up into everlasting life'" (**John 4:11–14**).

3. There will be geographic changes, and people will be healed. Yes, geographic changes are also coming to your world. Some of these changes include timely rainfall, changing deserts into fertile land, mountains melting (Reference **Psalm 97:5**), valleys becoming filled, and glaciers melting. Humans will drink pure, delicious water; families will be restored; and mental, emotional, and physical illnesses will be healed. Notice the awesome Scripture in Isaiah: "The wilderness and the wasteland shall be glad for them, and the desert shall rejoice and blossom as the rose; It shall blossom abundantly and rejoice, even with joy and singing. The glory of Lebanon shall be given to it, the excellence of Carmel and Sharon. They shall see the glory of the LORD, the Excellency of our God" (**Isaiah 35:1–2**).

Look at the healing that will take place:

> Strengthen the weak hands, and make firm the feeble knees. Say to those who are fearful-hearted, "Be strong, do not fear! Behold, your God will come with vengeance, with the recompense of God; He will come and save you." Then the eyes of the blind shall be opened, and the ears of the deaf shall be unstopped. Then the lame shall leap like a deer, And the tongue of the dumb

sing. For waters shall burst forth in the wilderness, and streams in the desert. The parched ground shall become a pool, and the thirsty land springs of water; In the habitation of jackals, where each lay, there shall be grass with reeds and rushes." (**Isaiah 35:3–7**)

God will finally restore your health. "'For I will restore health to you and heal you of your wounds,' says the LORD, 'Because they called you an outcast saying: "This is Zion; No one seeks her"'" (**Jeremiah 30:17**). Think of it—everyone will be healed, no matter what sickness they have or how old they are!

4. God will change the nature of wild animals. Imagine a world where the wolf and the lamb will live together. *How about a little child leading a young lion?* It is impossible in today's world, but during Christ's one thousand year reign on earth, all things will be possible. "But Jesus looked at them and said to them, 'With men this is impossible, but with God all things are possible'" (**Matthew 19:26**).

> The wolf also shall dwell with the lamb, the leopard shall lie down with the young goat, the calf and the young lion and the fatling together; and a little child shall lead them. The cow and the bear shall graze; Their young ones shall lie down together; And the lion shall eat straw like the ox. The nursing child shall play by the cobra's hole, and the weaned child shall put his hand in the viper's den. They [all the wild animals] shall not hurt nor destroy in all My holy mountain, for the earth shall be full of the knowledge of the LORD as the waters cover the sea. (**Isaiah 11:6–9**)

What inspiring and awesome words these are, and they are all true since God cannot lie!

5. God will give us a new and pure language. "For then will I turn to the people a pure language that they may all call upon the name of the Eternal to serve Him with one consent" (**Zephaniah 3:9**). No more confusion on how to worship God. No more language barriers. No more pronunciation issues. There will be one pure language that we all will speak to call on God's name. His name will finally be pronounced correctly by all. Everyone will finally worship God the way He wants to be worshipped, not the way we think He should be worshipped. And there will be many more wonderful gifts from God that we are not privy to know at this time. Notice the powerful Scripture: "But as it is written: "Eye has not seen, nor ear heard, nor have entered into the heart of man the things which God has prepared for those who love Him" (**1 Corinthians 2:9**).

Are you clearly seeing the entire picture of the giant jigsaw puzzle of God's extreme makeover? Whether we are ready for it or not, whether we believe it or not, the kingdom of God will come to this earth because "the mouth of the Lord has spoken it." Let's pray fervently and effectually for one another so that when God's extreme makeover comes to this world, we will be spiritually prepared for it.

7.7   HOW SHOULD A TRUE CHRISTIAN LIVE IN TODAY'S WORLD?

In today's hectic, chaotic, upside-down world, there are seemingly many things to worry about. People worry about people—kids, parents, neighbors, teachers, pastors, and friends. People worry about things— health, jobs, finances, church, house, school, tests, and clothes. They worry about food—what they should or should not eat and drink and how much of each. People worry about many other things.

What about you? Are you worried about something or someone? Should we live in fear of these things? What does the Bible say about being worried? And how should we handle the many worries each of us have today?

Webster's defines "worry" as "being uneasy or anxious, fretting" about people or things. Worrying is a form of thinking that is repetitive and nonproductive and can be very stressful if taken to the extreme. Christ gave an excellent example of worry as being nonproductive. "Look at the birds of the air, for they neither sow nor reap nor gather into barns; yet your heavenly Father feeds them. Are you not of more value than they? Which of you by worrying can add one cubit to his stature?" (**Matthew 6:26–27**).

Christ was asking people in His day, *"Will we get any taller by worrying about it?"* The answer is quite obvious. But this kind of thinking is an example of repetitive, nonproductive worry. Being worried or living in fear is not what God intended for us.

> So why do you worry about clothing? Consider the lilies of the field, how they grow: they neither toil nor spin; and yet I say to you that even Solomon in all his glory was not arrayed like one of these. Now if God so clothes the grass of the field, which today is, and tomorrow is thrown into the oven, will He not much more clothe you, O you of little faith? Therefore, do not worry, saying, 'What shall we eat?' or 'What shall we drink?' or 'What shall we wear?' For after all these things the Gentiles seek. For your heavenly Father knows that you need all these things. But seek first the kingdom of God and His righteousness, and all these things shall be added to you. Therefore, do not worry about tomorrow, for tomorrow will worry about its own things. (**Matthew 6:28–34**)

Christ is telling us to take one day at a time and not to worry about things; rather, we are to "seek first the kingdom of God and His righteousness." The top priority in this life is to put God first and to do what He tells us to do, and all other things will always work out for the better in the long haul.

I want to provide **four** steps that will help you not to worry.

1. Pray to God, and allow Him to handle your worries or problems over which you have no control. God will eventually correct the situation in His time, not yours. "My thoughts are not your thoughts; neither are my ways your ways" (**Isaiah 55:8**). God's ways of correcting a problem are far superior to our ways.

"Be anxious for nothing, but in everything by prayer and supplication, with thanksgiving, let your requests be made known to God; and the peace of God, which surpasses all understanding, will guard your hearts and minds through Christ Jesus" (**Philippians 4:6–7**). A supplication is a humble, heartfelt, and sincere appeal to God, who has full power to grant your request if it is in accordance with His will. Always pray to God, giving Him thanks daily for the things He has generously given you.

This first step reminds me of a story I read in the *Reader's Digest* a few years back about a young lady named Lisa Owens. Lisa was facing knee surgery. She was terrified and quite worried about it, so she asked her boss, a veterinarian at the animal clinic where she worked, if he had any advice for her. He was very comforting, and without hesitation, he told her, "Turn your worries into prayers, get plenty of rest, and don't lick your wound." This made Lisa Owens smile. It should make us smile too because that was good veterinary advice.

The Bible makes it very clear that in living a true Christian life, we should not worry but should constantly pray to God for help in our daily living. *Do you have good health?* Thank God for it. *Do you have healthy children?* Praise God for them. *Do you have a steady job?* Give God thanks for it. *Do you have a roof over your head and food on the table?* Be thankful for it. *Now that you have read some of God's truth in this volume, are you thankful for it?*

2. Meditate on the things of God. Take your mind away from worrying about yourself and others, and meditate on the wonderful things of God. "Finally, brethren, whatever things are true, whatever things are noble, whatever things are just, whatever things

are pure, whatever things are lovely, whatever things are of good report, if there is any virtue and if there is anything praiseworthy— meditate on these things" (**Philippians 4:8**).

What are "the things of God?" Since God is spirit, the things of God pertain to the spiritual realm. "The things which you learned and received and heard and saw in me, these do, and the God of peace will be with you" (**Philippians 4:9**).

The things you have read and learned from this book are the spiritual truths from God. Things like love, truth, peace, spiritual understanding, faith, and hope, among other things, are all things of God. The godly character that you are building in living your life on earth is much more important to God than the size of your wallet or the beauty of the house you live in. Meditate on God's Ten Commandments, His plan of salvation, His feast days, His love toward us, and the awesome destiny that He has planned for us. Meditate again on all the truths you have read in this book. They are all the spiritual things of God.

3. Ask God to help you put your worries in the right perspective. This step reminds me of a book written way back in 1961 by Richard Carlson, PhD, titled *Don't Sweat the Small Stuff ... and It's All Small Stuff*. The theme repeated throughout his book is don't make a mountain out of a molehill, or don't overly exaggerate your problem. There was a popular song by Bobby McFerrin a few years back that sums up putting things in perspective quite well— "Don't Worry, Be Happy"! This catchy song became a big hit.

Let's take a look at an example of an exaggerated problem. According to the National Bureau of Standards, a dense fog covering seven city blocks with a height of one hundred feet is composed of something less than ten gallons of water. The fog itself seems like a huge problem, but when placed in the right perspective, it is just ten gallons of water. *But what if you do not exaggerate your problem? What should you do then?* Back in Moses' day, there were perhaps three to four million

Israelites (maybe more) who had real physical needs. These were physical people who needed physical things, like food, water, and clothing. The quartermaster general of the US Army did a study on the account in Exodus and found that the Israelites had to have about 1,500 tons of food each day. It would take two freight trains, each a mile long, to carry that much food each day. Also consider that the Israelites were in the desert and needed water. If they had only enough water to drink for themselves, their children, and their flocks and herds and some water to wash clothes and do dishes, it would take eleven million gallons of water each day. The freight train carrying that much water each day would be 1,800 miles long.

In addition, the Israelites would need firewood to boil the water and cook their food. This would take four thousand tons of wood each day and a few more freight trains, each a mile long, to satisfy this requirement. Remember this is each day. Now multiply all these figures by 365 days per year, times forty years. *Do you still think God has a problem with taking care of your needs?* How great and powerful our God is! We need to ask God to help us put our worries in perspective and, at the same time, rely on Him to help us. God didn't even allow their clothes or sandals to wear out. "And I have led you forty years in the wilderness. Your clothes have not worn out on you, and your sandals have not worn out on your feet. You have not eaten bread, nor have you drunk wine or similar drink, that you may know that I am the LORD your God" (**Deuteronomy 29:5–6**).

4. If you think you can solve your own problem, make sure you pray to God about it first. This is to make sure that your resolution is correct. This fourth step leads us right back to the first step, which is to pray to God. These steps are circular, just like the Ten Commandments. One commandment leads to the next, and all are equally important.

This fourth step also reminds me of a letter I read by an unknown author. The letter portrays God as writing to all those who believe and trust in Him. It reads, in part,

Today, I will be handling all your worries. Please remember that I do not need your help. If the adversary happens to deliver a situation to you that you cannot handle, do not attempt to resolve it. Kindly send it up via prayer through My Son and it will be addressed in My time, not yours. Holding on to your problem or worry, will only cause delay in My resolution. If it is a situation that you think you are capable of handling, please consult me in prayer first just to be sure that it is the proper resolution. Because I do not sleep or slumber, there is no need for you to lose any sleep. Rest, my child, from worry.

1 Peter 5:6–7 tells us, "Therefore humble yourselves under the mighty hand of God, that He may exalt you in due time, casting all your cares upon Him, for He cares for you."

Let us pray to God Let us meditate on His things, and let us ask God to help us put our cares and worries in the right perspective. With the awesome God that He is, let's not worry but be happy as we live our Christian lives. Please thank God for the wonderful knowledge and future opportunity He has shown us in His Bible. May God abundantly bless each of you who read and heed the words found in your Bible.

Knowing and doing these spiritual truths expounded herein, will be the beginning of your new spiritual life. "I call heaven and earth as witnesses today against you, that I have set before you life and death, blessing and cursing; therefore, choose life, that both you and your descendants may live" (**Deuteronomy 30:19**).

Now that you know some of God's truth, you can begin your new spiritual life fully devoted to His plan and purpose.

WORKS CITED

Armstrong, Karen, (*A History of God*, 1993, 284)

Biblical Archaeology Review

Carlson, Richard, PhD, *Don't Sweat the Small Stuff ... and It's All Small Stuff* (1961)

Gideon International (2001)

Glueck, *Rivers in the Desert*, (24-25, 136)

Jewish Encyclopedia (*Immortality of the Soul*, Volume VI, 564, 566)

Lindsay, Michael, Rice University sociologist of religion

Pew Forum's Religious Landscape Survey, dated February 2008

Professor M. Montiero Williams from Oxford University (theChristianExpositor.org)

The Gospel of Matthew According to a Primitive Hebrew Text, Howard, 1987

The New Catholic Encyclopedia (1967, Vol. XIV, 299)

The New Strong's Exhaustive Concordance of the Bible (1984)

United Bible Society Scripture Language Report (2000)

US News and World Report, Jan. 31, 2000, 47

Wall Street Journal (December 13, 2008) commented in an article titled "Profit Sharing: The Good Book Is the Best Seller"

Scripture Index in Sequence

Author's Statement

- 2 Tim 3:16
- Isa 28:10
- 2 Pet 1:20
- 2 Pet 3:15–16

- Deut 12:8
- Rev 22:18–19
- Deut 12:32
- 1 Cor 14:33

- Acts 17:11
- 1 Thes 5:21
- Isa 28:10
- Rev 1:3

Chapter 1
God's Truth about the Bible
1.1 What Exactly Is the Holy Bible?

- 2 Pet 1:20–21
- 1 Thes 5:21
- 2 Tim 3:16–17
- 2 Pet 1:20–21
- Rom 15:4
- Titus 1:2
- John 17:17

- Psa 119:160
- 2 Tim 3:16
- Heb 6:18
- 2 Pet 1:21
- John 14:6
- John 8:44
- 1 Pet 1:16

- Ex 3:5
- Isa 40:8
- Matt 24:35
- Matt 5:18
- Isa 55:9–11
- Heb 4:12

1.2 Why Should the Bible Be Important to You?

- Acts 4:10–12
- 2 Tim 3:16
- Isa 40:8

- Isa 55:11
- Deut 12:32
- Rev 22:18–19

- Matt:24:35
- 1 Cor 15:21–23
- 2 Pet 1:19–21

- Isa 9:6–7
- Isa 7:14
- Micah 5:2
- Psa 72:9–11, 15

- Zech 14:4
- Isa 45:21
- Rev 1:8
- Matt 24:35

- John 4:10–14
- Heb 4:12
- Matt 4:4
- Psa 111:10

1.3 WHY IS THE BIBLE GOOD FOR YOU?

- 2 Tim 3:17
- John 3:16
- 1 John 4:19
- 1 John 5:3
- Psa 19:7–11
- Psa 111:10
- Prov 1:7

- Prov 9:10
- Jer 15:16
- Psa 119:105
- John 17:17
- 1 Thes 2:13
- Rev 21:5
- Psa 36:6

- Psa 50:6
- Psa 119:103
- Matt 5:12
- 1 John 3:2
- Rev 11:15
- Rev 22:12
- 1 Pet 1:6–8

CHAPTER 2
GOD'S TRUTH ABOUT GOD
2.1 UNDERSTANDING THE ONENESS OF GOD

- Mark 12:29
- Deut 6:4
- 1 Cor 8:4
- 1 Tim 2:5
- Gen 2:24

- Judges 20:1, 8, 11
- Gal 3:28
- 1 Cor 12:13–14, 20, 27
- John 17:3

- John 17:20–23
- John 10:30

2.2 IS GOD A TRINITY?

- John 1:1–3
- Acts 2:2–3
- Prov 9:1
- Rev 12:14
- Eph 5:27

- Rev 17:3–4
- Rom 15:18–19
- Rom 1:3–5
- Matt 1:20
- Matt 28:19

- Rom 8:16–17
- Eph 3:14–15
- 1 Cor 15:3
- Mark 3:28–29
- 2 Cor 13:14

- Acts 2:38
- 2 Pet 1:2–3
- Psa 104:30

- 1 John 5:7–8
- Rom 8:16
- Rom 6:3–4

- Rom 5:8–9
- Heb 2:10

2.3 Who Is the God of the Old Testament?

- Exodus 20
- Matt 22:36–40
- Gen 1:1
- John 1:1–3
- John 1:14, 17

- John 1:1–3
- 1 John 1:1–2
- John 1:18
- Phil 2:6–8
- Gen 32:23–28

- John 5:37
- Gen 3:8–10
- Mark 12:29–31
- John 12:49

2.4 Who Was Christ, and What Was His Mission on Earth?

- John 1:14
- Matt 11:19
- Mark 3:21
- Matt 16:13
- John 10:24
- John 9:29
- Luke 24:21
- John 1:1–3, 14–17
- John 8:58
- Ex 3:13–14
- Rev 1:8
- Rev 22:13
- Isa 44:6
- John 10:31
- John 17:5
- John 10:24–25
- John 10:30

- 1 John 1:1
- Matt 3:17
- Mark 9:7
- John 19:7
- 1 Cor 2:8
- John 10:35–36
- Matt 16:16
- Mark 15:39
- 1 Tim 1:15
- John 6:38
- John 3:16–17
- Rom 6:23
- John 12:46
- John 8:12
- John 15:22
- Rom 3:23
- John 1:29

- 1 Pet 1:18–20
- Isa 53:5–6
- Matt 15:17
- Matt 4:23
- Matt 9:35
- Luke 10:8–9
- Rev 5:10
- Matt 4:23
- Mark 1:1
- Mark 1:14–15
- Acts 1:3
- Mark 8:35
- Luke 9:1–2
- Luke 10:1, 9
- John 3:13
- Matt 24:14

2.5
WHY DOES GOD ALLOW SUFFERING?

- Matt 7:13
- Deut 30:19
- Rom 6:23
- Judges 21:25
- Deut 12:8
- 2 Cor 4:4
- Eph 2:2
- 1 Pet 5:8

- Job 1:12
- Job 2:6
- Eph 2:10
- Phil 2:13
- 1 Cor 10:13
- 1 Pet 3:18
- James 1:2–3
- Ecc 9:11

- Luke 13:4–5
- Heb 9:27
- John 3:13
- Heb 9:27
- Rev 20:11–14
- Rev 20:4–6
- Matt 9:36

2.6
COMMON MYTHS ABOUT GOD

- Hos 4:6
- Heb 11:6
- Heb 11:1
- 1 John 5:2–3
- Heb 11
- 1 Sam 16:7
- Mal 4:6
- Heb 13:8
- Exodus 20
- Ex 31:13
- Lev 23:31
- Lev 3:17

- 1 Pet 5:6–7
- Prov 21:4
- Heb 13:5
- Jer 23:23–24
- Heb 13:6
- Gen 28:15
- Matt 28:20
- John 18:36
- 2 Cor 4:4
- Rev 12:9
- Ecc 8:9
- John 3:16

- Jer 29:11–12
- 1 John 4:8
- Isa 55:8–13
- Isa 46:10–11
- 2 Pet 3:9
- Rev 3:20–22
- Job 24:10
- Psa 9:10
- Rev 21:6–7
- Num 23:19–20
- 2 Sam 22:31
- Jer 18:7–8

3.3 WHO IS THE "RULER" OF THIS WORLD?)

- John 18:36
- John 12:31
- John 14:30
- 2 Cor 4:4
- Eph 2:2
- Rom 1:28
- Rom 1:20–22

3.4 QUESTIONS AND ANSWERS ON THE FATE OF SATAN AND HIS DEMONS

- Jude 6–7
- Rev 20:10
- Ezek 28:13–14
- Rev 20:10
- 1 Cor 6:2–3
- Heb 9:27
- Luke 20:36
- Rev 20:11
- Dan 10:13
- Heb 2:7
- Psa 8:4–6
- Psa 148:2
- John 16:8–11
- Psa 89:6
- Rev 1:8
- Rev 22:13
- Isa 45:5
- Dan 9:21
- Dan 10:13
- Gen 17:1
- Rev 1:8
- Isa 41:26
- Isa 45:21
- Col 2:18
- Rom 1:24–25
- Ex 20:3
- John 4:23
- John 13:14
- John 15:16
- Matt 6:9
- Rev 21:4

CHAPTER 4
GOD'S TRUTH ABOUT MAN
4.1 THE ORIGIN OF MAN AND THE UNIVERSE

- John 3:16
- Deut 12:8
- John 1:3
- Heb 1:1–3
- Gen 1:31
- Rom 8:19–22
- Psa 8:7–9
- Gen 1:26–28
- Heb 2:8
- Jer 29:11
- Ecc 12:13–14

4.2 What Is Man?

- Gen 2:7
- Ezek 18:4
- Rom 3:23
- Ezek 18:4
- Rom 6:23
- Col 2:8
- Rev 2:18
- Rev 1:14–16
- Job 32:8
- Zech 12:1
- 1 Cor 2:11
- Eccl 12:7
- Matt 10:28
- 1 Cor 2:10–12

4.3 Why Was I Born?

- Psa 111:10
- Rom 2:13
- Gen 1:1,21,25–26
- Gen 3:1–5
- Gen 3:6–7
- John 8:44
- Titus 1:2
- Lev 26:3, 6, 12
- Lev 26
- Deut 28:15–18
- Deut 28
- Heb 5:8–9
- Matt 22:35–40
- Ex 20
- Rom 8:16–17
- Eph 1:22
- Gal 3:29
- Gal 4:7
- 1 John 3:2
- Rev 20:4
- Rev 21:1–3
- 1 Cor 2:9
- Jer 29:11–12

4.4 What Exactly Is Repentance?

- Rom 3:23
- Rom 6:23
- Mark 1:15
- Acts 2:38
- 1 John 3:4
- Rom 5:12
- Rom 3:23
- 1 Sam 16:7
- Psa 51:1
- Joel 2:12
- 2 Cor 7:10
- Acts 5:31
- 2 Tim 2:24–26
- Acts 11:17–18
- Acts 20:21
- Acts 2:38
- Rom 6:23

4.5 What Exactly Is Baptism?

- 1 Cor 14:33
- John 3:23
- Acts 8:38–39
- Matt 3:13–17
- Psa 51:1, 9
- Rom 6:3–4

- Matt 18:3
- Eph 4:20–24
- Rom 12:2
- Acts 2:38
- Rom 8:6
- Gal 5:22–23
- Rev 21:8
- Lev 23

4.6 IS THERE MORE THAN ONE HEAVEN?

- Gen 1:20
- Gen 1:1
- Gen 27:29
- Isa 45:8
- Gen 1:15
- Psa 8:3
- Heb 8:1–2

4.7 DO GOOD PEOPLE GO TO HEAVEN WHEN THEY DIE?

- Acts 13:22
- Acts 2:29
- Acts 2:34
- Jer 30:8–9
- John 8:52
- Rev 20:14
- Heb 11
- John 3:13

4.8 DID THE PROPHET ELIJAH SKIP DEATH AND GO TO HEAVEN?

- John 3:13
- 2 Kings 8:25
- 2 Kings 8:16–18, 25
- 2 Kings 2:1, 3, 11–15
- Heb 9:27
- 2 Kings 2:16
- 2 Chron 21:12–15
- John 3:13
- 1 Cor 15:21–23

4.9 DO WICKED PEOPLE GO TO HELL WHEN THEY DIE?

- 1 John 4:10
- John 14:21
- 2 Pet 3:9
- John 3:16
- Matt 5:44–45
- Psa 16:10
- Acts 2:27
- Heb 9:27–28
- Rev 20:5
- 2 Pet 2:4
- Rev 20:12–15
- Psa 118:29
- Eph 2:4
- Psa 19:9
- Psa 111:10

4.10 HOW DID HUMANITY GET TO THIS PRESENT CHAOTIC STATE?

- Rom 1:28
- Psa 19:7
- John 18:38
- John 8:45
- John 17:17

- Gen 2:17
- Gen 3:5
- Rev 12:9
- 1 Sam 8:7
- Rom 3:18

- Prov 1:7
- Isa 59:8
- Rom 1:28
- Rom 1:21–23

CHAPTER 5
GOD'S TRUTH ABOUT SALVATION AND RESURRECTIONS
5.1 WHAT EXACTLY IS SALVATION / BORN AGAIN?

- Isa 28:10
- Acts 17:11
- Rom 6:23
- Heb 9:27
- Rom 3:23
- Rev 11:15
- 1 Thes 4:14–16
- Rev 5:10

- 1 Cor 15:50–54
- Rom 5:9–10
- 1 Cor 15:50
- Rev 20:5
- Rev 20:12
- Rev 21:8
- Mal 4:3
- Rev 20:14–15

- Heb 5:9–10
- Rev 7:10
- John 3:3–5, 6
- 1 John 3:9
- 1 John 5:12
- John 14:6
- John 10:9
- Rom 6:23

5.2 WHAT STEPS ARE NEEDED FOR SALVATION?

- Rom 3:23
- Rom 6:23
- 1 Pet 1:20
- 2 Pet 3:9
- Rev 3:19
- Rom 3:23
- Act 2:38
- Acts 3:19
- Matt 18:3

- Eph 1:7
- Psa 51:1
- Rom 6:6
- Col 1:14
- Rom 5:8
- Acts 2:38
- 1 John 2:1–6
- 2 Cor 1:22
- Rom 8:9, 14

- Acts 8:18–19
- 1 Cor 6:11
- Rom 5:9
- Rom 8:30
- John 17: 1–5, 20–23
- Mark 13:13
- Matt 24:13
- Lev 23

5.3 A CLOSER LOOK AT REDEMPTION

- Psa 49:6–9
- Heb 4:15
- Heb 2:9–10
- Mark 14:16
- Luke 22:19
- Ex 12:14
- Lev 23:4–5

5.4 THE BIBLICAL TRUTH ABOUT CHRIST'S DEATH

- Matt 16:21
- Gen 1:4–5
- Gen 1
- Gal 4:4
- John 17:1
- John 7:8
- Matt 12:38–40
- Jonah 1:17
- John 2:19–21
- Dan 9:27
- 1 Cor 11:23–24
- Matt 27:46–50
- John 19:31
- Lev 23:4–8
- Lev 23
- Mark 2:28

5.5 WHO SHOULD WE TRUST TO SAVE US?

- Prov 25:11
- Psa 146:3–4
- Mic 7:5
- Jer 17:5
- Ex 20:3
- 1 Thes 5:21
- Jer 7:3–4
- Isa 5:20
- Gen 26:6
- 2 Cor 1:9–10
- Prov 14:12
- Hos 10:13
- 1 Kgs 11:1–7
- Psa 44:6
- Psa 49:6–9
- Mark 10:24–25
- Psa 37:3–4
- Prov 3:5
- Psa 31:19
- Heb 11:6
- Nahum 1:7

5.6 IS JUST "BELIEVING IN CHRIST" ENOUGH FOR SALVATION?

- Acts 16:31
- James 2:19
- John 7:31
- Luke 6:46
- Matt 27:22–23
- John 8:40

5.7 Is Just "Having Faith In God" Enough for Salvation?

5.8 Is Just "Doing Good Works" Enough for Salvation?

Chapter 6
God's Truth about the Law
6.1 Have the Ten Commandments Been Done Away With?

6.2 Two Often Quoted/Misapplied Scriptures

6.3 ACCORDING TO GOD'S LAW, WHICH DAY IS GOD'S TRUE DAY OF REST?

- Rom 3:1–3
- Gen 1:2
- Gen 1:3–5
- Mark 2:27
- Gen 2:1–3

- Rev 1:18
- Ex 20:11
- Isa 58:13–14
- Ex 20:8–11
- Matt 15:9

- Rev 12:9
- Luke 6:46
- Deut 5:33

6.4 WHY SHOULD GOD'S HOLY DAY SABBATH BE IMPORTANT TO YOU?

- Isa 58:13
- John 6:44
- Matt 23:35
- 2 Pet 2:5
- Gen 5:22
- Gen 26:5
- Psa 119:172

- Acts 17: 2
- Luke 4:16
- Mark 2:27–28
- Ex 31:13–17
- Gal 3:28–29
- Isa 58:13
- Rom 7:22

- Rom 7:12
- 1 Cor 7:19
- Heb 4:1–3
- Psa 95:11
- Heb 4:8–11
- Rev 20:6

CHAPTER 7
GOD'S TRUTH ABOUT THE KINGDOM OF GOD
7.1 FIVE COMMON MISCONCEPTIONS ABOUT THE KINGDOM OF GOD

- Rom 14:17
- 1 Cor 4:20
- Ecc 8:9
- Isa 59:8
- James 4:1–3
- Rev 11:15
- Matt 25:31
- Rev 2:27

- Rev 1:16, 20
- Micah 4:2
- Zech 14:4
- Mark 1:14–15
- Matt 24:22
- Matt 24
- Rom 3:23
- Micah 4:3

- John 3:3
- 1 Cor 15:50
- Luke 10:8–9
- Luke 17:20–21
- Dan 2:44
- Dan 7:14
- Micah 4:4

7.2 What Exactly Is the Kingdom of God?

7.3 Is Baptism Necessary to Be in God's Kingdom?

7.4 Seven Biblical Truths That Lead to Your Awesome Destiny

7.5 Character Traits of Our Future Spiritual King

- Mal 3:6
- Heb 13:8
- Psa 25:8–9

- Num 12:3
- James 4:6
- Micah 6:8

- Isa 9:6
- John 15:13–15

7.6 GOD'S EXTREME MAKEOVER

- Jer 29:11
- Isa 2:3
- Zech 14:8
- John 4:11–14

- Isa 35:1–2,
  3–5, 6–7
- Jer 30:17
- Matt 19:26

- Isa 11:6–9
- Zeph 3:9
- 1 Cor 2:9

7.7 HOW SHOULD A TRUE CHRISTIAN LIVE IN TODAY'S WORLD?

- Matt 6:26–
  27, 28–34
- Isa 55:8

- Phil 4:6–9
- Deut 29:5–6
- 1 Pet 5:6–7

- Deut 30:19

INDEX

143, 195

C

Christ 11, 15, 18, 19, 20, 21, 22, 27, 29, 30, 31, 34, 35, 36, 37, 38, 39, 40, 41, 42, 43, 44, 45, 46, 47, 48, 49, 50, 51, 52, 53, 54, 55, 58, 59, 60, 61, 62, 64, 66, 74, 76, 77, 79, 80, 86, 87, 88, 90, 91, 93, 94, 96, 100, 102, 107, 108, 109, 112, 113, 116, 118, 121, 125, 127, 128, 134, 139, 140, 141, 142, 144, 145, 147, 148, 150, 151, 152, 154, 155, 156, 157, 158, 159, 161, 165, 166, 167, 169, 170, 171, 172, 173, 174, 175, 177, 178, 179, 180, 181, 183, 186, 188, 189, 190, 191, 194, 195, 196, 197, 198, 199, 200, 201, 202, 203, 205, 206, 207, 208, 210, 211, 213, 215, 217, 218, 227, 234

Christian vii, 2, 31, 55, 82, 86, 100, 108, 111, 113, 114, 117, 119, 126, 129, 149, 155, 166, 168, 181, 184, 197, 216, 218, 221

Christianity 2, 4, 39, 46, 71, 100, 111, 128, 129, 137, 143, 145, 152, 157, 165, 168, 194, 245

Christians 2, 31, 36, 37, 38, 39, 40, 44, 46, 61, 100, 102, 118, 125, 138, 140, 142, 149, 150, 151, 156, 157, 164, 166, 168, 169, 170, 171, 172, 174, 175, 176, 178, 180, 186, 188, 190, 192, 193, 194, 198, 212

Commandments 25, 40, 44, 62, 64, 107, 111, 117, 135, 142, 171, 172, 173, 174, 177, 179, 184, 219, 220

Confusion 3, 25, 29, 57, 84, 113, 128, 174, 194, 216

Conversion 117, 118, 145, 201

D

Daniel 10, 72, 73, 74, 77, 86, 91, 92, 155, 194, 200

David
did not go to heaven 121, 122

Death 18, 38, 42, 48, 51, 52, 55, 56, 57, 59, 60, 61, 62, 69, 73, 78, 94, 100, 102, 107, 110, 111, 112, 113, 114, 116, 118, 119, 120, 121, 122, 125, 126, 127, 128, 131, 132, 133, 137, 139, 140, 141, 142, 143, 144, 146, 148, 149, 150, 151, 152, 154, 156, 158, 159, 162, 172, 173, 177, 178, 189, 191, 201, 205, 206, 208, 221

Debased mind 88, 134, 136

Deceived 40, 46, 66, 85, 89, 135, 138, 141, 162, 163, 185, 213

Demons 67, 71, 77, 84, 85, 86, 87, 89, 90, 91, 94, 129, 131, 165, 166, 169,

Joseph De Capite is a dedicated Bible student who has a passion for the truth of God. The love of God and His Word began over thirty-five years ago when he was challenged about heaven, hell, the purpose of human life, God's plan of salvation, His law and the coming Kingdom of God. Joseph then began an extensive study into all of his beliefs as a Catholic. He was astonished to find that the majority of Christianity's beliefs and teachings are not biblically based. His passion for the Word of God, as well as leaving a legacy to his children and grandchildren, has brought him to compile this collection of essays on truths found in the Holy Bible.

Joseph also has a deep love for music and holds two bachelor's degrees: one in vocal performance and one in music education. He loves to garden and is an avid reader. He is a devoted husband, a father of two daughters and a son, and has three grandchildren.

Joseph lives in Warner Robins, Georgia, with his lovely wife, Regina.

CPSIA information can be obtained
at www.ICGtesting.com
Printed in the USA
BVHW030031301121
622778BV00019B/964/J

9 781638 370970